D0384657

ANYTHING GROWS!

ANYTHING GROWS!

SHERYL LONDON

**Ingenious ways to grow more food
in front yards, backyards, side yards,
in the suburbs, in the city, on rooftops,
even parking lots**

 Rodale Press, Emmaus, Pennsylvania

Dedication

For Susan Lone, who loves the earth and all that grows upon it.

And for Flora Roth, whose long friendship has nourished me like the best of edible gardens.

Book design by Jeanne Stock

Illustrations by Kathi Ember

Library of Congress Cataloging in Publication Data

London, Sheryl.
    Anything grows!

    Includes index.

    1. Vegetable gardening. I. Title.
SB321.L754 1984   635   83-24782
ISBN 0-87857-498-0 hardcover
ISBN 0-87857-500-6 paperback

2   4   6   8   10   9   7   5   3   1   hardcover
2   4   6   8   10   9   7   5   3   1   paperback

Contents

Acknowledgments   **vi**

Introduction   **1**

Chapter 1   Mary, Mary Quite Contrary, Where Does Your Garden Grow?   **7**

Chapter 2   Finding New Growing Space—Options for Earth Gardeners   **26**

Chapter 3   Containers—Go Anywhere, Grow Anywhere Gardens   **48**

Chapter 4   Designing Your Garden—The Add-a-Garden Plan   **69**

Chapter 5   The Plot Thickens—Planning the Plantings   **82**

Chapter 6   Deciphering the Catalogs—
Choosing Vegetable, Fruit and Herb Varieties   **93**

Chapter 7   Getting Ready for Gardening   **142**

Chapter 8   The Secrets of the Soil   **154**

Chapter 9   The Gardener's Magic Wands   **168**

Chapter 10   It Ain't Necessarily Sowed—Seeds vs. Transplants   **184**

Chapter 11   Nurturing Nature Along—Tips on Helping Growing Plants   **193**

Chapter 12   The Good Guys and the Bad Guys   **206**

Chapter 13   Making the Season Last Longer   **229**

Epilogue   **234**

Recommended Reading—Digging Around for Information   **235**

Index   **236**

Acknowledgments

I am indebted to the following people who took the time and effort to help me cultivate this book and make it grow: My thanks to my editor Anne Halpin and her assistant, master gardener Debbie Fry, for their talent and ability to select and organize, and for their insights in knowing what was needed and what should be eliminated. My assistant, Tina Gonzalez, whose enthusiasm, support and patience allowed her to decipher my penciled scrawl from reams of yellow legal pads. She gave me much moral support, and some day she might even get to like worms. My husband, Mel London, who has lived with me for 38 growing seasons, who turns the compost faithfully and who has shared in every harvest.

"If you want to be happy for an hour, get drunk. If you want to be happy for a weekend, get married. If you want to be happy for a whole week, kill your pig and eat it. But if you want to be happy all your life, become a gardener."

David Burpee
(W. Atlee Burpee Co.)

Introduction

Gardeners come in as many shapes and colors as the flowers and vegetables they grow. There are lifetime urban dwellers who live in large cities or small towns. There are those who live in "bedroom communities" in the suburbs, and there are the true country people who usually have enough land for a large garden. It seems that all gardeners, no matter where they originate, have at least one thing in common. By nature, the universal characteristic of gardeners is generosity of spirit: a willingness to share not only their bounty but their knowledge as well. It is in this spirit of exchange of information and sharing of ideas that this book is written.

Why Do We Garden?

In this book you will meet people from various regions of the country and from all walks of life who prove that it can and has been done, that gardens can thrive despite limitations of space and time. Like us, these gardeners live in big cities, small towns, the suburbs, and on big farms. They are imaginative, inventive people who have devised ingenious solutions to problems they've encountered. They have discovered ways to overcome environmental limitations and they have found all sorts of nontraditional spaces to grow food, and most of all, they have taken seemingly inhospitable places and turned them into monuments of their own determination. Theirs are personal triumphs over hostile forces. I have often wondered why we all do it, and what gardening does for us; I believe our reasons for gardening are as varied as we are.

For some of us, a garden is a link to the passing seasons that gives us a needed kinship with the universe and a chance to express our relationship with living things—birds, insects and other creatures—that inhabit it. A garden also appeals to our senses: it has color, shape, texture, fragrance, and even sounds that can be heard when leaves rustle in the wind. It is a kind of blank canvas of self-expression on which we leave our marks. For others, a garden environment that is hardly ideal represents a challenge, and the garden instills a sense of achievement when it succeeds. And there may be yet another reason for gardening, one of which many of us are not even consciously aware. The United States is composed of various disenfranchised ethnic groups who have a deep, basic need to carry on their cultural heritage by having control over some piece of living land. Somehow the sense of security provided by growing one's own food on a little plot of land has been lost in the new world, and some of us need to find it again.

For most of us, however, gardening is a kind of self-prescribed preventive medicine, good for all ills. A new leaf forms. A flower unfurls, then fades and becomes a fruit. We dig in the soil and coax life from a seed. The growing plants we tend are constantly changing and never static. The garden has curative powers we may not even be aware of, but suddenly, when gardening, we seem to unwind. Tensions slip away. Our muscles don't feel quite so tight. We are soothed by the touch of a cool breeze on our hot faces, we breathe deeply the fragrance of the earth and feel a sense of well-being and harmony with the world. If we feel lonely, there is solace. If we wish to be alone, there is solitude, too. If we let it, the garden becomes a retreat, an oasis.

My first experience with gardening, 25 years ago, was like emerging from a misty dream. There was a sudden realization that I was on my knees with my blue jeans wet and muddy. Glancing at my carefully manicured nails, I saw that they were chipped and ringed with brown earth. I felt wisps of damp gray hair covering my eyes, blurring my vision. I was a happy, free kid again, playing in the dirt. I had accidentally, secretly rediscovered some joys and pleasures I had not been allowed since I was a child. Gardening, I realized, is only a grown-up "cover," an acceptable adult way of recapturing those happy childhood moments. I knew all at once that I was hooked forever.

Speaking with friends and acquaintances, I discovered other urban and suburban gardeners who, like me, had never seen a real farm up close. For most of our lives, we all took our food supplies for granted. But in recent years, as we've become increasingly concerned with high petroleum costs and the distance our produce must travel to reach us in the cities and towns, we have reinforced our survival instincts. As home gardeners, each of us can, in his or her own small way, experience the satisfaction of fighting the system by avoiding the packaging, transportation and advertising costs that are tacked on to every item of food we buy. We become less dependent on commerce and more self-sufficient when we don't have to rely upon a source hundreds of miles away to supply us with fresh food. Perhaps it is time to rethink, for example, how necessary it really is to ship broccoli or tomatoes in refrigerated trucks all the way from California to New York during the summer. When we grow our own, we can have access to fresher, tastier, cheaper food. But, besides freshness and better flavor, we develop a respect for food growing,

plus a better understanding of and empathy with the farmer and his agricultural problems. There is also less waste on the table, for who would want to leave on his plate a sprig of parsley that he himself grew?

Who Gardens?

If statistics can be believed, the rewards of gardening are attracting more of us than ever before. According to a Gallup poll conducted in 1981* we are in the midst of a gardening revival, the like of which has not been since the Victory Garden era 40 years ago. Many of today's new gardeners may not recall the time after Pearl Harbor was attacked, when massive home efforts were begun and sustained through the four years of World War II. It was a period when people planted food gardens as their personal contribution to the war effort, while farmers went off to fight and food became more scarce. It was an inspiring communal effort, a national involvement for a fundamentally good reason. By 1943, an estimated 18 million such gardens existed, according to a *Life* magazine article of that time. People found all sorts of unexpected and unused places for growing vegetables. Even Boston's famous Copley Square was plowed and planted.

Today, in the 1980s our gardens are "Victory Gardens" of another kind. Our enemy this time is a faltering economy. According to the United States Department of Agriculture, more Americans talk about gardening and participate in some form of it than our national sport of baseball: some 80% of all households. Also, the Gallup survey mentioned earlier discovered that 47% of the households in the U.S.—that's 38 million households—planted food gardens in 1981, an increase of 4 million over the previous year. The survey also showed that in addition to those with traditional food

*The survey was conducted for Gardens for All, a national association for gardening.

2

gardens, 7 million households grew some vegetables in containers or along with their flower beds. And so, gardening is gaining a foothold once again.

Of course, the economics of small space gardening can become hazy if you factor in the cost of your time. But records show that raising vegetables for home consumption is still less costly than buying them. That same Gallup poll found that in 1981 an investment of about $20 for seeds and supplies returned approximately $400 worth of produce in an average garden. One other statistic gives further impetus for this book: many people in the survey, instead of stating that they had no desire to garden, indicated that their major problem was that they had no *time* or *space* for a garden, and if they had more time and/or space they would indeed have a garden. Well, where there's a will I hope this book can show a way. A good gardener can grow about 1 pound of vegetables *per square foot*, and intensive methods can triple that yield.

My own development as a gardener has occurred over the years in the midst of tremendous limitations of environment, the amount of time I had to spend and a lack of gardening knowledge. Twenty-five years ago, I was a complete novice. I thought peat moss was spelled "Pete Morse" and was the name of someone's gardener. The only grass I saw grew out of cracks in the broken city pavement. Vegetables always came covered in plastic wrap and were purchased at the local supermarket. I thought tomatoes were *supposed* to be mealy textured and tasteless. Herbs, I suspected, were grown in far-off exotic parts of the world, somewhere perhaps on the Oriental or African spice trade route, and by the time they reached me, they had to be dried and brittle and packed in those little glass bottles. The Earth I considered only as a planet. Dirt and soil were things that had to be removed from my clothing at the dry cleaners. Gross exaggerations? Partially, of course. Never-

theless, the true urbanite, the complete "city mouse," may still hold fast to some of these views.

The City Gardener

Toughened by the realities of a hostile environment for both people and plants, we have become something of an army of gardeners all across the country. We have begun our gardens, and they have flourished and become a tribute to the indomitable spirit, ingenuity and resourcefulness that makes us all survivors who grit our teeth and refuse to quit. And isn't it wonderful how we have been able to create these oases in the midst of all kinds of encroaching blight? Some of us have enriched the lifeless, compacted soil on unloved and unlovely litter-strewn city streets and transformed these places into secret gardens that struggle into life. Some of us have planted in unlikely cold, lightless places that appear to spell certain death for growing things, but we find that with care, they thrive. In fact, it has always amazed me that so many plants do actually flourish where only neglected space had been before.

The Country Gardener

On the other side of the coin, the country gardener may have plenty of space for a food garden and most likely is blessed with more experience than his urban brothers and sisters. Country people are not gardening novices; in fact, they generally have abundant space in the back of the house where there is a large traditional garden with neat rows of produce properly spaced as advised on the back of the seed packets. But these people may never have experienced the joys and advantages of one or several smaller gardens. Though for some of us the first step is finding enough room for a garden, others who have lots of space should consider boosting their total production by gardening on the idle bits of their land. It is less wasteful to learn methods of producing greater yields and continuous harvests from a small garden than to neglect a larger one for lack of time. And time is always of the essence.

The Key to Keeping the Garden Manageable

In our busy contemporary lives, whether we live in the city, the suburbs or the country, we all feel pressed for time. Small space gardening allows for more attentive care and gives us more control. It doesn't seem to get out of hand. The person with lots of space, then, must learn to "think smaller," for the rewards to be gleaned from a miniplot are evident: a smaller expenditure of money for seeds or seedlings and fertilizers; less space to weed and water; the satisfaction of carrying out a careful plan to extend the seasons; learning new techniques, like how to grow things vertically; no more wasteful overproduction of bountiful crops like tomatoes or zucchini that have to be given away as surplus; less work, and therefore more time for other things. Most of all, a garden should be fun and cost-effective. It should not be a chore.

Whether we are busy or just naturally lazy, most of us don't want to participate in the burdensome physical effort required to care for a large, wide open space. Newspaper reports tell us that the trend for the 80s in gardening is that smaller is better. But the idea of a small garden has been with us for a long time. Charles Dudley Warner, a collaborator of Mark Twain's, was one who never belittled small spaces. He once said of a garden, "However small it is on the surface, it is 4,000 miles deep and that's a handsome property!" Anyone can grow sprawling fields of watermelons and plots of corn in large spaces, but the special techniques of "farming in a flowerpot" may be something we've neglected. Perhaps abundance has made us wasteful, and country gardeners may well learn a few tricks from their city cousins who

have to make do. With this in mind, the ideas and gardening techniques throughout this book can apply to smaller, potentially productive spaces that country people, as well as city dwellers, may never have considered using before.

Gaining Experience and Confidence

In the intervening years from "Pete Morse" to peat moss, I have picked brains, asked millions of questions and read lots of books about gardening. It has been a most humbling experience, for I have found that when it comes to gardening, *everyone* is always somewhat of a novice. We can always learn more from each other. I found that a rooftop gardener may know a lot about container gardening, but nothing about growing directly in the earth. By the same token, an expert truck farmer with a large traditional garden may never have had a small intensive garden, or gardened in spot pockets or containers. I have also discovered that we are like foreign exchange students who learn from one another the ways of creating or adapting ideas for our personal trial and error experiments.

Another discovery that I've made on my journey from novice to pundit is that definite rules and exact formulas are practically nonexistent, particularly in the sphere of organic gardening. All accomplished gardeners swear by their own exploratory procedures and formulas, which inevitably contradict the methods of their equally successful neighbors. Every good gardening book, therefore, is only an accumulation of personal experience, a baton in a relay race, passed on to the next person, who then carries it further. By that token, this book is the result of my own attempts (plus the personal experiences of others) to find solutions for gardening problems. Passed on to you, I hope that what I have learned in my own gardens—one on a windswept rooftop in the city, and the other in the sand and salt spray of the seashore—will inspire and encourage you to leap over your own pitfalls and turn them into pleasures. The size of your garden, wherever it may be, is restricted only by how involved you wish to get. There is as much delight in eating fresh lettuce or that "dream" tomato grown in a rooftop container in the city as there is in eating lettuce or tomatoes that arc grown on a farm or in the suburbs. When one is inspired to be ingenious, one can find ways to grow almost anything anywhere.

Anything, you say?

Yes, I say.

But you can't grow corn in a flower pot.

Or can you?

What Neophytes Need to Know

Just a few words of encouragement to the novice: growing vegetables is a lot easier than most information may lead you to believe. The fact is, I successfully grew all kinds of things before I learned that you couldn't possibly grow them in my area. Although the stumbling blocks that may be encountered are overemphasized in this book, I have stressed them purposely, so you can more easily recognize and avoid them.

Besides striking an inspirational spark, I also want to give you reasons for the various procedures and techniques presented here. Knowing the "why" behind the "how to" of growing procedures is what turns brown thumbs into green ones. Just as great chefs rarely follow a recipe to the letter once they have mastered the basics of cooking, so too should gardeners adopt this attitude. In the same way that chefs develop a "feel" or sensitivity for dishes they create, gardeners also learn to temper the rules once they know them. As soon as we understand the basic requirements of a vegetable we can then take

liberties and experiment with its culture.

So please take all my advice with some reservations and tailor it to fit your own garden and climate. Common sense can be the best antidote for confusion. Garden terms and garden language are not standardized. A drill, a furrow and a row all mean pretty much the same thing. You will also note a lack of uniformity in most of the planting specifications on seed packets. Burpee suggests planting carrots 12 inches apart, while Comstock, Ferre Co. recommends 14 to 16 inches. Then, too, when you choose among the various intensive planting methods, instructions for spacing seeds may change again.

Don't be afraid to experiment—it's part of the joy of gardening. We can afford to take a few risks by planting early for we stand to lose only a few seeds and some time at most, and we can replant easily when weather conditions are more favorable. Besides, as we shall see, on a smaller scale there are many more options for circumventing the weather to make it work for the gardener. The chance of having those first tender peas or that first homegrown salad a few weeks earlier is worth the risk.

The two keys to success in gardening are (1) understanding how plants grow and what they need to grow, and (2) understanding what environmental conditions you have to offer and how you can modify them to provide a better home for your plants. The so-called green thumb is not much more than an appreciation of these simple facts:

The main purpose of any plant is to reproduce and propagate itself by making more seeds. When you grow a plant for its fruit, like a tomato, you want to encourage nature to take its course. But when you're growing a plant for its leaves or roots, you try to postpone or prevent its eventual maturity (like when you pick the flowerbuds off your basil to prolong leaf production).

Plants grow at different widths, heights, depths and thicknesses of stalk, in order to support their final mission in life—their seed pods.

When a plant reaches maturity and becomes strong enough to support the additional weight of flowers and fruit, it gathers its energy and blooms.

A plant will continue to blossom and bear its fruit until it creates enough seed for the following generations, or until its normal life cycle is interrupted for any of a variety of reasons, such as frost.

Seed germination and root growth are stimulated by soil conditions. The roots develop to supply moisture and food to fuel the plant's growth, and to help anchor the plant.

Root growth and the release of plant foods from fertilizers are hampered by tightly packed, waterlogged, airless soils.

Each vegetable, fruit and herb has its own favorite combination of heat, light, water and soil.

Where these preferred combinations exist in nature, plants will be found growing in abundance.

When we approach vegetable gardening with enough curiosity to find out what combination of environmental conditions is best for each vegetable, and to duplicate those conditions as closely as possible with our own climate and soil, we can produce the best vegetables we ever tasted and have lots of fun doing it.

Just look again at your thumb as you begin to turn the pages of this book. It's starting to turn green already, isn't it? And remember, in the words of M.C. Goldman, Executive Editor of *Organic Gardening* magazine, "No amount of planning can take the place of dumb luck."

Mary, Mary Quite Contrary, Where Does Your Garden Grow?

Gardens do not come in standard sizes. They are found in all kinds of places, on the earth and even in the sky, as we'll see. All you need to do is seek, and ye shall find a space for your own. Most likely it's been right under your nose all the time. Finding a place for a garden can be just like a treasure hunt, for all around us there are potential gardens.

Those of us with access to some land (who I like to think of as "earth gardeners") usually have more to start with. Living near any piece of terra firma that is either owned or rented is a decided advantage when you're looking for garden space. A garden can grow on a little bit of land in the city, the suburbs, the country or the seashore. The best spot for yours may be in a dooryard, next to a porch or by the side of a pool. If you're very lucky, you may enjoy the triple blessing of front, back and side yards to use for gardening. Or you could plant your garden in a lawn, or what was once a parking area, or even in a neglected former garden plot. Your garden could be a tiny patch outside your mobile home. It could be a row of plants trained to grow vertically next to a fence. In short, your garden might be in any spot you've been avoiding because you thought that growing conditions there were not ideal. But few of us are blessed with ideal gardening conditions. "Ideal" is a myth.

Making the Front Lawn Productive

Traditionally, most of us have maintained what is regarded as a respectable relationship with nature: we have a front lawn. We could, of course, dig up a sunny part of that lawn to make room for a vegetable garden. But traditions die hard. "Besides," we mutter, "what will the neighbors say?" No doubt the neighbors won't mind at all once they see that you can create a garden on your lawn that's pretty enough to take the place of a flower bed. (I'll explain how in Chapter 4.) And you needn't stop there, either. Some of your ornamental bushes can produce fruit as well, and you can tuck some parsley or lettuce alongside that path to your garage. Of course, you may have to break with a few accepted traditions along the way, but that has always been a part of any true creative process. Besides, it's time we change our antediluvian thinking about that old sacred cow—the lawn—and start to turn these useless energy gobblers into food-growing spaces.

We don't have to give up *all* of our lawns at once to grow vegetables, although some of the gardeners mentioned in this book, as you will see later, have indeed done so. But it is certainly true that the equipment, fertilizers,

Self-Sufficient Town Gardeners

Joe and Joyous Mahaffey live in the last private house that is still standing on the main thoroughfare of a business district in downtown Denver. The building boom that's been going on in this thriving city has placed their standard suburban tract house in this most unique position.

Joe and Joyous are both retired, and Joe is the gardener of the family. His garden rambles along both narrow sides of the house where it started. Over the years it has crept into the front and back lawns as well.

"We like living in the city now, but we also like what grows easily in the country," Joe says. "Now that we have both, we never have to go to the supermarket for fresh produce. Nobody had a food garden here in the inner city when we started ours in 1975, quite by

seed, insecticides, tending, mowing, trimming, irrigation—even the man-hours alone—that we lavish on our lawns could be better spent growing something we can eat. Especially since after giving those immaculate lawns so much tender loving care we don't like to use them for fear of ruining the grass. Instead, why not turn that plain old front yard into a new kind of landscape that combines some lawn and flowers with food? Now that we are all learning how to get along comfortably with less— less energy, limited resources and smaller spaces—it is time to reassess our basic lawn and landscape designs to incorporate edibles and treat them in an ornamental fashion.

Other Places for Gardens

Another idea whose time has passed is that the vegetable garden must be all of one unit or one plot. Spread the wealth. You can group vegetables alongside a house foundation, tuck them into spots with flowers, line them up as path borders, have them make a ring around a tree. You can take out some groundcover on a sloping hillside and terrace an area there for growing herbs, vegetables or strawberries on several levels. Look under your bed, or in your closet or under the kitchen sink—no burglars may be lurking there, but you'll find a good spot to grow bean sprouts or (if it's damp and dark) mushrooms. Even accident. We decided to replace a deteriorating hedgerow with peas and beans alongside the iron fence on the side of our house, and it just grew from there." Today their garden includes two basic sections, one that's 6 feet wide by 20 feet long, and the other 8 feet wide by 15 feet long.

"Originally," explains Joe, "we didn't start the garden for economic reasons, but just for the fun of it. Over the years it has really slimmed down our food budget, although that wasn't our intent. Do you know that just from our tomato patch, after we've eaten our fill and given some away, we put up 60 quarts of fresh tomato juice a year—and that ain't hay!" The tomato patch is a 6 by 10-foot plot that holds about 24 plants. There are a few other plants scattered around the rest of the garden. Joe and Joyous grow six different varieties of tomatoes: Burpee Big Early, Burpee VF Hybrid, Ace, Jubilee, Rutgers and Super Steak.

"I grow everything from seed except rhubarb and asparagus. That comes back every year, you know," explains Joe. He starts his own tomatoes and peppers indoors, and sows seeds of cabbage, corn, lettuce, beets and spinach directly in the ground.

"We grow six varieties of lettuce all different colors," Joe continues. "I think it looks as pretty growing as flowers. Our corn patch over there is 8 by 8 feet and it really produces the best, sweetest table corn. We replace some of the sugar snaps, after they're harvested, with pole beans and some cucum-

bers. We also grow hot and bell peppers and lots of fruit. We have three fruit trees: a plum, a cherry and an apple. We have hedges of raspberries that we have to confine or they'd take over the place. But oh, that homemade raspberry jam—it's worth the extra care considering that they're $3.00 a pint when they're store bought!"

Joe says they haven't had much luck with their beets, but their lettuce (especially Black-Seeded Simpson, Grand Rapids; Green Ice and Ruby) does fabulously. So does their spinach (they grow Avon).

Does such a bountiful garden take a lot of time to maintain? Not really, Joe says. The most he ever puts in, during the peak of the season, is a couple of hours a day. Usually it's less.

And what about the climate in Denver, I wanted to know. Does that limit what the Mahaffeys can grow? Responded Joe, "Here in Denver, because of the drought restrictions we can only water every third day, but that's no real problem with mulches. We have a short growing season, too. Our last frost is around the middle of May so our hot-weather crops, like the tomatoes, go into the ground at that time. We really do have capricious weather here, though. Why, last week there were a few tornadoes, and one year we were almost wiped out by hail. Some plants were wind-damaged, but they came right back up and started to grow and produce again. Sure makes you have faith!"

these unused "problem spaces" that don't seem able to support any life can be resurrected for producing food. The best way to find garden space you never thought you had is to be flexible in your thinking about what and where a garden should be. Be eclectic, try some new approaches. Growing space is everywhere.

Here are just a few examples of what's possible, to get your imagination started on ideas for your own garden:

If the soil is compacted in a narrow side yard, build a series of raised beds.

A skinny strip of soil near a garage can accommodate a whole season's worth of

tomato plants if you grow them on a trellis.

A woven wood or wire mesh fence with a mere 12 inches of space in front of it can support a crop of succulent sugar snap peas that you can't buy in any store. And when the weather gets warm you can replace the spent pea vines with a crop of burpless cucumbers that are sold in markets at prices that hover around $1.00 a piece.

Low food prices are now ancient history, and prices are still climbing. Boosting your total production by creating more usable space, even when you already have an established standard garden, can only help in your pri-

Vegetables can grow in plenty of places besides a backyard garden. In this yard, lettuce borders the walkway, tomatoes are trained to grow up strings in a narrow patch beside the garage and other vegetables share the flowerbeds.

vate war against food prices. It might also give you the option of making your main garden smaller. In any case, the more you can grow, the better off you are. You might want to use the extra space for a special garden, such as a little "test kitchen" garden where you can experiment with growing some of the more exotic and gourmet vegetables. You will have more control with the garden close to your house, under your watchful eye, and you will find that this garden will be easier to care for.

Where to Garden When You Don't Have Any Land

For some people, finding space in the earth for a garden may first require a break with past traditions while others need to play hide-and-seek for growing room. On the other hand, apartment dwellers and other people with no access to land (I like to call them "sky gardeners") have one seemingly major disadvantage: they must buy or make their own soil. But what seems like a disadvantage at first can really be a blessing in disguise, for sky gardeners (or anyone else who gardens in containers) have speed on their side. They can prepare, at once, a rich, custom-blended soil mixture, without waiting to gradually improve problem soil.

Walk along any street in any town, city or suburb and look up, and you will find a wealth of acreage waiting to be claimed by sky gardeners. Here are just a few of the gardens I've seen where people don't have any land at all:

Rooftops on residential and office buildings filled with containers.

Boxes tucked behind water towers on city rooftops where vegetables thrive.

Balconies filled with clay pots, clinging to the sides of high-rise apartment buildings.

A "sky" garden above a garage.

Another garden on top of a theater marquee.

A window box garden fastened to the windows of a townhouse.

A container garden suspended from a street light, and another from a tree in a backyard.

A roof ledge lined with plastic garbage cans from which dangled scarlet tomatoes and a few zealous zucchinis.

Old rubber gloves planted with herbs and clipped to a wash line on a city tenement rooftop.

Behind every granite facade there is room, at least for a lettuce plant in a pot.

No matter where you live, then, your garden can be as elaborate as you can afford to make it, or as modestly ingenious as you can devise. Vegetables have no color or class prejudice; they are very democratic—they grow equally for everybody. No matter what your budget, where you live, or how you can afford to live, you can have a modest container garden with an individual charm. A container garden need not be the province of only sky gardeners who have no land. For example, here are some ways containers and space-saving structures can be used in conjunction with a large vegetable garden:

Why walk to the back garden in the rain for parsley when it can grow as a border for a rose bush or around an annual flowerbed near the front door?

Why not plant a tub with your favorite kitchen herbs and place it near the back door of the kitchen? It's wonderfully convenient for the family cook.

Beans can be beautiful; they shouldn't be banished to the backyard only. Beans growing in an ornamental concrete urn with a wire teepee for support can be equally elegant on a penthouse terrace or by the doorway of a tract house, especially when you grow a variety like the scarlet runner bean with its beautiful red blossoms.

Kuster's Parking Lot Inflation Garden

My husband and I are partners in a documentary film company. On one of our assignments we were filming at television station KBTV in Denver. We left some necessary pieces of equipment in the van and I went out to get them. However, instead of walking through the parking lot from the rear door, where we entered, I walked out of the front door and found myself face to face, right in the parking lot, with an oasis of greenery in which stood a printed sign that read: Kuster's Inflation Garden. Bill Kuster works as a weatherman for the TV station and he is a charming, friendly and dedicated gardener.

Bill originally came from Fernville, Pennsylvania, a town of 100 people, "if you count the dogs, cats and children." He's a born country boy. He told me that he had worked as a weatherman in Philadelphia for thirteen years and had his first small food garden right on Independence Mall. When he came to Denver to work at the station he needed to have another food garden. Four years ago he cut out a piece of the blacktop from the parking lot and made this one. A load of good topsoil was trucked in by a local contractor. Bill has a thorough soil analysis done every other year, and then prepares the soil accordingly. He spends about 6 hours a week working in the garden, between his noon and 5 P.M. broadcasts.

Bill Kuster is so enamored of small food gardens that he has done two things to promote them. At 5 P.M. every evening he gives a progress report on his own garden to his viewers. "Weather and gardens go together, so my audiences can garden along with me," he explains. The Burpee seed company also supplies sets of four packets of vegetable seeds and Bill gives them away to anyone who requests them to start their own garden. The station has sponsored the giveaway program for three years now, and they've given away more than 50,000 packets of seeds to interested viewers.

The parking lot garden is divided into two areas. One is for sitting, and contains a small wooden table and bench; the other part is a minuscule, exquisitely laid out food garden about 16 by 20 feet. There is a path of hexagonal stepping stones winding through the middle of the food garden, allowing the gardener to tend his plants from both sides. The focal point of the garden is a dwarf crabapple tree. It creates the effect of a well-landscaped miniature park with a view of a neighboring farm—but the entire scene is of lilliputian proportions! Nevertheless, I listed onions, beans, eggplant, zucchini, cucumbers, carrots, squash, tomatoes, radishes, parsley and chives growing in that "farm." The garden blocks are marked with large pictures of vegetables showing what, one day, will be harvested. Bill's garden is living, thriving proof that you can indeed grow anything anywhere.

This apartment balcony holds tubs of tomatoes, eggplant and squash; hanging pots of strawberries and herbs; and boxes (securely fastened to the railing) of leaf lettuce and flowers.

Grapes trained over an arbor can shade a picnic table or a carport, and can be a practical shade-making device for a city rooftop garden, a large country garden or a suburban backyard.

Small spaces, with the addition of a little imagination and knowhow, are capable of producing prodigious quantities of vegetables, herbs and fruit. New planting techniques take into account the growing habits of individual vegetables, so you can plant more crops in a given space. And a whole range of new compact varieties now on the market seem to expand even the smallest spaces. Therefore, you no longer need a large tract of land to have a productive garden. It is possible to create the tiniest sanctuary where you can nibble a freshly pulled carrot if that's all you want, or to harvest bushels of edibles for your table from several minuscule gardens scattered all over your property.

But even after the space is found, you may hear other grumblings from your nagging inner voice:

...but, I can't grow anything, I don't have a green thumb.

There's no sun where I live.

The rooftop is too windy.

My soil is too hard.

The water table is too high.

The sun is too hot.

It's too much work.

I don't have the time!

However, when you begin to really examine these problems, one by one, the excuses and rationalizations fade and dissolve into the atmosphere like vapor. *There are no excuses for not gardening.* There are solutions for everything, even the problem of "no time." Although in all honesty I can't tell you that a garden will grow completely by itself, it almost will, if you plan it well and keep it small and devote to it a bit of weekend time or a few minutes before or after work. Remember, plants grow in profusion all by themselves in nature, so with a little help your garden plants will reward you a thousandfold. And the rewards are well worth the effort.

So, whether you want to be a front porch farmer, a backyard gardener or a rooftop recluse, whether you want to grow peppers or peppermint, you can do it, with a little ingenuity. Mary, Mary, then become contrary. Contrary enough to break a few rules—or at least bend them—and find your own untraditional garden space. Give up all your old excuses, for inflation makes our gardens grow. In the next several pages I will give you some criteria for choosing the best of the garden locations available to you.

How to Outwit the Weather

The weather. It's a universal subject, one that everybody comments about. When we say that everybody talks about the weather and nobody does anything about it, in truth we are saying that we must gracefully accept along with sunshine and balmy breezes the fog that rolls in from the sea, the rain that pours down from the heavens and the wind that lashes at our windowpanes. Much easier weather to accept, of course, is the gift of a bright, clear, sunny day.

Macroclimates and Microclimates

All of these unchangeable conditions are part of large-scale weather patterns that are influenced by the movements of cloud covers, the locations of mountain ranges, valleys, and rivers—the topography of the entire area. This "macroclimate" is what the TV weatherman is talking about when he says something like "there's a cold front coming in from the Rockies . . ." The farmer, like the TV weatherman, is also a macroclimate maven. He constantly looks up at the sky for his weather indications. He checks the wind direction and looks to see if the clouds are white and puffy or dark and ominous. The meteorologist, although using more accurate and scientific tools, studies the same conditions the farmer assesses with his skyward glances. Often, the farmer's deductions are almost as accurate as the meteorologist's. Yet, however accurately they can predict the weather, like us they can't do anything to change it.

Although we can't change the large weather patterns rolling over our gardens, we *can* influence climatic conditions in selected areas of our gardens. The parts we can change by modification, when we understand them, are microclimates, small pockets formed by the unique interactions of the sunlight, heat and cold and the various objects that either radiate, absorb or reflect the heat and light. An oasis in a desert is a dramatic example of a microclimate. But these pockets of unique climates also occur right where we live and sometimes are referred to as the "little weathers." They can be caused by the confluence of hilly slopes and low-lying areas, the direction of the prevailing winds, the sun and cast shadows. All of these factors are major influences in the creation of the microclimates which present us with specific (and often less than ideal) conditions for growing vegetables.

Microclimates are everywhere and not only down on the ground. Sky gardeners, too, are affected by the wind and sun, although their conditions differ somewhat. Modifying our microclimate allows us to knock the weather down to size, so we can handle and control it.

Identifying the Microclimates in Your Garden Spot

The first thing you need to do in planning the garden is to walk around your potential garden spots and locate your own microclimates, then analyze them and decide on the best way to handle them. Take a notebook and pencil with you to jot down any information you want to remember. It's best to take this walk three times a day—morning, noon and late afternoon. A yardstick or tape measure will come in handy to find out how large your potential growing spaces are. Write down the numbers—you'll want to use them later.

When I strolled through the places where my own gardens would be established, I took along several plant identification labels (wooden ice cream spoons or Popsicle sticks will also do nicely). I marked the following symbols:

☼　Full Sun

◐　Part Sun

◓　Shade

on the labels with a waterproof pen, and plunked the labels down where the conditions matched their symbols, noting the times of day. At the end of the day I collected all of the labels and totaled up the number of hours of sun in each location. I have found this method a fairly easy and accurate way to establish the total hours of sunlight available in different spots. It will help you know *what* you can grow as well as *where* it will grow best. Here are some other things to note on your walks:

Check the angle of the sun and observe which areas get the maximum amount.

Remember that the angle of the sun's elevation changes with the seasons: the sun is lowest in winter and highest in summer. Try to keep that in mind, especially if you're taking your walk early in spring. As the days get longer in the summer, it may indeed be possible to get enough sun in tiny hidden corners.

Note, too, that your house or a neighboring building, as well as nearby trees, will cast shadows at certain times of the day. On a rooftop some shade would be welcome, of course, but in a small backyard it can be a disadvantage.

Familiarize yourself with the exposures of your garden-to-be. Notice that the north side is almost always in shade, and the south side gets the most consistent sun. The east and west sides also receive a good amount of light. However, the east side may be somewhat cooler, since part of the sun's warming energy is used in overcoming the cold of the previous night. And you may find extra warmth along a south wall by late afternoon.

Be aware of temperature changes as you walk. Note where it feels warmer or cooler. Cool spots could be caused by deep shade from a tree above, or a lower-lying area or a constant cool breeze. Warm spots could be caused by sloping ground (higher ground will be warmer than lower ground), the presence of natural windbreaks like shrubs or vines or simply because areas in unshaded, direct sunlight will have warm spots.

Farmers use the same sort of information you are gathering on your walks. The farmer's scale is larger, but the microclimates on his land contain the same elements as yours. For example, the southern slope of a hill is warmer and drier; the northern slope is cooler and moister. The farmer knows from experience that each side of the hill will support different plant life, or may at least require different planting times. He knows that slopes affect water drainage, as well as exposure of plants to the sun and wind. His land is usually open to the sky on all sides, and in seeking the very best growing area, he looks for a gentle slope away from the direction of the prevailing winds. The farmer knows that constant winds stress his crops and cause rapid evaporation of moisture from the soil. He is aware that flat or sunken spots get bogged down in heavy rains and collect mist and frost on still nights. The farmer may compensate for his microclimates in several ways. He may build windbreaks called "berms," mounds of earth, to baffle the prevailing winds. He might take advantage of the higher ground to plant tender, heat-loving crops. And he might delay planting on the north side of a hill for a few weeks in spring.

On a smaller scale, we gardeners can modify our microclimates, no matter where they are, with a lot more ease and control. We can snare the sun and collect warmth in places where it's cool, and harness and tame the winds where they are a menace. We can light up the shadows and filter the burning sun. And we can cool the air with moisture and shade where it is too hot.

When newspaper headlines proclaim on a hot day that "it's so hot that you could fry an egg on the sidewalk" what they're really telling us gardeners is that a concrete surface can collect and radiate enough heat to cook an egg. And from our own experience we all know that different surfaces and colors vary in the way they absorb and reflect heat and light. I once had a pair of fancy tennis shorts with one black leg and one white leg. When I wore them, the black side was always too hot while the white one was always comfortable. Needless to say, I learned a firsthand lesson not only about tennis players' preference for white clothes but also about the ability of white surfaces to reflect, rather than absorb, heat. Before you tackle the task of microclimate modification, you should write down a few more things in your notebook.

How to Judge Your Growing Season

Vegetables couldn't care less about subzero winter temperatures. With a few excep-tions, most of them are annuals in our gardens and, as the term implies, they don't last the winter anyway. We start them anew from seed each spring, and they die when the first hard autumn frost gets to them or not long after. As the nights get longer the spent corpses of this year's plants are laid to rest on the compost pile, to be resurrected a few months later in the form of soil enrichment for the next generation of freshly planted seeds. What is important to vegetables is the number of days between the last frost of spring, the time when the earth begins to stir, and the first hard fall frost, when they succumb and meet their destinies. This period of time, of course, is known as the growing season. Since it varies all over the country, zone maps, which are usually found in seed catalogs, can be helpful in locating your area and depicting the *average* period of time which falls between the frost dates for your zone. Alas, zone maps offer only the most general of guides, because weather conditions vary from year to year and because the maps can't take into account the multitudes of microclimates within each zone.

The climate and geography of the United States creates weather patterns that are vastly different from one another. They are capricious and filled with so many variables that it is possible for a growing season in one location to vary by as much as twenty days from the growing season in another spot only a few miles away. This sort of variation might be caused by a significant difference in elevation, for example. And there are many other factors that come into play, such as whether your area is coastal or inland. The zone maps, then, should only be used for overall reference and to familiarize you with weather-related plant hardiness. Since growing zones are usually mentioned on the backs of seed packets, knowing your zone also will help you decipher some of the cryptic information found there. Meanwhile, to pinpoint information for your particular county and its local influences, con-

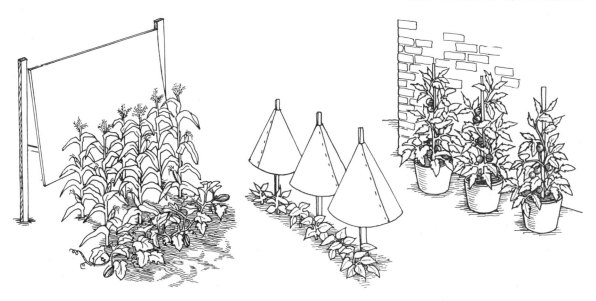

Reflect more light into shady spots for sun-loving crops like corn. A cone of roofing paper (tarpaper) elevated on a stick can create a warm spot for a tender young plant. Plant heat-loving crops like tomatoes to the south side of a masonry wall.

tact your United States Department of Agriculture Cooperative Extension agent. (More details about their wonderful services appear in Chapter 8.)

It is a fact that some vegetables thrive in the heat while others flourish only in cooler weather, with a certain number of daylight hours. In addition, the variation between day and night temperatures influences planting time and growth habits. With these few things in mind, let us consider some specific ways to help modify different sorts of microclimates.

Sky and seashore gardeners particularly should note the suggestions in the following pages for remedying conditions such as burning hot sun, severe winds, cast shadows and sea spray or smoke in the air. They are applicable to and can be easily adapted for your particular growing environment.

How to Snare the Sun and Light Up the Shadows in a Cool Garden

First, here are some suggestions for dealing with a location that is shady or cool, to make it more hospitable to vegetables and herbs:

If the area gets sun for a few hours a day, try storing heat for tender plants. Paint the inside of any kind of clean metal container—storage drum, restaurant-size food tin, washtub—with black paint and fill it with water. The water will absorb as much as 95% of the heat it receives from the sun during the day, and then slowly radiate it back to the surrounding area at night. Place the drums between plants or as close to them as possible. Try this to protect tender plants on sudden cold nights and to extend the growing season.

Depending upon their color and density, solid stones, rocks, masonry and concrete surfaces of walls and floors in the vicinity of the garden will absorb the sun's heat and give back about 50%. These same materials, when built with openings, can also serve as windbreaks to divert cold air or allow better air circulation.

In cool climates, plant heat lovers such as tomatoes and eggplant against a south-facing wall to catch the low-angled spring sun. It will be several degrees warmer there than in a more open area just a few feet away.

Black roofing paper fashioned into a cone and placed on a stick can create a hot spot which collects the sun's warmth for cold-sensitive vegetables. Use the cones like umbrellas over seedlings for protection (but be sure the sticks are long, so the cones don't cover the plants and keep them in the dark).

Cold frames angled to face south also catch any available sun. They will serve as a nursery for tender seedlings and can also extend the growing season in areas where it is short. Details for building and using cold frames appear in Chapter 13.

Since temperatures differ with latitude and elevation, earth gardeners must pay particular attention to the physics of warm air rising and cold air falling. Therefore, plant warmth-loving and/or early and late crops on higher ground where they get the most sun. Avoid planting in low spots where frost usually settles. As a rule, rooftop gardeners can usually start their vegetables earlier because of higher elevation.

Planting heat lovers in raised beds is another trick to use. The soil warms up faster and dries out earlier in the spring than when

vegetables are planted in an unraised garden, making it possible to plant sooner. Of course you have to remember that when the weather gets hot in summer these beds will still dry out faster; keep them well mulched.

Raised beds also enable northern gardeners to extend a short growing season. Planting early-maturing varieties of seedlings, rather than seeds, is also helpful when the season is short.

Take a tip from the British. They plant many tender heat-loving vegetables in tubs and place them on wheeled platforms. The plants can be easily moved indoors to a sheltered place if you expect a sudden frost, and then rolled back into the sun the next day.

Plant protectors, those invaluable, many-shaped devices, not only trap heat and help keep the soil warm and moist, but they can protect against the hazards of frosty winds as well. They are also useful for preventing a washout of freshly planted seeds or delicate tiny seedlings. (See Chapter 10 for more information.)

A sheet of *black* plastic placed atop a garden bed can absorb the sun's heat and smother weeds while allowing speedier germination. But remember to remove it when seeds germinate. *Clear* plastic allows the sun's rays to penetrate but stimulates weed growth also. (Neither is biodegradable and I do not recommend using them for mulching.)

Paved sidewalks, brick or concrete patios, enclosed gardens, black tar roofing material or dark quarry tile flooring (which is commonly used for rooftop living areas) are all materials which collect and radiate solar energy.

Here's a surprise for city gardeners. Dust and smog retain heat for longer periods, and it takes more time for the heat to disperse after the sun goes down. These atmospheric conditions often create city temperatures which are higher than suburban or country areas with cleaner air. Thus, an advantage to city gardeners is a longer growing season for heat-loving plants.

In cloudy regions, shady places and wherever summers are cool, a white wall facing south reflects light and heat. For real heat lovers (melons, for example) place a thin piece of painted wood or a house shingle painted white close to a plant to create a warmer, brighter spot.

Another way to reflect light is to tape aluminum foil to a piece of plywood or any kind of stiff panel and use it to bounce light into northern, eastern or western exposures, or wherever you need more light. Caution: when the sun is really bright, remove the panel so you don't cook your plants.

Less industrious gardeners can try the drugstore for a reflector. They sometimes carry ready-made sun reflectors designed to intensify the sun for suntan worshippers. These reflectors fold in two places and form a three-sided structure which is really more beneficial to plants than to people.

Light-colored walls, mirrorlike silver Mylar sheeting or the type of ready-made light reflectors used by still photographers and filmmakers can also be used to brighten shadowy areas. Tilt them up and place them on the east and west sides of the garden area for concentrated light.

When you are shortchanged on sun by advancing shadows, frequent coastal fogs

A row of blueberry bushes forms a living windbreak for a garden planted where there are strong prevailing winds, top. A permeable fence, like this picket fence, slows wind better than a solid wall, center. For rooftop and patio gardens, a row of trellised cucumber or squash plants in containers makes an effective windbreak, bottom.

or shade for part of the day, give that space over to leafy vegetables, root crops and some herbs such as chervil and parsley. Since early varieties of vegetables have a somewhat different genetic makeup from later-maturing varieties, they require shorter days or fewer warm days to mature. Select these early varieties, too, if you receive only partial sun.

Containers and hanging baskets offer the big advantage of mobility. They can be moved from shade to sun and back again, whenever conditions warrant a change.

Harnessing and Taming the Winds

There is nothing quite so refreshing as a cool breeze on a hot day. Yet a summer storm can transform these delightful wafts of gentle air into high-speed gusts that are capable of knocking down tall, unstaked plants. But the prevailing winds, the cold ones that come from the north or west, are the winds to worry most about. In spring and fall particularly, constant wind can cause stressful conditions— rapid transpiration of water from leaves and quick drying of soil—that can slow down the growth of sun-loving crops. In extreme cases, strong wind can cause total devastation, snapping off the stems of growing plants. But there are several ways to intercept the chilling and drying effects of strong prevailing winds.

A windbreak can make the change in the environment that will vastly improve your garden's performance. To be effective, windbreaks should be placed between the source of the constant wind and the plants you want to protect. Generally, the most effective and most attractive way to tame the wind is to plant a row of trees or shrubs some distance from your garden in the direction from which the prevailing breezes blow. This technique works particularly well both in large, open spaces and as a shield for smaller gardens. Fences also make effective windbreaks, but a permeable type of fence, such as a picket fence, works far better than a solid fence or wall. A permeable fence slows the speed of the wind passing through it. But a solid wall will simply divert the wind up and over it, without really slowing it down.

Try some of the following ideas for rooftop, seashore, urban and country gardens, wherever the wind menaces the well-being of your vegetables and flowers:

When choosing plant material for natural windbreaks, always select trees and shrubs that are wind tolerant. These are usually the thicker, leathery-leaved shrubs and trees such as Japanese holly or privet. Tamarisk, bayberry, juniper, barberry, and Japanese and black needle pines also make excellent wind barriers.

Staggering the trees or shrubs and planting a double row breaks the force of the wind more effectively than single row planting.

Filter the wind with lattice, a trellis or mesh screening. Use it to support flowering or food-producing vines and create a living fence. Grapes, pole beans or climbing varieties of peas are all good choices. (These trellises are also indispensable for saving space in narrow rooftop terraces or tiny balconies or backyards. More about that in Chapter 11.)

In coastal areas rugged, low-growing shrubs that harmonize with the line of the sea and horizon are less vulnerable to the ravages of ocean winds than tall plants with a strong vertical shape. The beach plum is one of my favorites, and jelly or jam made from its fruits is a rare and special treat. A good, hearty tree to plant near the coast is the gray-leaved Russian olive.

For clues to seaside windbreaks, look at what grows naturally in the area. Look for those wildlings which have gray, silvery, tough, leatherlike leaves. Dig up small transplants and transfer them where you need to block prevailing winds. But be sure the plants you want to move are not endangered species.

Group vine-planted containers with trellis support to provide a quick, movable hedge on a patio, balcony or anywhere. This kind of plant grouping buffers the wind while creating a soft, leafy background, and it can be used as a screen to create privacy or hide a view of a garage, compost heap, nearby building or other eyesore.

Sometimes tall buildings may cause problems for townhouse gardeners. Drafts peculiar to the city, with its high and low buildings, can turn a narrow backyard into a wind tunnel, a situation for the gardener that's much like living in a canyon where winds become trapped. Windbreaks help slow the rush of drafts into the yard.

Another idea to try where strong, gusty winds may blow vegetables over is to make the plants mutually supportive by setting them close together. This can work well for corn, peppers and tomatoes, for example. But be sure to allow for proper air circulation around the vegetables to prevent fungus from forming.

If you garden on a windy rooftop or balcony with great amounts of afternoon sun, you will find that kitchen herbs such as sage, thyme and rosemary are wind tolerant and rewarding plants to grow.

Fruit trees are also very tolerant of the wind. In fact, the wind acts as a pollinator for their flowers.

Among the most charming and inexpensive wind modifying barriers which can be used anywhere in the country or city are rows of mammoth sunflowers. Sunflowers share their bounty of seeds with birds and people alike, making them a delicious, edible windbreak for all.

How to Filter the Sun and Cool the Air When It's *Too* Hot

Although vegetables love and cannot, in fact, live without the sun, they can also get too much of a good thing. A key point to remember is that a combination of heat and moist air is very different from a combination of heat and a dry breeze. When the sun burns overhead and it's dry, the two best ways to protect your vegetables from sunburn are to provide some sort of filtered overhead structure and to cool the air with moisture. If you live near the ocean, a stream, lake or river, you have observed how moisture drawn into the air cuts down solar heat and cools through evaporation. If your garden spot gets *too* hot, and your plants seem to wilt frequently, try some of these suggestions for creating a cooler climate by giving shade or moisture:

Overhead shade trees that are not too dense and not too close to the garden, and vines planted on some sort of special structure, allow air circulation while providing relief from the heat. For example, pole beans can be planted on the west side of the garden to screen the hot afternoon sun.

Plant lettuce or other crops that bolt in the heat under the dappled shade cast by trees and shrubs.

Choose the heat-loving vegetables for the hottest spot in the garden—okra, eggplant, melons and lima beans all need lots of heat to grow best.

Overhead lattice or snow fencing will shield and shade crops from the hot sun in places where there are no trees.

Also for these treeless spots, plant tall-growing sun lovers like corn. In hot weather let them provide the filtered shade for nearby lettuce and cabbage, which prefer cooler growing conditions.

In hot climates, planting vegetables in containers near a swimming pool or a running stream will provide them with some cooling by evaporation.

Try planting on the north, or shadier side of your property in a hot climate. A northern exposure is a good place for growing mint, broccoli or boysenberry bushes.

Since heat and light bounce off bare walls, try covering a wall near the garden with a vine crop, like spaghetti squash or cucumbers. Supported on a trellis against this kind of wall, cucumber and squash vines will reward you with their cool green foliage, followed with bright yellow flowers and then fruit. Note that as young squashes mature you will need to devise slings to support them, or their weight will snap the stems before the fruit is ripe.

Watering in places open to the hot sun, like rooftops, is a must-do daily chore for cooling the air and your vegetable plants. But water in the early morning or evening to revive them. Watering in the noonday heat is not as effective, since the sun is at its strongest and the water evaporates too quickly.

Frequent hosing down of the flooring of a roof, terrace or concrete patio helps to cool the atmosphere. Overhead misting can also help cool the air around your plants.

Mulch everything in sight. It's the best protection for keeping roots and soil cool, where plants need it most. When you put your wrists under cold water or dangle your feet in a cool running brook on a hot day, you lower your body temperature enough to stay comfortable. That's what plant roots want, too.

Pollution: How Big a Problem Is It?

When he was asked by the host mayor of Denver what he thought of the crisp, clean air of that Colorado city, ex-mayor John V.

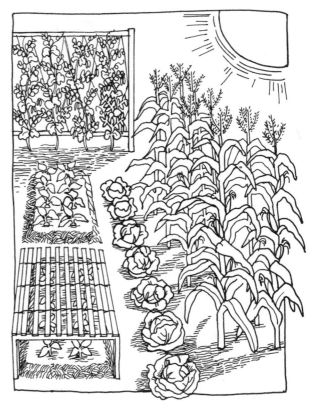

Three ways to filter the sun when it's too hot (clockwise from right): plant sun-loving corn on the north side of the garden to create some shade for crops like cabbage, which prefer cooler conditions; cover a raised bed full of new transplants with snow fencing to provide dappled shade until they adapt to the outdoor environment; plant climbing peas on the west side of the garden to give relief from the hot afternoon sun.

Lindsay of New York gallantly defended the reputation of his own hometown by retorting, "I guess it's nice, but I just don't trust air I can't see." However witty the answer, pollution is no laughing matter. Gardeners are rightly concerned when they question whether contaminants can reach them through the vegetables they grow and eat. In truth, all types of pollution are the negative by-products of what is called "progress." A mobile society pays its dues from exhaust emissions, soot, smoke, dust and the careless, thoughtless villains of industry who have buried toxic wastes, and who have created the unseen, creeping consequences of America's "Love Canals."

And none of us is immune to pollution problems. The farmer in the open countryside may suffer from contaminants that seep into the ground water from runoff of the chemical fertilizers and insecticides he sprays on his fields. Suburban and city gardeners, in turn, have to contend with automobile exhaust wastes and other airborne particulates, as well as contaminated soil.

As home gardeners, as well as private citizens, we do not have to give up our gardens. But what we must do is develop an awareness of our garden environment, plus a combative spirit and a knowledge of the precautions we can take if we garden in an "iffy" environment. Just heed the following precautions before starting any new garden:

Know what is in your soil. Have it tested by sending a sample to your local USDA county extension agent.

When locating your garden site, keep it away from a heavily trafficked road to avoid pollution from car exhaust. These pollutants do diminish with the distance from the road.

Start a compost heap to build up soil fertility. Good, rich organic soil that is constantly improving dilutes pollutants that could be present.

Do not add sewage sludge from urban areas; it may contain heavy metal contaminants. Also, don't use clippings from lawns treated with weedkillers.

Even though pesticides aren't used in your garden, wash all vegetables thoroughly, particularly leafy greens.

Cabbage, lettuce, broccoli, and cauliflower are protected by outer leaves which are discarded. Corn kernels are protected by husks, peas and some beans by pods. All are good choices for vegetable gardens where there may be airborne pollution.

Fruiting vegetables, such as tomatoes and eggplant, usually escape soil contamination since they are sheltered by leaves. So are the fast-growing edible pod peas. All root crops should be washed and peeled.

Don't spread rock salt around icy walks and driveways in winter. The dissolved salt seeps into the ground and can pollute growing areas.

Do choose a substitute, such as sand, ashes or kitty litter, and keep a few buckets handy to de-ice walks, steps and driveways safely. Litter and sand actually improve the soil texture by aiding drainage and aeration.

Never take soil or leaves from the sides of busy roads to bring home and use in a garden or container or compost pile.

Rooftop gardeners should replace the top 3 inches of soil every other year to eliminate any build-up of soot and other city pollutants that inevitably accumulate.

The hose is your friend. Frequent showers, when nature does not perform, help wash away damaging grime.

Voice your concern long and loud. Become active in supporting those who are working to save our environment. Help stop pollution before it stops our gardening.

Choosing Your Garden Site

When zeroing in on your actual choices for potential garden spaces, the primary guide to keep in mind is that the best space receives 6 to 8 hours of sun a day. Most vegetables need at least a half day of sun to flourish. Without it, they will grow slowly and become puny specimens. They will look spindly and sparse, and eventually the leaves will yellow, then drop off and die. If your climate is foggy, cloudy, or in constant smog, you will need more like 8 to 10 hours of direct sunlight daily. However, don't despair if you don't have this much sun. There are a slew of vegetables such as lettuce and cabbage, and herbs like parsley and chives, that do nicely on 4 hours of sun a day. If your garden is partially shaded, careful placement of your plants is essential for success. Here are some basic rules of thumb:

☼ **Full Sun:** Direct sun from morning till dusk, or at least 8 hours a day, most likely facing south or southwest. Plant the flowering and fruiting vegetables such as tomatoes, peppers and eggplant in this part of the garden.

☽ **Part Sun:** Four to 6 hours of direct sun, or partial sun with some protective covering such as tree leaves or latticing in very hot climates. Usually an eastern exposure which catches morning sun, or western with afternoon sun. Root vegetables and leafy greens such as radishes, beets, spinach and lettuce will do very well here.

⊜ **Shade:** No direct sunlight, or possibly just a bit in the early morning hours. The exposure here is a northern one, but what you can grow here depends upon whether that northern exposure is in California or New Hampshire. In California, I met a woman called Granny Green Thumb who grows boysenberries along the shady north side of her house. In New York I have a thriving mint patch in a shady corner. You might try capturing reflective light, as described earlier in this chapter. If all else fails, this is a good place to put the compost pile!

The direction your garden site faces doesn't always determine the amount of light you receive. A southern exposure doesn't mean much in the city when buildings to the south of you block the sun. And a northern exposure doesn't mean you can't garden, provided you do have open sky or bright reflected light. Remember, too, that the summer sun is higher in the sky and the days are longer; therefore, there will be more overall light than at other times of the year. Total available sunlight is measured in terms of the length of the exposure. A longer or shorter day can influence the growth patterns of some plants even more than temperature does.

Other Considerations

When you select your planting spaces, make sure that a nearby tree doesn't become an unseen enemy. Tree roots can extend under the soil to the garden area and compete for moisture and plant food. If you do anticipate this problem, you will need to compensate with additional food and water to keep both your vegetables and trees happy, and select shallow-rooted, shade-tolerant vegetables such as lettuce if you plant in containers or pockets under a tree. The lay of the land is another matter to which you should give some thought. Slopes affect surface drainage. Flat or sunken spots get bogged down in heavy rains and may collect frost, too. A simple drainage test, if you have any doubts, can be done as follows in suspect places. Dig a few holes 18 inches deep. Fill them with water and allow them to drain. Then refill a second time. If the holes have not completely drained after 12 hours, the soil needs some care before planting. To improve drainage, add lots of organic matter. You can work in some builder's sand, too (don't use beach sand, though, it's too salty).

If you are a sky gardener, you may have a few additional points to think about.

Keep in mind that a cubic foot of soil weighs roughly 25 pounds and that most balconies are built to bear a maximum of 55 pounds per square foot.

To avoid any undue stress, place large containers against load-bearing walls, since most rooftops were not designed to bear the heavy loads an elaborate garden may impose. If you have ambitious plans it is best to consult a structural engineer or an architect who can suggest ways to distribute the weight so it doesn't exceed safety limits.

To lighten the weight load, both for carrying soil to its site, and to prevent detaching the balcony from the building or adding unnecessary stress to the weight-bearing areas (to say nothing of mobility) try using a lightweight mixture in your containers.

The easiest way to lighten soil and improve the texture of a potting mix for container plants is to add perlite, an expanded volcanic material, or vermiculite, which is puffed mica, plus peat moss to your topsoil. (See page 165 for some tips on lightening soil mixes.)

Another safety consideration is roof parapets. By law, penthouses are required to have 45-inch-high safety walls. If yours does not, it is smart to install them before any accident occurs. High winds and flowerpots are a lethal combination without protective walls.

Make sure, if you live in rented quarters, that the rooftop is yours to exploit. The rooftop always belongs to the landlord and his permission, in writing, should be extracted before you plant your flag.

There are a few simple things to remember when planning a rooftop garden that most people forget. Somehow, it's always the most obvious matters that we overlook.

How do you get onto the roof? Remember, everything for your garden has to go up the same way you do. Nurseries will usually deliver free of charge to houses with elevators. If there are stairs to walk, there is an extra charge.

Also, measure your building's elevator if you plan to buy tall fruit trees. Sometimes the only roof access is a hatch at the top of a fire ladder; if that is the case, you'll probably have to lug everything up by yourself.

There is sometimes an additional problem in urban areas—pilfering and vandalism. According to the type and location of your garden, you may encounter this nuisance and have to deal with it. Gardens in more open public spaces may be a temptation to passersby. But being forewarned is being forearmed. Here are a few precautions you can take:

Camouflage what you are growing by creating a heavy visual barrier that will conceal the interior—such as a border of tall flowers or berry bushes with thorns.

Interested neighbors, particularly children, who are outdoors a great deal will take pride in your efforts if they are involved in some way. You might give an occasional gift of a squash or tomato to your junior "watchdogs."

If stealing becomes a real problem, buy a sign with a picture of a snarling German Shepherd, which reads CAUTION: Attack Dog on Premises. Signs warning of snakes are also said to be effective.

On rare occasions pranksters may uproot or smash growing vegetables. But a psychological barrier like a sign is sometimes more effective than a spiked iron fence or barbed wire.

The hows and whys of growth and life cycles remain mysteries of the universe. Having a garden is a way to experience the magic of the continual process of birth, growth, death and rebirth, and it is an experience that should not be missed for any reason.

Like all of life a garden has its obstacles and unexpected problems. But with problems also come the joys and challenges of finding the solutions. Having a garden is a pleasure that all of us should experience whatever obstacles we need to overcome before we start our gardens. The rewards are worth the effort.

Finding New Growing Space— Options for Earth Gardeners

No one says that if it is your preference, and you have the time and space as well as the inclination, that you should not have a single large, conventional row garden behind your house. But this traditional manner of gardening requires a season-long commitment to hard work—which is fine as long as you have the time and enough energy and ambition stored up from the winter. Somehow, though, when the July heat and weeds and summer vacations begin to take their toll, that big garden gets to be too much work, and many people become vegetable garden dropouts.

Newer small-garden techniques make it possible, in a minimum amount of space, to get all the hard work over with at the outset. A convenient, walk-around garden that is designed to allow you to do routine garden work in odd moments of spare time can enable you to fit a garden into your busy work-a-day life. The methods that I'll be discussing in the pages that follow can be used either individually or in combination with one another—whichever makes the best and most productive use of any bits of idle space available to you. In this chapter and the next one, we will be exploring the possibilities of five basic alternatives or adjuncts to the large row garden.

Raised Beds: Generally associated with the "intensive method" of producing big yields in small spaces, raised beds are also a blessing in gardens where drainage is poor. They are sometimes used in conjunction with bottomless boxes.

Bottomless Boxes: A modification of the intensive method, these structures are sometimes used to make a garden on top of a hard surface (such as a rooftop or paved patio) and are also used to contain the sides of raised garden beds. Bottomless boxes can follow any shape.

Freeform Beds and Spot Pockets: There are many alternatives to a manicured lawn or a large row garden. When your soil is enriched with organic materials, you can employ intensive methods of gardening in an array of shapes, such as curves, freeform shapes, wide rows, small spot pockets or larger circular planting spaces. Fitting these small gardens in odd corners of your yard or close by your kitchen door makes for greater economy of effort than more traditional gardening plots.

Food among the Flowers: Vegetables and herbs can be tucked into the landscape among the ornamentals to create an edible "vegescape."

Containers of All Kinds: They can be used anywhere by themselves or in combination with any of these other options. We'll discuss container gardening in the next chapter.

Raised Beds and Bottomless Boxes

The idea of growing beds was originally conceived on farms where land was poorly drained. Farmers learned to plow furrows between the rows of crops to improve drainage, which left the crops growing on raised ground. If raised growing areas hadn't been one of the oldest ideas in gardening history, if they hadn't been used with some variation in ancient China, during the days of the Roman Empire, in old Babylon and all through the ages in various European countries, the gardeners of today would probably have invented raised beds out of necessity. The raised bed adapts perfectly to today's need for small, highly productive gardens.

Today, raised beds have become practically synonymous with a precisely detailed organic technique of gardening that is known by the rather cumbersome name of "The Bio-Dynamic/French Intensive Method." Sometimes it is simply called "The Method" and some gardeners know it as "The Chinese Method," which is actually a variation on the same basic theme. The idea behind intensive, raised-bed gardening is to get three to four times more produce from the amount of space that normally would be used for a traditional row garden. The increased yields are obtained by spacing plants very close together in deeply cultivated, organically enriched soil. It is work to prepare raised beds for the first time, but once constructed, the beds mean a lot less work in caring for the garden. Permanent pathways are established between the beds and, because you never step on the beds and compact the soil, heavy digging and deep tilling is no longer needed each year.

"The Method" relies on basic organic principles that were introduced to this country by J. I. Rodale in the early 1940s and developed into a growing system in 1966 by the late Alan Chadwick, a British horticulturist working at the University of California at Santa Cruz. The basic elements are as follows:

Deep or "double" digging. This is the hardest work involved in intensive gardening. The soil is loosened to a depth of 24 inches and improved with large amounts of compost or manure. (See Chapter 9 for details.)

Making of raised beds. These raised areas occur naturally after the soil in the bed areas is loosened and large quantities of organic matter are added. The beds are

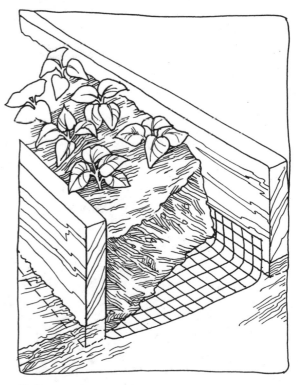

To keep moles out of your carrots and beets, excavate the bed where you want to grow root crops to a depth of 18 to 24 inches, put down a layer of wire mesh and replace the soil before planting.

narrow enough so the gardener can tend the vegetables from both sides without standing on the loose, friable soil. This loose soil allows plant roots to reach deep down for nutrients and moisture.

Close planting replaces conventional, widely spaced rows. In addition to allowing more plants in a given space, weeds have little room to grow and the overlapping leaves of the closely spaced plants shade and cool the bare soil so less watering is required.

Intercropping plants. Intercropping encompasses several different ways of accommodating growing plants together to take advantage of small spaces. A knowledge of the plants' growth habits, nutrient and cultural needs is necessary to intercrop successfully. You can, for example, intercrop plants with different maturation times; deep- and shallow-rooted plants; sun lov-

ers with lower-growing, shade-tolerant plants; and different kinds of plants that have similar nutrient needs.

Succession planting. These repeated sowings of vegetables keep the harvest coming more continuously. The idea is to plant a new crop as soon as the previous one is harvested, so that the soil never lies idle during the growing season.

Strict intensive gardeners prepare their raised beds so that the sides are exposed to the air and slope gently down to form unrestrained, moundlike shapes. But other gardeners prefer to confine the beds with some sort of enclosure to get neater and more varied shapes. These enclosures are bottomless boxes.

Bottomless boxes can be considered either as frames for raised beds, or as bottomless containers placed on a hard surface to

There are lots of ways to plant raised beds. For example, you can plant in rows, left, or in blocks, right, or with trellises installed to support climbing plants, page 29.

hold soil. You can design them in any shape or size you like and plunk them down wherever there is enough sun for growing vegetables. You can also use them in an area where you can modify a microclimate to capitalize on previously unused garden space.

Vegetables are wonderfully adaptable and will grow happily in any geometrically shaped space: long rectangles, squares, triangles or circles. These shapes, used alone or in combination, can extend the garden or elevate it. They can create a beautiful, orderly garden that's too lovely to be hidden, a garden that sits proudly in front of the house. In Chapter 4 I'll show you an easy way to design and combine shapes.

Advantages of Raised Beds and Bottomless Boxes

There are many advantages to raised beds and bottomless boxes. Consider these:

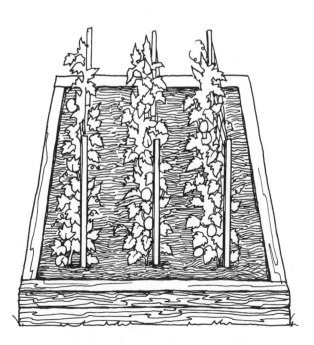

Good garden habits are encouraged because the gardener has a sense of being able to control a concentrated area.

The soil in each box or bed can be mixed to meet the special requirements of certain vegetables that are light, medium or heavy feeders.

Raised beds, contained or not, offer an extra bonus in the spring. The soil warms and dries out earlier in the season, meaning that you can plant earlier in raised beds than in ground level gardens. Just remember to keep them well-mulched during summer dry spells.

Protection from nibbling wildlife is easier to manage. You can enclose smaller areas individually rather than building a big, expensive fence to surround a whole huge garden. If gophers or moles are a problem, for example, you can put wire mesh on the bottom and up the sides of the bed before filling it with soil, so they can't find an opening to squeeze through (see illustration on page 27). It would be nearly impossible to put wire mesh under an entire 20 by 30-foot garden!

Garden beds can be measured exactly, so it's easier to target the amounts of fertilizers and water. You won't waste as much.

Making exact measurements of the beds and numbering each one allows you to keep easier records and notes of your experiments. Crops can also be rotated more easily through a system of numbered beds.

Paths between beds can be covered with wood chips or pebbles to keep your feet dry and free of mud when you work in the garden.

Because your soil is not compacted by being walked on, you won't need a tiller or other heavy machinery. You can do all your gar-

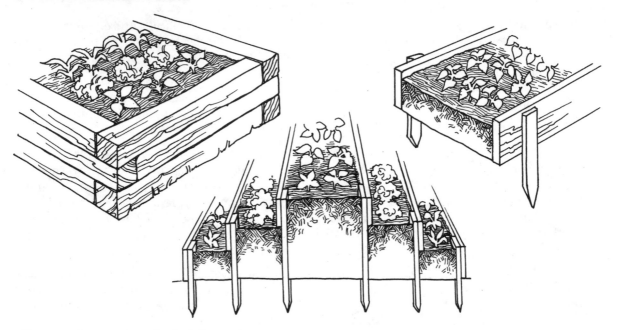

Here are three options for building raised beds contained with wood sides (left to right): lay boards horizontally on top of one another with corners interlocking; make a multi-level bed to accommodate plants on several levels; hold the boards in place with simple wood stakes driven into the ground.

den work from the perimeters of the beds, with long- or short-handled hand tools.

Creating a special microclimate within each confined area is simple—you can use collapsible, temporary structures to filter intense sun or reflect additional light or protect vegetables from the wind.

Removable plastic structures can be used as little greenhouses to speed germination during chilly weather. The sides of bottomless boxes serve as supports to which a sheet of plastic is easily stapled.

Bottomless boxes make it easier to overcome obstacles of the terrain. You can use the boxes to create a terrace garden on the side of a hill, or fill them with topsoil and rich compost in a yard where the soil is compacted or needs improvement. They also work well where the soil is very sandy.

You can create a garden in an "ungarden-able" spot, like a pavement or rooftop, with a bottomless frame to hold soil.

The bold good looks of contained geometric shapes add interest to the landscape on a front lawn, along the side of a house, or anywhere.

Creating changes in level or height of the beds, where none naturally exists, adds an important design and scale element.

With bottomless boxes, your garden design is flexible. It's easy to incorporate additional beds into the original design for a larger garden.

The walls of bottomless boxes deflect pets, children, garden carts, and hoses from crushing or trampling vegetables.

When the sides of the raised beds are reinforced by boxes you will not have to reshape your raised beds every year. Heavy rains will not erode them.

The boxes can be made of any sturdy material and with a broad top edge can double as benches—you can sit while you plant, cultivate or weed. It's not necessary to kneel—unless you prefer to—and it's a great help to people with bad backs.

Raised beds can be designed at wheelchair height or boxes can be stacked to make waist-high planters.

Best of all, because of the flexibility of their sizes and shapes, bottomless boxes are adaptable to every garden location—rooftop, balcony, front yard or entry, backyard or patio.

How to Build
Contained Bottomless Boxes

Here are some pointers on designing and building your bottomless boxes:

Plan the design of your whole garden first, if you intend to use more than one or two boxes. But however many boxes you expect to have, start only one or two at a time, so you're not overwhelmed by a major undertaking.

Box frames can be any length and the height can range anywhere from 4 to 36 inches. If the box is sitting on a hard surface, it needs to be higher. If it sits on soil prepared to a depth of 24 inches, it can be lower and still allow enough space for roots to grow.

Whether your boxes are square, rectangular, triangular or circular, they should be small enough so that you can reach into the center from all sides. The average person's reach is 30 inches, so 5 feet should be the maximum width of any box.

Trace the shape of your box-to-be on the ground before you build it. Use white agricultural lime in a funnel to draw the shape on the ground. That way you'll be sure the box will fit the space, and you can

determine whether the shape you've chosen will work well in the surroundings.

The width of the paths between the beds should provide enough room for you to kneel comfortably outside the boxes to work in the gardens. The paths should also be able to accommodate a wheelbarrow if you plan to use one.

Choosing Construction Materials

Here is a chance to assert your individuality by selecting a construction material that will give your contained raised beds a very personal style. Don't be afraid to create your own unique combination of materials and design. You can achieve a rustic look, a tailored formal arrangement, or the charming informal look of recycled materials.

Don't write off recycled materials as "junk." They can be quite attractive, and they are terrific money savers. There are lots of creative ways to use materials like broken concrete paving, used railroad ties (make sure they are old so they no longer bleed creosote, which is toxic to plants), old telephone poles, old barn beams (about 8 by 8 inches), large rocks, used bricks and pressure-treated timber ends to build bottomless boxes and retaining walls for garden beds.

New materials to choose from include concrete blocks, new bricks, new railroad ties, pressure-treated lumber* or pine planks treated with copper naphthenate. If you choose wood for your boxes, there are some things you should consider. Wood is easier to use than brick, but brick is more permanent than wood, since brick must be tied together

---

*Pentachlorophenyl is sometimes used on pressure-treated lumber—if you use pressure-treated lumber, place a sheet of plastic between wood and soil surface, since the material is somewhat toxic to plants. Do the same for new railroad ties that are treated with creosote, which is another substance toxic to plants. Copper or zinc naphthenate is a wood preservative that's not harmful to plants.

and anchored with mortar. Building a retaining wall of brick is a more costly and elaborate project. (For information on how to build a brick wall, see *Plan and Make Your Own Fences and Gates, Walkways, Walls, and Drives* by E. Annie Proulx; Rodale, 1983.)

Constructing the Boxes

It's not a difficult task to build bottom-less boxes. What you are really doing is just constructing a low wall around four sides of a raised bed to retain the earth. Sometimes, when the bed is against the side of a house, fence or garage, it will only require three sides. When you construct a three-sided box, just consider these few tips:

Damp soil piled up against a surface will eventually cause the surface to rot or mildew.

Allow for air space of about 3 inches between the garden bed and the wall or fence, and stick a few pieces of pressure-treated plywood or heavy polyethylene sheeting between wall and garden for protection. Make sure the sheeting extends several inches underground.

If the box is to be placed against a house, a few coats of protective asphalt waterproofing compound on the wall that will be next to the garden is also helpful.

The box sides must be strong enough to withstand the weight of the soil which presses up against them.

Remember that wood is easier to dismantle than brick if you should move.

Wood will decay in time (but what doesn't?). Try to use lumber that is naturally rot resistant (such as cedar or redwood) or stain it with Cuprinol, not creosote which can be damaging to plant life. You can also use pressure-treated lumber.

Wood should be a minimum of 2 inches thick (when laid horizontally) to prevent buckling.

If the frame is only 1 board-width high (4 inches) it can rest directly on the ground. If the box is more than one board high, it will need interior structural support. Deeper frames should have corner and side posts (see illustration on page 30).

You can place bracing stakes behind the wall boards in the inside, or on the outside, as you prefer. But the braces are stronger

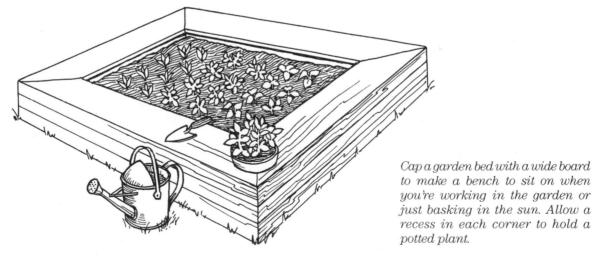

Cap a garden bed with a wide board to make a bench to sit on when you're working in the garden or just basking in the sun. Allow a recess in each corner to hold a potted plant.

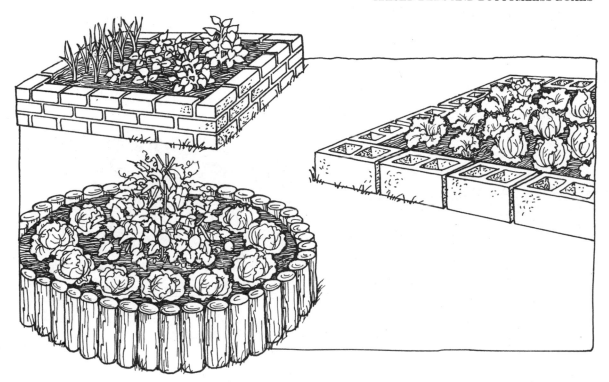

Just a few of the many ideas for retaining raised beds with different kinds of building materials: small circular post ends left over from a terracing project; bricks, cinderblocks. For more growing space, fill the holes in the cinderblocks with soil and plant herbs in them.

when used outside. Use 2 by 4-inch stakes with galvanized steel nails that won't rust out. Drive the stakes 1 foot into the ground.

For a wall 18 inches high, space the stakes 4 feet apart for support. A higher wall will require stakes 3 feet apart. Also, set the bottom board 2 inches into the ground for extra strength.

Capping the tops of the retaining walls allows you to sit down to do gardening chores. Use a 1 by 6-inch plank nailed flat to the top edge.

Another way to make a frame is to use short boards, which are available in 2 by 2, 2 by 3, or 2 by 4 planks. Set the boards on end vertically, edge to edge and drive them at

least 1 foot into the ground. This type of box will use up more lumber; however, it's a great way to frame circular beds. Short pieces of logs can also be used in this manner.

Railroad ties are an excellent material to use for garden beds and they are very popular. Although railroad ties make an extremely strong wall, they are quite heavy to move around. A typical size tie is 6 by 8 inches and 8 feet long.

Pressure-treated timbers can be used more easily since they are smaller and more lightweight. They are usually 4 by 4 inches and are sold in several lengths.

When working with pressure-treated lumber or railroad ties, set the bottom tie into the ground to half its depth to make a firm foundation. Then lay the others on top, interlocking them at the corners of the bed. As you build the wall, use 12-inch spikes to hold the ties together so they don't slip off.

Making Paths

Use whatever is available and attractive for the paths between your beds. One thing I've found is that black plastic sheeting laid

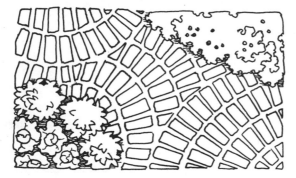

Bricks laid in patterns on a layer of sand make beautiful, durable paths in a garden.

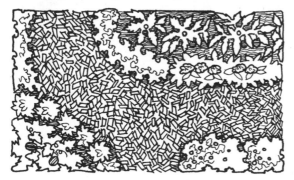

For a weed-free path, lay down sheets of black plastic and cover with bark chips or straw

down first smothers the weeds and keeps them from growing through your path. The materials listed here add attractive textural contrast and do not need to be joined or grouted in any way. Most of them are paving materials which are easy to use; all you have to do is just pour them on. Consider making paths with bark chips, gravel or stones, marble

chips, sawdust, straw, small flat rocks, pine needles, or grass clippings. You can place old bricks in a pattern on top of a layer of sand for a very attractive and permanent path (see illustration), or you can lay down old wood planks.

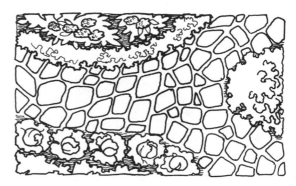

If you live where the ground is rocky, pave your paths with flat stones.

Freeform Beds and Spot-Pocket Gardens

We Americans love our lawns. But what gardener hasn't felt enslaved to that expanse of useless green grass, at least once in a while? If you want to bind yourself to a life of unrewarding, unceasing manual labor, if you want to engage in a horticultural battle that requires more machinery and hand tools than your dentist uses, then grow grass.

However, with increased energy costs in recent years, along with some shifts in American priorities, the time has come to question the worth of a manicured lawn, and many gardeners have already done so. Bernie Katz in Denver is one of them (read his story on page 40). This is not to say that all mowed turf should be abolished (unless like Granny Green Thumb, on page 44, you wish to do so). But parts of your lawn can be carved out and converted into most appealing and decorative herb and/or vegetable gardens. If you rent a house and decide to move, it's a simple procedure to convert the garden back to a lawn with patches of sod or grass seed. And if you build them right, trellises and other plant supports can be collapsed and taken along with you. It just seems wasteful and silly to grow only grass when for the same expenditure of effort, energy and money, you can produce something to eat right at your front doorstep. Even if you have a large garden or truck patch, the convenience of having a small garden of kitchen herbs or salad greens close by the house can save many a weary footstep during dinner preparations.

If you have always had a conventional row garden in the backyard, the only obstacle you need to overcome is the psychological barrier to get vegetables out into the open, right up front, where they can be admired and easily attended to. A vegetable garden *can* be attractive, and you'll have the double pleasure of all that fresh food to eat. Splitting up the garden area into more than one plot can still give you the same amount of growing space as that one large garden out back, but smaller spaces encourage experimentation and you can more easily cast a watchful eye on the progress of a new or exotic vegetable or herb variety. You may encounter some initial objections from less daring neighbors who will disapprove of your breaking with the traditional front garden of ornamental shrubs, flowers and grass. But I say just assert your individuality and ingenuity. Chances are that when your neighbors see how attractive a well-thought-out vegetable garden can look in the midst of a front lawn, they will follow suit.

Things to Consider

The key to such a garden, of course, is very careful design, plus careful selection of plants. The creation of these freeform and pocket gardens is completely possible (and even fun) when you forget about traditional row planting and spacing, and practice some of the intensive gardening techniques. Intensively planted pocket gardens in handsome shapes will keep your front or side lawn looking beautiful while producing constantly. Here is some general advice to follow:

To design an informally curved bed, stretch a length of hose or rope on the ground to give you the ideal sweep and curve you wish, then proceed to dig within this shape.

Plant and keep extra seedlings in a flat to have them ready when needed for succession plantings, so you never leave a "hole" when a beet or turnip is pulled or a lettuce plant is cut.

Replace harvested crops either with these seedlings or with edible flowers such as nasturtiums. Chapter 5, on planning what to plant in small gardens, discusses the techniques for planning intercroppings and successions, and the timing necessary to enable you to put them into practice easily.

Discard the advice on the back of the seed packet about seed spacing. Planting in wide rows or bands, "block" planting or sowing seeds in triangular or circular modules all use small areas more efficiently than single rows.

When gardening in more than one area, you have the option of choosing several "best" locations for the specific needs of each vegetable: you can group the heat lovers together or find some partial shade that the leafy greens love.

Rotating your crops is simple: just move what you grow from patch to patch.

Spot Pockets

Growing a spot-pocket garden, simply put, means placing vegetables and herbs wherever there is a small pocket of soil and sunshine, simultaneously making use of the principles of companion planting and taking advantage

Who says a garden has to be rectangular? In this front yard, a circular garden holds strawberries, carrots and a blueberry bush in a tub; a freeform bed along the sidewalk has leaf lettuce, cauliflower and nasturtiums; and a semicircular bed in front of the house contains tomatoes, bush beans and herbs.

of microclimates. This is indeed limited-space gardening. For the newcomer who wants to dip his or her toe before taking the plunge, and for whom vegetable gardening is a new adventure, spot pockets are an excellent introduction to the techniques of gardening. Trying your hand at growing small pockets of herbs and vegetables in among the existing flowers and ornamental shrubs will create an awareness of the basic requirements and growing habits of edible plants. Starting out small will also guarantee you some measure of success. When you decide to expand your garden into more beds or containers or even an edible vegescape, you will have a good idea of the amount of time and work involved, and you'll be able to judge how much more you're ready to handle.

To repeat, the plan's the important thing. The only disadvantage, if you want to call it one, is that harvesting involves a bit more footwork. But you already knew that gardening is a sneaky way to exercise, didn't you? Here are some ways to discover and then plant spot-pocket gardens:

Study your landscape with specific crop choices in mind, reserving the spots that receive generous amounts of sun from spring through summer for peppers, eggplants and tomatoes, and locations that are sunny in spring and fall but shady in summer for leafy greens, cole crops, root vegetables and some herbs.

Forget the space hogs—those rambling, spreading crops like zucchini and mint that take loads of space. Choose vegetable varieties that are specially bred for small spaces; these are the same compact and midget varieties that also thrive in containers and are the greatest boon to small space gardeners. (See the chart, Vegetables for Containers and Small Spaces, in Chapter 6.)

Consider the surrounding plants in relation to the crop you plan to grow in a given location and try to select a vegetable with the same soil, sun and cultural needs. For example, shallots and okra will rot if they are overwatered, but melons are always thirsty. Eggplant loves full sun, and so do nasturtiums; therefore, a good combination for a spot pocket would be eggplant and nasturtiums.

Be aware of the compatibility of the pocket crop and its flowering buddy. If a certain ornamental plant is normally bedeviled by slugs for example, then lettuce, which slugs love, would be devoured overnight if you planted it in the same pocket.

Finally, you can experiment with companion plantings to your heart's content on a small scale. Spot pocket gardens offer the ideal conditions in which to match up herbs and flowers that have a beneficial effect on each other. For example, a tomato plant in a pocket garden can be surrounded with pots of marigolds, or beans with summer savory. Chapter 6, on planning your crops, will explain all about these plants that help each other.

Now that you know what to consider, where should you look to find the spaces? Anyplace. Anyplace where you would enjoy the surprising charm of a crinkly, crisp, emerald path of parsley next to a clump of butter-yellow daffodils; or a chaos of fiery nasturtiums cascading over the ruffled edge of a patch of fragile, ice-green leaf lettuce. Or, imagine the dark green crinkly leaves of young spinach wreathing tall, lavender blue spikes of iris; or the delicate tracery of rich green carrot tops and crimson-veined beet greens intermingled with the expectant faces of confetti-colored pansies. These are just some of the combinations to try. Container gardeners, please note; for if you have no pockets in the earth, you may contain the earth in a pocket that can go and grow anywhere, as we'll see in the next chapter.

Circle Gardening

If you'd like to try a garden in a shape that's more strictly defined than a freeform bed or pocket but that still is a change from the usual rectangular garden, consider a circle garden. The circle is a particularly pleasing shape for a small garden carved out of a lawn. Circle gardening techniques were originated in the 1950s by a horticulturist named Derald G. Langham, who was invited to Venezuela to work on plant genetics. He was seeking a way to maintain the purity of seed strains without having them get mixed up during heavy rains. Instead of using long rectangular beds, he adapted circular shapes to contain, yet isolate, one growing space from the other. Instead of planting in rows, he used the Chinese method of ridges and furrows.

Although a garden carved out of a lawn can be any shape, the use of the circle creates many other options (and can be used as a shape for container groupings as well as on a lawn). You may add to the overall size of a circle garden by increasing the number of circles. Or you may design just one very large circle, and divide the interior into interesting freeform patterns or wedges separated by paths (which would be necessary to reach all sides of the beds). A circle is the least traditional of garden shapes, but a circular shape has the potential to meet the requirements for small, found-space food gardens. In fact, when you think of a circle garden reduced in size, you will find it is the same shape as a half-barrel or other round container, which somehow we don't consider to be as radical a garden shape.

Circle gardens offer the advantages of good management for less labor. Here's a rundown of their major benefits:

A large circular garden is a visually attractive and psychologically enticing space. The gardener can stand in the middle, surrounded by his or her plants. Sensitive

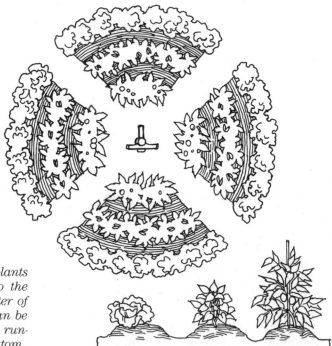

A circle garden can be planted with shorter plants along the outer edge and taller plants to the center. A revolving sprinkler is in the center of this garden, top. In dry climates, plants can be set on ridges with furrows between to catch run-off rainwater as shown in the side view, bottom.

gardeners may find themselves seduced by a feeling of intimacy with the plants, which may in turn lead them to tend the plants more lovingly. Thus, the circle garden becomes a magic circle of sorts.

Tall and short plants can grow together with the tallest ones in the center, grading down in height toward the outer edges of the circle.

A circle up to 39 inches in diameter can be tended from the outside, therefore no paths will be necessary.

Kitchen scraps and plant wastes can be dug into the central core of the growing circle and so provide on-the-spot compost.

Watering can be done in two ways. If the circle is small (39 inches across, or less), a hose bubbler can be laid in the center of the circle for ground watering with plants placed along the outside rim. If the circle is a large one, then an overhead revolving sprinkler with a Rain Bird head (which has an adjustable pulse) can be mounted on a central stand and will spray a full circle automatically.*

Preparing a circle garden is simple. Here's how to start:

Select a suitably sunny spot to make your circle. The goal is to prepare a saucerlike depression in the soil with a ridged mound 8 inches wide around the circle's perimeter.

To make the circle, tie a length of string half the desired diameter to a stake and plunk it into what will be the center of the proposed circle. Tie a narrow-necked bottle filled with agricultural lime, flour or sand to the other end of the string. Keeping the string taut, turn the bottle upside down and start to walk in a circular path, leaving a traced outline. (You can use a large funnel instead of a bottle if you like.)

Starting from the center stake, use a hoe and rake and draw soil from the center to form the outer ridge. The inside of the circle is now a saucer or basin about 4 to 6 inches below the original surface level.

If you wish to use a larger circle (6 feet 6 inches or more) then raise the central core into a mound, creating the Chinese ridge and furrow system in a concentric circle. You can plant in the central mound or hide your compost pile there.

If your circle is 8 feet across or larger, cut four paths dividing it into quarters, for easier access to the wedges that are formed within the circle.

It's fun for each member of a family of four to take his or her own garden wedge to care for; it encourages a gentle competitive spirit between family members who vie for the best patch. (For design details on expanding a circular garden, and making the circle work with other shapes in your garden landscape, see Chapter 4.)

When planning crops for your circle garden, a rule of thumb to use is that a 39-inch circle accommodates as many plants as a 10-foot row. The depth and spacing of plants will, of course, depend upon the kind of vegetables to be grown. A circle this size can support nine to ten pepper plants or four large tomato plants or six cabbages or seven cauliflower, or an herb garden or a small salad garden.

A circle twice that size (6 feet 6 inches) provides a very feasible way to grow corn in a small garden (corn normally requires lots of space). Twelve cornstalks, planted close together for better pollination and mutual support in strong winds can yield 24 ears of

---

*Several kinds of sprinklers are carried by A. M. Leonard and Mellinger's. See the list of tool suppliers at the end of Chapter 7 for addresses where you can write for catalogs.

Bernie Katz's garden is planted in curved rows that follow the shapes of the garden beds he designed to fill odd corners of his property.

Having It All, Grass, Flowers and Vegetables

Bernie Katz has carved a small curved garden bed out of part of his front lawn in Denver—and he's growing a tremendous amount of vegetables there. On the opposite side of the yard, there is another bed of the same shape in which he grows flowers. The two designs are balanced, compatible, and equally colorful and beautiful. The entire lawn is surrounded by a lovely wrought iron fence—and even that is used to support a crop of sugar snap peas. The vegetable rows are planted not in a straight line, but following the curves of the bed, which gives it additional charm to passers-by on a main street. Many people stopped to enjoy it as I did the day I happened to walk by.

Bernie manufactures chemicals for industry and dabbles in real estate. The old house behind the garden is one that he owns and recently converted to small condominiums. He lives in one of the apartments and does all the gardening by himself, although he generously shares his bounty with his tenants. When I asked him why he started his food garden, he replied that he gardens because he loves it. It's good exercise and he enjoys the fresh produce.

The garden, he said, is about 120 square feet. To enrich his soil he uses peat moss and sheep and cow manure that he trucks in from nearby farms. Bernie mulches his vegetables with recycled grass clippings from his lawn and he plants both seeds and seedlings. Lettuce grows under the oak tree, where he manages to harvest it all summer long without it bolting. He also tucks some herbs in among his flowers, "because they look beautiful together."

When I asked Bernie if he had any advice for his fellow gardeners, his dry sense of humor cropped up. "Hire somebody else to do it, it's damned hard work," he told me. But he obviously loves gardening or he wouldn't do it. I wondered if he suffered any theft problems since his garden was right by a main street. He answered, "Not since I spent $5,000 for this new iron fence. I figure that this year each head of lettuce should cost me only $200." Cost effective? Who knows, in ten years, $200 a head could be the going supermarket price.

corn.* Early catch crops of spinach, beets or lettuce can be planted in the same space before and after the corn harvest. That's a lot of food from only a 6½-foot circle.

Vegetables taste just as good and grow just as well in casually formed or circular spaces as they do when marshalled into rigid military formation, so try something different if you haven't yet done so.

Food among the Flowers

Combining edibles with ornamentals is another idea for self-sufficiency that's as modern as today. It takes the same amount of space, sunshine and fertilizers to produce a healthy vegetable plant as it does to grow a flower. The solution for a limited space is to make your vegetable garden and your flower garden the same—to grow food among your flowers in an edible vegescape.

Creating a vegescape or edible landscape is a step beyond tucking little pocket gardens of vegetables among your flowers. In a vegescape, the food *is* the flowers, as it were. It's a larger scale project but it merely requires a change in the thinking that only ornamental trees, shrubs, vines and flowers are decorative. You think flowers, but you plant food instead. Vegetables, herbs, fruiting vines, fruit trees and berry bushes can be quite decorative in their own right when you use them creatively. Here are some ideas for starting your own edible landscape:

Think of pretty flowering vines on a fence, but instead, plant dangling purple-podded beans, jade green sugar snap peas, yellow-flowering cucumbers, or a minivineyard bejeweled with clusters of blushing carmine and indigo grapes.

Think of tiny, starry white flowers with golden pinpoint eyes hanging in a basket

outside your dining room, but plant tiny *fraises des bois* (wild strawberries) and get the same white flowers along with thimble-sized perfumed, scarlet berries.

Think of sitting in a grove of blossoming trees, but plant dwarf fruit trees whose beautiful spring flowers will turn into luscious fruit. You will be able to enjoy their beauty twice.

Think of flowering hedges encircling your house, but make those hedges that will later reward you with ultramarine blueberries or ruby raspberries to make the pies and jams you dreamed of as a child.

Think of pleasing both your eye and your stomach. That's what vegescaping is all about.

Now, down to the nitty-gritty, and how you can go about creating this edible wonderland. First, forget the idea that garden success is measured solely by the volume of food produced. With vegescaping you can create a casual, natural, enjoyable setting that will produce food for the needs or tastes of a small family, but in moderate amounts with minimum care and maximum beauty. Remember that you are not running a roadside produce stand, but just want enough delicious vegetables, herbs and fruit, freshly picked at the point of perfection, for your family's delight. Your primary goal is *quality* rather than quantity. The real trick is to adapt the plants to their environment so they require less care, and to plant dual-purpose plants that are attractive in the landscape while they produce food.

Planning for Aesthetics and Nutrition

Here are some tips on planning your vegescape:

Create a vegescape in the same manner that you would create a landscape. Keep tall vegetables in the rear, then those with medium growth habits, followed by the lowest growing or creeping plants toward

*Midget corn varieties can be spaced more closely and thus produce a greater yield.

41

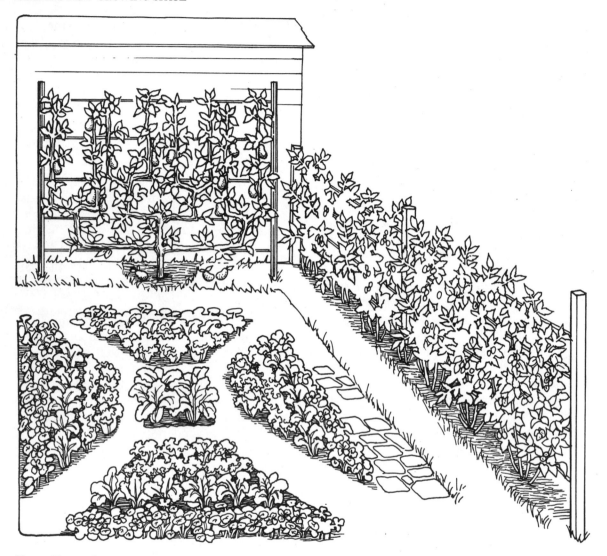

Vegetables replace ornamentals, creating a colorful, edible landscape in this backyard. A dwarf pear tree is espaliered next to the garage wall, the hedge on the right is formed by raspberry brambles, and the neat geometric garden holds handsome red-stemmed Ruby Swiss chard, two different kinds of leaf lettuce and a border of sunny marigolds.

the front, anticipating their height and spread. (You can get this information from seed and nursery catalogs that list plant dimensions at maturity.)

Note other growth habits besides height and spread, such as fruit and blossom color, and leaf texture—just as you do when planting flowers.

Plant deep-rooted crops next to shallow-rooted, spreading vegetables or creeping herbs. When the roots are harvested their "holes" are quickly covered.

Accent the landscape: A few vertical-growing points of interest are essential to good design. Vertical emphasis can be achieved with dwarf fruit trees or vertical structures that support climbing vegetables such as melons or tomatoes. Or you can really get creative and discover the surprise and charm of cucumbers or peas trained over a discarded beach umbrella frame, or a dead tree. Or let your vegetable vines clamber over and cover the stalks of giant sunflowers.

Fences and walls can support vine crops, heat-loving bushy plants such as eggplants and peppers, and fruit trees, which can be placed against a wall and espaliered by training and tying their lateral branches. If the wall is brick or stone, the fruit will also benefit from the heat absorbed and retained by the wall.

Berry bushes such as blueberries and brambles, such as blackberries or dewberries and raspberries, can be trained to form lovely hedges; grapes, too, can be pruned and trained in this manner.

When planting, allow access for maintenance chores and picking the crop.

Now, here are some suggestions for replacing ornamentals with edibles:

Foundation areas around a house are usually planted with the same uninteresting bushy evergreens. Why not plant a "cole hedge" instead? Start with tall Brussels sprouts in the rear—they look like miniature palm trees with tiny green cabbages growing up their stalks beneath a canopy of gray green leaves. In front of them, plant deep green curly kale, and in front of that a border of alternately planted red and green cabbages.

Create a feathery, ferny glade with carrots or with asparagus (after the spears are harvested the plants grow into delicate, soft lacy foliage). Intercrop bush beans or large-leaved bush zucchini, and have some sunny, colorful, round-leaved nasturtiums, for a salad, spill over around a border.

Don't give up your barbecue area if the neighbors complain. As a windbreak that will help control drifting smoke, plant in a U shape three rows of different varieties of corn—early, middle and late maturing, or plant giant sunflowers and snack on their seeds. You'll have an edible fence.

Perennial rhubarb's large, bold leaves can pass for showy, expensive tropical ornamentals. Surround them with strawberries and you have the makings of a perfect pie, growing together.

Grow borders of vegetables everywhere for definition, for a border does to a garden space what a ribbon does to a package: it dresses it up. Line walkways with Ruby chard or purple bush beans, or exquisitely flowering okra.

Substitute a few edible apple trees for ornamental crabapple trees.

Shade your front entryway as they do in Yugoslavia, with grapevines, or build a covered structure for them to twine on. I have a neighbor who had an outdoor lattice-enclosed shower covered with grapevines. He picks and washes the fruit and eats it while he's showering—a sybaritic pastime, if ever there was one.

Five or six different varieties of leaf lettuce with their various textures and shades of green can be grown together. Their forms, colors and contrasting shapes look as beautiful together as any flower bed. For example, you could combine several of the following varieties:

Ruby—light to deep green frilly leaves

Granny Green Thumb's No-Lawn Garden

"You'll know the house when you see it 'cause it's the only one on the street without a lawn," said Ruth Linter, who is better known as "Granny Green Thumb" to the readers of *Vista,* the Sunday Supplement to the Ventura County *Star Free Press* in California. Following her directions, we found Ruth and her husband Clarence standing among the cabbages and kumquats on what *should* have been a front lawn on a typical suburban tract house. But there wasn't a blade of grass in sight!

This diminutive, spunky lady calls herself "a casual, lazy but organic gardener" who is "always experimenting and trying new things." She is also

obviously not afraid to break with a few traditions that she finds impractical. "I don't believe in lawns," she says. "A lawn just can't do you that much good. It's silly to waste land, time and energy on grass if you don't have much space. It's just not ecologically correct." Granny Green Thumb, from the looks of her garden, is definitely not a space waster. Every inch of growing room is utilized on her property, and the garden wraps around all four sides of her house. Gardening is right in line with her personal views about "living a balanced life on all levels," and she believes that everyone should have a food garden. A trip to Holland in the 60s, she claims, inspired her to grow vegetables, fruit and flowers like the Dutch do, in small yards in front of their houses.

"The dirt we have here is called adobe," she said, "a kind of fine clay that needs lots and lots of humus to make it friable and able to hold moisture."

Even though Ruth claims to be a very casual gardener who works in her garden "whenever I have the time," the almost continuous growing season of this subtropical area of southern California's citrus belt allows her the choice to be casual. "Cool weather crops can go in from September to December and are ready two to three months later. Hot weather vegetable seedlings can go into the ground anywhere from March through June, depending on whether they are early or late varieties, and the harvest starts about July.

"We don't keep our garden full all the time, because our freezer usually is. We're just two people, you know, and we have plenty for two; with the fruits and berries there's more than enough. Do you know that if you have a place in the shade where nothing else will grow, you can try boysenberries?" Granny Green Thumb does. On the north side of the property, the house itself casts a shadow and that's where the boysenberries grow, supported on a wood and wire trellis which makes them easier to pick. Elsewhere in the yard, Concord and Thompson Seedless grapes climb a fence, and gooseberries flourish in a pot next to the sidewalk, with a supporting stake to keep them out of the way.

Besides the berries, Granny Green Thumb's "yard" is home to about 30 fruit trees. A loquat tree is espaliered against the south wall and seems to flourish in a 1-foot-wide strip of soil. The only other two full-sized trees are an avocado and a walnut tree. The rest of the trees are dwarf or semidwarf. Cherries, peaches, apricots, nectarines, persimmons, plums, lemons, mandarin oranges, kumquats, tangerines and figs all luxuriate in this coastal location, even here in the middle of the city.

There is an ornamental hedge of edible natal plums defining the front yard. Red currants, *feijo* (or pineapple guava) and a passion fruit vine are scattered in sunny spots. There is a Zaiger dwarf almond and a Beverly Hills apple, a variety that grows well in this area and which produces three crops a year for Ruth. There are three Nanking bush cherries, which "taste something like cranberries and make great jam" and a "fun tree," a Golden Delicious apple onto which three other varieties of apple have been grafted. On the side of the house where the ground slopes toward the driveway is a thriving strawberry patch terraced simply with a retaining wooden structure. Even the driveway is graced with a narrow border of herbs.

How does Granny grow this veritable fruit salad of a garden and this abundance of vegetables in such small space? Easy, she says. "We have access to aged, weed-free steer manure, mushroom compost and redwood compost with added nitrogen, besides our own continuous compost pile. We get lady bird beetles and praying mantises from the Rincon Vitova Insectary in Ventura. I use lots of Tanglefoot for ants and bugs on the fruit trees and we have three young hens that we let out when the occasion warrants to eat snails in our garden. You have to remember, the experts don't know it all. If it works for you, do it. If it grows, that's all I care about. It's the nature of the plant that it *wants* to grow, you don't grow it. You just help it along, in your own way, and in harmony with the good earth."

Every inch of Granny Green Thumb's lot is devoted to growing food. In the photo on page 44, Granny stands next to a loquat tree that thrives in a 1-foot-wide strip of soil. The photo above is a view of the front "yard" planted with vegetables, fruits and herbs.

Double-Duty Landscape Plants

This chart presents a selection of suitable edibles based on their uses in the landscape. P indicates perennials; V indicates plants that can be grown vertically for height, or trained against a wall. Many of the plants (like leaf lettuce) are available in a variety of foliage shapes and fruit color.

Ground Covers and Low Border Plants

Beets
Midget Cabbages
Carrots
Cauliflower
Red Chicory
Cranberries P
Leaf Lettuce, all kinds
Peanuts
Radishes
Rucola
Sorrel P
Spinach
Strawberries (wild and domestic) P
Turnips

Edible Flowers

Carnations
Chive Flowers
Daylilies P
Marigolds
Mustard Green Flowers
Nasturtiums
Pansies
Roses P
Squash Blossoms
Sunflowers (seeds) V
Violets

Herbs

Basil (green and opal)
Borage
Camomile
Chives P
Lovage
Marjoram
Mint P *
Oregano P
Parsley
Rosemary P †
Sage P †
Tarragon P
Thyme P

Spiky Growth

Garlic ‡
Leeks
Onions ‡

Vines

Pole Beans V
Cucumbers V
Grapes V, P
Melons V
Squash V
Sugar Snap Peas V
Tomatoes V

Bushy Shrubs

Artichokes
Asparagus P

Bush Beans
Brussels Sprouts
Cabbage (red and green)
Swiss Chard (both red and white stemmed)
Collard Greens
Dill
Eggplant (purple and white)
Horseradish P
Kale
Mustard Greens
Okra
Peppers (yellow, red, green, both hot and sweet)
Rhubarb P
Squash (bush type)

Hedges

Blackberries P ‡
Blueberries P
Corn V
Currants (red and black)
Gooseberries P §
Raspberries P §
Rose Hips P §

Fruit Trees

Most dwarf specimens of fruit and nut trees (most P, V)

*Mint is best confined to a container.
†Rosemary and sage grow into shrubs in warm climates.
‡Although mature onion and garlic foliage dies before the crop matures, the plants also produce beautiful purple flowers. Grow a few for their flowers. Green onions can be pulled before they're fully mature, while the tops are still green.
§Thorny bushes can define and fence in an area, since they are not easily penetrated.

highlighted with dark red and purple

Oak Leaf—medium green, oak-shaped leaves

Black-Seeded Simpson—pale yellow green leaves

Green Ice—frilled, light green foliage

Bibb—rosettes of lush green oval leaves

Romaine—upright, torpedo-shaped heads shaded light to dark green

As you can see, harvesting the landscape and thinking of edibles as flowers can become an absorbing, irresistible challenge for both the novice and sophisticated gardener. There is only one major hazard—you may create a picture that's much too pretty to disrupt. So here is some advice on how to have your plant and eat it, too:

Select crops that bear over a long season and which also remain attractive while growing: the cut-and-come-again types such as Swiss chard and Ruby chard; all kinds of peppers—sweet and hot, green, red and yellow; leaf lettuce; bush beans and bush squash; and vine crops.

Learn to follow vine crops with vine crops; intercrop cucumbers just as the sugar snap peas are fading. Vines are a good bet for production that goes on and on.

When you grow plants that mature rapidly and are harvested by total removal, such as radishes* or beets, keep them going by having a ready supply of backup seedlings to replace those that are pulled. The chart titled Double-Duty Landscape Plants will help you to visualize and translate ornamental plants into edible ones. The edibles are listed in categories based on their uses in the landscape.

Hanging baskets should be used freely as accents, for they add another dimension wherever you suspend them. So do containers—they make a strong architectural statement while they accent the landscape. With their great flexibility, they can be enlisted to fill in any empty space left by vegetables that have been harvested. When containers are lightweight and brimming over with good things to eat, they are indeed a movable feast, accenting the landscape with good taste (pun intended).

*Thompson and Morgan sells a packaged assortment of four radish varieties—French Breakfast, Scarlet Globe, Sparkler and White Turnip Globe—that mature at different times and are different shapes and sizes so you don't have to harvest them all at once. Ask for "Radish Salad Mixed Varieties" if you order from Thompson and Morgan (you'll find their address in the list of seed sources at the back of Chapter 6). Or you can buy several varieties and mix them yourself.

CHAPTER 3

Containers— Go Anywhere, Grow Anywhere Gardens

A container, by definition, is anything that holds something. By its very nature, a container suggests mobility and impermanence—unless, of course, the container is so large and weighs so much that it cannot be moved easily. In some places extremely heavy containers can be a decided advantage as on city sidewalks where containers sometimes manage to "walk away." Container gardens also lend themselves to the impermanent attitudes of transient apartment dwellers, house renters, or mobile home occupants; you *can* take it with you when you move.

Containers make gardens possible where they would not otherwise happen. On patios, entryways, decks, balconies, rooftops, where weather conditions are extreme or soil and drainage poor, container plantings are the perfect, and sometimes, the *only* solution. So, along with the permanent edible landscape, there is the changeable, movable container garden to consider.

The types of containers you choose do not have to be limited by your budget, but can be as diverse and creative as your imagination allows. (See A Scavenger's Manual of Castoffs and Remakes, later in this chapter, for some very inexpensive container ideas.) Containers for gardening need to fulfill just two basic requirements:

They must be large enough to accommodate and support the desired plant when it is fully grown.

They must be able to hold soil and must allow drainage of excess water.

With the absolute requirements so simple, just about anyone willing to spend a little time caring for a growing vegetable plant can have some sort of food garden. Even the smallest budget can support a few containers!

Besides affording you better control over the growing environment, container gardens add pizzazz wherever you place them. You can create a showcase by grouping containers together on different levels to create height (and save space). You can highlight a drab or dull spot, or hide a problem area along a driveway or walkway. Front, rear, and side entrances are enhanced and say "Welcome" when dressed up with a well-groomed container of something fresh and good to eat.

Of course, there are different challenges for every location. For example, although horticulture was surely the last thing urban architects had in mind when designing balconies and rooftops, many green-thumbed high risers have used containers to overcome the special environmental obstacles presented to them. Although two-footed vegetable "poachers" and four-footed garden marauders are left below on ground level, skyscraper gardens have the violence of the elements to contend with. They are whipped by leaf-tearing winds and baked by the searing summer sun, while a steady rain of city soot pours down. But these problems can be dealt with. No one ever told a cucumber or a tomato plant that it is really supposed to grow only at ground level. If you give contained plants what they need in the way of water, soil and sun, if you choose the proper varieties and provide the plants with the correct size container, they'll be happy to grow and produce wherever you put them—even on a rooftop in the sky.

Further, the portability of a container garden means that you can move your edible landscape around, making use of sunny spots in out-of-the-way places, despite space limitations.

Some Helpful Tips on Selecting Containers

Because of the limitation of the soil depth, such as confined plant roots, "out-of-ground" plantings are completely dependent upon what *you* give them and how you care for them. Thus, there are some special things you must pay attention to, whether you grow vegetables in a found, bought or self-built container in an earth garden or sky garden. Before the container receives the plant, here are some suggestions to follow:

The size of any container must accommo-

Here's a handsome assortment of wood containers you can make or buy (clockwise from right): a tub set on a wheeled platform for portability, a square redwood box with notched sides, a box made from wood strips stacked and glued together and two simple wood boxes decorated with strips of lath. Boxes don't have to be square—a triangular box is perfect for a corner, and rectangular boxes fill narrow spaces nicely.

Modular boxes can be grouped and arranged in many different ways for flexibility. Shown here are rectangular boxes of leaf lettuce grouped around a dwarf fruit tree, a tiered arrangement of boxes full of herbs, and smaller boxes set on the stairs to the deck.

date the depth of the roots and size of the mature plant, just as you can't cram a size 9 foot into a size 5 shoe. In no way can corn, with its deep and spreading roots, be made to bear its ears and show its silks in an 8-inch flower pot, although it might be an attractive foliage plant. The right variety of corn, however, can be grown in a large container. (See the chart Vegetables for Containers and Small Spaces at the end of Chapter 6 for more information on vegetable varieties and container sizes.)

If your container garden will include fruit trees, know that except for figs, which like the smallest pot into which their roots will fit, you should use a thick-walled 80-gallon barrel (33 inches deep and 35 inches in diameter) for each dwarf fruit tree. If you will espalier the tree, the container will need to have a 48-inch-high trellis to support the trained branches. Berry bushes can be accommodated in half-barrels at least 24 inches deep.

Wood containers are preferred by many experienced container gardeners. Wet wood swells and helps to retard evaporation (a greater concern in container gardens than in ground-planted gardens). It has the ability to survive temperature extremes, and it comes in a vast array of ready-made styles, shapes and sizes. (See illustrations.) Wood is also an easy material to handle when building your own containers. Although redwood and cedar will last the longest, they are also the costliest woods to use. Pine is an acceptable replacement choice.

To extend the life of any wooden box, barrel or other container, paint the wood inside and out with Cuprinol.

Two or three coats of silicone rubber coating (a weatherproof sealant and protective film with great flexibility) painted only on the inside of any wooden box will make it last much longer than it would otherwise.

Whether you build or buy wooden containers, take advantage of different shapes. Hexagonal containers can interlock, forming a neat design grouping; triangular boxes are especially useful in corners.

Make sure that the corners of boxes are reinforced with angle brackets and brass screws, not nails, as containers will fall apart when nails and hardware rust out.

Iron or aluminum bands on tubs and barrels are usually the first parts to go. Therefore, to double the life expectancy of the barrels give them a protective coat of rust resistant paint. Keep the retaining bands or hoops from slipping with L-shaped cooperage nails. If brass hoops or strips are used to bind the wooden staves together, these should be coated with varnish. If metal bands have disintegrated but the wood is still good, a hardware store or nurseryman may be able to reband an old barrel for you.

Even if you cannot wield a hammer and nails, you can still glue stacks of 2 by 2 lumber together to make wooden plant boxes. (See illustration on page 49.)

Concrete planters are rugged but their weight is a strain on rooftops and terraces. Concrete planters are best used at ground level.

Fiberglass and nonporous hard and soft plastic containers do not dry out as quickly as clay pots, but they usually come without drainage holes, which you will need to provide. To provide drainage in a plastic tub or pot, heat an ice pick or a screwdriver in a flame for a few minutes and then use it to puncture the sides of the container 1 inch above the bottom. Put one or two holes in the bottom as well. Wear gloves to protect your hands.

Adequate drainage is imperative for all containers, regardless of the material they are made of. Make sure that there are ½-inch drainage holes at 6-inch intervals on the bottom, whether you buy, build or find containers.

Both plastic and clay pots will last for several years, although the plastic material eventually dries out and will crack from the heat of the sun. Clay pots are handsome and their natural colors complement plant foliage. They do, however, dry out more quickly than plastic containers. Clay pots may crack in cold weather if left outdoors.

Avoid *thin* metal containers since they will absorb heat rapidly and can "cook" plant roots on a hot day. They also rust out quickly from contact with moist soil.

Some of the handsomest containers I've seen have been adapted from chimney flue tiles and sewer pipes. If you don't want to settle for the limited shapes and sizes of clay pots but you'd like to have inexpensive, durable and handsome containers with the look of clay, chimney flue tiles and sewer pipes can open a whole new range of options to you. They are available vitrified (glazed) or unvitrified, in round, oblong, rectangular, square or "camelback" shapes, and can be found at lumberyards or building supply dealers. (See page 57 for more information.)

Cinder blocks are highly porous and will dry out quickly, so if you want to grow plants in them, glaze them with polyurethane before filling with soil.

If you are reluctant to invest in containers of hardier, more permanent materials, you can try pressed-paper tubs. These inexpen-

Just a few of the many kinds of containers manufactured commercially (clockwise from upper right): a glazed clay pot, unglazed terra cotta pots, a half-barrel, a redwood tub, plastic pots, assorted sewer pipes and chimney flue tiles and paper pulp pots.

sive containers are available in several sizes and are lightweight and easy to move around. The disadvantage is that they may not last more than one season.

Another kind of lightweight container that's especially good for roof gardens is a reusable Styrofoam pot. The pots are white, so they do not collect heat around plant roots. Styrofoam pots are available from a number of sources, including the Geo. W. Park seed company's catalog (see the list of seed companies at the end of Chapter 6 for the address).

Containers made of dark-colored materials absorb more heat than those of light color. Dark containers can help seedlings get a faster start, and they also retain heat for vegetables such as tomatoes. Auto tires can be turned into little warm spots for plants. In hot, dry climates, though, extra heat can be harmful. If you live where it's warm, use light-colored containers.

On paved surfaces (patios, rooftops or driveways), raise the bottoms of large containers so that they rest on cleats at least an inch or two above the pavement. The space is needed so air may circulate, water may drain properly, and so that you can sweep under the containers.

Slightly elevated containers also prevent rambling roots from growing into the surface of a rooftop and causing cracks that

A Garden in Garbage Pails

For years I knew him as "Mike Downstairs"; we gardened on our city terrace, while twelve stories below on a tenement rooftop he grew the lushest, most exquisite vegetables in cast-off garbage pails. Eventually, I met Mike Tyna, a structural steel and bridge painter who is an avid, dedicated gardener, and we began to exchange garden information and tips, even though our problems were somewhat different.

"I started fifteen years ago on city fire escapes," he says, "with a wooden box full of basil and tomatoes that a neighbor had started. She was afraid that the fire inspector would give her a summons and she asked me to carry the box on the roof. I looked around and the rooftop just seemed like a lot of wasted growing space and that's how it all started." His rambling garden is composed of containers of a variety of shapes and forms, all of them culled from around the city and from his jobs.

He uses 5-gallon plastic pails taken from completed construction jobs, 4-gallon containers from commercial delicatessens (that once held cole slaw and potato salad). He also recycles containers from industrial cleaning supplies—especially the containers for hand soaps. They last about five to six years, he says. Mike drills two to four holes about 1 inch above the bottom of all his containers, to provide drainage. He gets soil from outdoor jobs and street excavations and adds vermiculite to lighten it.

Mike has managed to combine his fishing hobby with his gardening, by using fishing tackle to support his climbing vegetables and for a novel form of pigeon protection. "The pigeons are a real problem," Mike complains. "I call them flying rats." To keep them out of the garden, Mike weaves fishing line into a sort of "cat's cradle" webbing around the perimeter of the rooftop garden area. This woven "fence" forms an almost invisible barrier that pigeons can't fly through. His fishing hobby also comes in handy for fertilizing his plants. He keeps a covered bucket filled with fish scraps and water, and after each fishing expedition he adds to it and lets it stand until the end of the growing season. Then he adds a little to each of his 50 containers to winter over. The can is kept covered so there are no odor problems.

In fact, all of Mike's organic kitchen waste goes back into the soil. He makes his compost by just digging it into the soil in the pails. Considering the fact that Mike works but one hour a day on his garden, watering with a long hose, the output is amazing. He companion plants with garlic and marigolds, and rotates crops by marking the pots with what grew there the year before, then growing something different the next season. The crops include broccoli, lettuce, squash, cauliflower, Egyptian bunching onions, elephant garlic and fresh herbs for Italian cooking, including parsley, dill, basil and oregano.

As we walked toward one of the containers, he laughed. "I don't grow zucchini, I grow weapons! Here, take this one—it's one of the smaller ones." I took it upstairs and weighed it. It just topped 2½ pounds!

turn into leaks in the neighbor's apartment below.

To avoid mud washing out of containers when you water, and to save yourself a lot of cleanup chores, fill your containers in the following way. For a bottom layer in all containers, place 1 or 2 inches of broken clay shards, gravel, or lightweight Styrofoam pellets and cover with a layer of porous fiberglass cloth insulating material (such as Landscape Mat, available from Brighton By-Products, Box 23, New Brighton, PA 15066) or several layers of old nylon stockings or curtains. Over this add 2 inches of peat moss, to help moisture for the roots where it is most needed, and fill the container with the desired soil mixture, leaving a 2-inch space at the top.

The Art of Scrounging for Garden Containers

The people you sometimes see in the countryside or on suburban or urban streets rummaging through someone's discards are not all vagrants or eccentrics. What they may be is gardeners unself-consciously picking their way through a recycler's paradise. Scrounging, for plant containers, as for anything else, is an ingenious way of accepting a challenge. First, you must have an eye and a mind that can separate an object from its usual function and second, you must be able to envision how you may adapt your lucky find to a new use. One of the chief joys of scrounging containers to use for gardening is the serendipity of uncovering these lucky finds, for they can be either ready-made, adaptable containers or assorted used materials from which you are able to fashion entirely new containers or other garden structures.

Scrounging is an art that needs no practical reason, such as lack of funds to buy new materials. But if you must justify the fun of it to yourself or your skeptical friends, just say

Some recycled containers for resourceful gardeners.

you are engaged in the noble pursuit of recycling. It's much the same as the concept behind composting—not wasting usable materials of any kind, even though you may be a millionaire (like Stewart Mott, whose gardener, Robert Wong, relies on recycled containers for his employer's rooftop garden).

If you spread the word around your neighborhood that you are looking for salvageable materials, you may get a lead which uncovers a wealth of it at places like recent demolition sites, boat docks and railroad yards, or

housewreckers' salvage yards. These are the glorious freebies, the building materials that you gather and haul away yourself. From these materials you can improvise garden paths, terrace pavings, windbreaks, garden furniture, cold frames, containers and boxes, grape arbors—anything you can envision and build yourself to enhance your garden.

Expensive containers and garden structures do not guarantee any better harvests than found objects. Remember, the fashionable French, who have a world reputation for

The Author's Chimney-Flue Herb Garden

In my seashore garden I grow herbs in flue tiles 8½ by 8½ by 24 inches deep, sunk into the ground halfway and at an angle. Only the containers holding mint are enclosed on the bottom to confine the vigorous roots. The other flue tiles are left open at the bottom. Using these containers lets me custom-blend soil mixes for the needs of individual herbs. When I initially prepared the soil for the herb garden, to fill 75 square feet I used 6 cubic feet of peat moss plus 25 pounds of dried cow manure and a generous shovelful of wood ashes. You could also use 5 pounds of agricultural lime plus 5 pounds of bone meal plus 100 pounds of compost, lightened with sand or vermiculite.

All the perennial herbs are left in place, and various annual herb varieties become an experimental learning project that changes yearly. Only peppermint is grown in a separate area because of its spreading growth habit. The angled tiles act as a border for a raised growing bed for vegetables which may then be companion-planted near the proper herbs. A brick path bisects the bed and separates herbs that require full sun from those which need filtered sun or mostly shade. The path also allows "foot-room," access to work from the sides of the vegetable bed.

The herb selection chart in Chapter 6 outlines the basic needs of my favorite herbs.

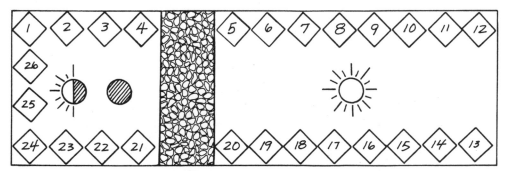

1 lemon balm, 2 chervil, 3 lovage, 4 curly parsley, 5 rosemary, 6 oregano, 7 chives, 8 dark opal basil, 9 French tarragon, 10 thyme, 11 green basil, 12 borage, 13 fennel, 14 sage, 15 leaf coriander, 16 rose-scented geranium, 17 sweet marjoram, 18 dill, 19 French sorrel, 20 summer savory, 21 Italian parsley, 22 garlic chives, 23 garden cress, 24 chamomile, 25 spearmint, 26 peppermint.

A Scavenger's Manual of Castoffs & Remakes

Where to Look	What You Are Likely to Find	Tips for Improvisation
Housewares and hardware shops	Bowls, washtubs, pots, laundry baskets, colanders, Styrofoam picnic coolers.	Styrofoam picnic coolers covered with plastic wrap are also good for starting seeds.
Wallpaper shops	Plastic water troughs, used for wetting rolls of wallpaper.	A 32" x 6" x 4" deep trough makes a perfect lightweight window box or sill container.
Liquor stores	Wooden packing crates.	Line crates with plastic before using them as planters, so the soil doesn't escape through the cracks.
Restaurant equipment suppliers	Heavyweight plastic garbage cans, pails, and plastic bags, huge pots, bowls, storage bins.	
Commercial bakeries	Butter tubs, egg crates, plastic milk cases.	
Institutional kitchens (restaurants, hospitals, schools)	Gallon-sized cans, plastic tubs, pickle tubs, cooking oil tins.	
Stationery supply stores	Waste paper baskets, damaged file cabinet drawers.	File cabinet drawers are good, deep boxes.
Building supply yards	Concrete blocks, ceramic chimney flues, drain and sewer pipes, old railroad ties, bricks, slate.	Concrete blocks can be used to contain the compost pile.
Garages and used car dealers	Old tractor and auto tires, oil cans.	Tires used as planters attract and store sun's heat—perfect for melons, tomatoes, peppers and other warmth-loving crops.
Wholesale and retail food markets.	Wooden produce crates, bushel baskets of all sizes and shapes, plastic milk delivery cases, berry baskets.	Line open baskets with heavy black plastic bag and slash for drainage. Some supermarkets will charge you, others are happy to get rid of their excess containers.

Where to Look	What You Are Likely to Find	Tips for Improvisation
		Lettuce plants can grow in a berry basket—use as a table centerpiece and harvest at the table for a truly fresh salad!
Housewreckers' salvage yards	Bathtubs and sinks.	Use a layer of gravel for drainage in tubs and sinks.
	Toilets, washbasins, refrigerators.	Remove refrigerator door and turn on its back for a fine plant container.
	Used bricks, plumbing pipes.	Pipes can be used for vertical garden support structures.
Streets, discards from closets, garages and attics	Old shoes, boots and gloves, old bureau drawers, cooking pots.	Whimsical containers for pepper plants and small tomatoes.
	Plastic or clay pots discarded with dead plants.	Scrub, dry and sterilize old clay pots; place in cool oven and bring heat to 220°F. Bake for 1 hour and let stand overnight to cool before reuse.
	Pieces of broken pavement.	Use for garden paths.
	Old umbrella frames, umbrella stands.	Train vines on umbrella frames.
	Gallon plastic milk and cider jugs.	Cut off tops of plastic jugs with scissors to make small containers.
	Stepladders.	Lay flat, plant herbs in each division.
	Wire bicycle wheels.	To train vines on.
	Wire bicycle baskets.	Line with moss and hang.

being connoisseurs of art, refer to any rebuilt, recycled object as *l'art trouvé* or "found art objects." So when you are rummaging through other people's trash and are mistaken for an eccentric vagrant, look up confidently and speak French. Somehow it sounds more chic to say, "Je cherche l'art trouvé," than "I'm a garden scavenger looking for castoffs."

Making Portable Planters from Chimney Flues and Sewer Pipes

Chimney flue tiles or sewer pipes make terrific containers for a garden planted in a geometric design. I used them to create my herb garden at the seashore. Here's the procedure for making the planters:

Use a diamond blade masonry saw to cut the pipe to whatever length you wish.*

Once the pipe or flue tiles are cut, trace the inside contour on a 1-inch-thick piece of wood (preferably redwood or Cuprinol-treated pine) and saw it out. For large planters you may need to glue two cut pieces

*Sometimes, if you ask nicely, your dealer will cut them for you.

together.

Drill two to five ½-inch holes for drainage. The number of holes depends on the size of the pot.

Insert the wooden bottom into the pipe to the desired depth (depending on the size of the intended plant's root system).

Glue the bottom in place with epoxy bond or a silicone glue.

How to Move Heavy Containers

Large containers made of durable materials and filled with soil will support several vegetable plants or even a fruit tree or berry bush. Big containers also need less frequent waterings than small pots. But their mobility is hampered unless you know how to move these heavyweights—or any container for that matter—without throwing your back out of whack. Here are some strategies to make moving them easier:

For moderately heavy pots a burlap bag or piece of old rug or carpet can act as a skid to cradle the pot and pull it.

Always move a container *before* watering, when it's lighter. A 12-inch pot filled with soil can weigh 65 pounds. An 18-inch-square wooden box filled with soil can weigh 200 pounds. A tree in a 4 by 4 by 2-foot box with 32 cubic feet of soil can weigh over a ton. When wet, they are considerably heavier.

Build a movable wooden platform 1 inch thick for very heavy containers. The platform should have three pieces of board

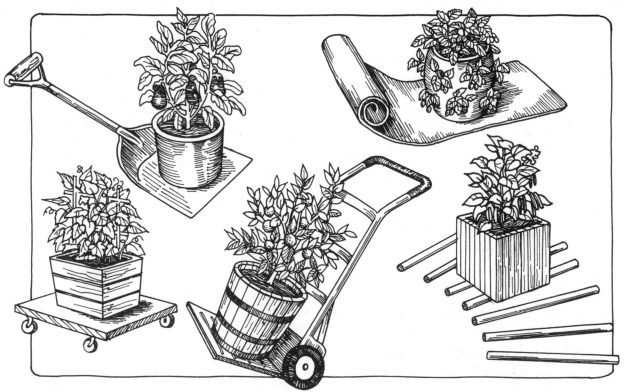

Strategies for moving heavy containers include sliding the pot on a rug, rolling it on poles or broom handles (fan them out as shown to go around corners), using a dolly, putting the tub on a platform with casters and sliding the pot on a broad spade.

nailed to the top, as shown in the illustration. Mount the platform on 2-inch industrial rotating caster wheels (preferably nonmetal). Keep the container on it for air circulation, extra strength on the bottom and for easier mobility.

The best way to move a potted shrub or tree is to use a heavy-duty two-wheeled hand truck. A hand truck can be rented or purchased, or perhaps borrowed from your neighborhood food store or local furniture movers, or sometimes from an apartment building superintendent. The wide base slides easily under a heavy pot, the handles tilt toward you, and "you're off" on two sturdy wheels.

A wide-bladed shovel, wedged under a tub, will help to lift and slide it across the ground.

To build the pyramids, Egyptian slaves rolled heavy stones from quarries to building sites on rollers. This method, in a less grandiose form, will let you move even the heaviest containers. Place three or four 2-inch metal rods or pipes, wooden dowels or broom handles parallel on the floor surface. Wedge a wide shovel under the tub, lever the tub up onto the pipes and slide it over the pipes until you get to the end. Move the pipe in the rear up to the front and repeat the process until the container, slowly but surely, is where you want it to be. When turning a corner, fan out the rollers into the direction you want to go.

The Care and Feeding of Container-Grown Produce

The soil mixture is considerably more important for container plants than for those grown directly in the ground. It must be light but rich, and it must drain easily yet still hold moisture and nutrients in place for plant roots. These are the same requirements as for in-ground vegetables, with one big exception: plants in containers have access to far less

soil. It's up to you to provide for all the nutritional and moisture needs of container plants. Their confined roots and restricted soil volume can't supply enough for good growth. The soil must be chosen very carefully, replenished regularly and kept in peak condition for good yields.

The following tips could make the difference between contained vegetables that grow and produce well, and puny plants that merely exist:

Success starts with a specially blended, lightweight soil mixture. (See Chapter 8 for more information.)

When filling the container, allow 2 to 3 inches at the top for adding soil amendments like compost, to accommodate a layer of mulch and to prevent surface runoff when watering.

In an established container garden you should restore the soil seasonally or add more compost or manure or other organic fertilizers for additional succession crops.

In the fall, after crops are spent, pulling them out loosens the existing soil. To each pot, add a combination of organic fertilizers containing the three major nutrients (nitrogen, phosphorus and potassium): ½ trowel blood meal, 1 trowel bone meal, and ½ trowel of greensand. Add any fallen disease-free leaves to decompose over the winter along with some peat moss and dehydrated cow manure. Additional vermiculite or perlite will also help to lighten compacted container soil. Work well into soil and leave the soil surface rough and uncovered over the winter.

Supplemental feeding with a liquid fertilizer such as fish emulsion every week to ten days during the growing season ensures that a good supply of nutrients will be available to plant roots. Nutrients leach out of pots easily with the drainage water, and

Recycling on a Rooftop

He refers to himself as "an elevator farmer," and indeed he is, since his farm in the sky is a lofty, narrow, windswept city penthouse wrapped around three sides of a seventeen story building, reachable only by an elevator which leads directly into the apartment. He is also obviously the King of Container Gardening, since containers of every conceivable size, shape, color and material are utilized to hold soil in which to grow vegetables. Although the unconventional Stewart Mott—philanthropist, political activist and the largest stockholder of General Motors—can well afford to buy exquisitely handcrafted redwood boxes for growing his vegetables, he is a practical-minded person who believes in recycling wasted urban materials scavenged from the city streets. Old tires, wooden panels, doors, milk boxes, crates—all are refashioned to be used as garden containers.

Because Stewart Mott is extremely busy with his other business interests, he hired a dedicated young Cornell University horticulture graduate, Robert Wong, to take his place in the garden. Stewart Mott believes, along with many other people, that rooftops are potential food growing spaces that are wasted acreage, and he and Robert Wong are obviously out to prove that city people can grow a large amount of their food very close to home, without great cost.

The rooftop is a veritable cornucopia which bears out that premise. I counted several different varieties of some 30 vegetables, 33 different herbs and 7 kinds of fruit trees, along with some grapevines and assorted berry bushes. All the plants are grown from seed. Seeds are started in cat food cans, recycled from the dinners of three huge cats that roam freely on the premises. In fact, Robert Wong has had to devise a mesh covering for the growing boxes to prevent the cats from digging up the soil and destroying the seedlings. The mesh netting performs double duty—it also supports cucumber vines.

The north side of the roof, the most windswept area, is partially sheltered by a stockade fence. Here, enclosed by cinderblocks, sits the heart of the recycling operation—the compost pile. The compost is fed with spent soil from potted plants and the household table wastes of a staff of nine, plus chopped up waste material from the many ornamentals and flowers that also share container space on the terrace. "But I have to make sure," Robert says, "that no plant material is diseased or it will spread. One year, someone carelessly put some tomato and squash vines which had succumbed to a virus on the pile and the next planted crop for which we used some of the compost wilted.

"Another problem we once had was with mildew." Robert continued. "We plant things very closely together and in hot weather, with the parapet enclosure, and probably not enough circulating air, our melons died of a bacterial wilt. We've learned since then to plant them in a more open area where air can circulate better and now we're O.K."

The compost heap is about 3 by 3 by 6 feet high and is contained on three sides. In spring, one side of the wall is taken down and the newly made compost is scooped up from the base and added to the boxes. "We have a source of real manure, which is like gold in the city; we get it from a stable that houses the police constabulary. We bring burlap bags, our own shovels, our own muscle power and a truck. The price is right, too; it's free for the taking. We use salt hay as a mulch for some things and when it's wet down it doesn't seem to blow away. And speaking about wind, although there's a smoke-belching incinerator nearby, the wind blows most of it away and a hose washes down any sooty fallout that may remain."

Both Robert Wong and Stewart Mott feel that "urban rooftop gardening is lots of fun, although with the amount of things we grow in a season, it's hard work too. It's also a challenge to be able to produce enough vegetables, berries and herbs for nine people with enough extra to make gift baskets of fresh produce and never have to take the elevator down to the street to go to the supermarket and buy those inferior, tasteless vegetable reproductions. Each meal we eat of our produce confirms our belief that the hard work is completely worth it."

need to be replenished more often than in an earth garden.

Water, water, and more water. That's another big difference between container and in-ground gardens. Of course, watering frequency depends upon the size and kind of container, the needs of the individual plants, the environmental and regional conditions and the miniclimate you create to conserve moisture and shield your plants from wind or too much sun. But in any case, container soil dries out very quickly outdoors, and watering may become a daily chore.

Check the top inch of soil daily by pressing your hand or a piece of newspaper or paper towel on the surface. If it becomes damp at once there's no need to water.

When you do water, make sure you water thoroughly, so that the soil is saturated and water starts to drain from the container bottom.

A fine spray from a hose will not only wash off rooftop soot, but can revive a wilting plant.

Grouping containers together increases the humidity around them and prevents rapid evaporation. Mulches, too, will help maintain soil moisture for a longer time. But remember, the smaller the container, the more frequent its need for water.

Beware of overcrowding plants in containers. Crowded plants will shade each other and stifle flower production. When grown directly in the earth, plants can spread out in other directions, but in containers all they can do is spill over the sides.

Meticulous grooming is a must since containers are usually placed in conspicuous places such as terraces, steps or doorways.

Special Tips for Growing Herbs in Containers

Most culinary herbs will grow in a pot

that is 5 inches in diameter and 5 inches deep, taking approximately one quart of soil. This size is the very *minimum* size to use except in a few cases (specified on the herb selection chart at the end of Chapter 6).

Larger size containers and in-ground plantings, of course, will produce larger plants with more vigorous growth.

Some top-heavy herbs require sturdy flat-bottom pots or containers that will not tip over easily.

When choosing containers, remember that clay pots absorb root moisture and are especially good for some herbs that prefer drier or sandy soil. Wooden or plastic pots will keep soil moist longer for herbs that require more root moisture.

When designing any herb garden, plan to plant perennials first as a framework and then group containers of annuals around them if their needs are the same. Take into account that movable containers cater to the finicky sun needs of herbs. Some herbs prefer bright sunshine; others will thrive only in filtered sun or mostly shade.

An easy way to winter over tender perennials or perennials outside in containers is to place a Styrofoam pot over the plant, pierce a plastic bag in several places to let in air, and wrap the entire plant.

Now that you know the basics of container gardening, let's look at some creative ways to get those containers up off the ground to save even more space.

The Upwardly Mobile: Getting Plants Up off the Ground

You'll discover lots of new places for containers when you begin to look up and start to think vertically instead of horizontally. A large variety of specially designed containers can help your gardens to grow upward. One classic design is the window box, which can perch on a balcony, porch, or deck railing, or hang out of a kitchen window within easy reach of a watering can. Also, the highwire hangers-on— hanging baskets of all styles, shapes and materials—can provide the needed decorative accent, lend a special charm and enhance any garden space. There are barrels, pyramids and strawberry jars, which have traditionally been used for strawberries, but which can just as easily hold lettuce or herbs. You can create a "growing wall" garden to hang over a fence or stand against a wall (see page 67). Here are some things you should know about each of these types of airborne containers.

Window Boxes

Inch for inch, window boxes deliver more impact for less effort, giving a lift to both the outside and the inside of a house (and usually, to the entire street). You may be tempted to think that anything as charming as a window box must be illegal. Although they are *not* illegal, in some cities there are certain ordinances governing the use of window boxes (in some cases they cover tub plantings as well) when they are placed on the front of buildings. If you are contemplating installing window boxes, you may need to get clearance, usually through the buildings department of your city. A sampling of some of the guidelines from New York City will help you realize that they are not difficult to comply with, and for the most part they are considerate of the safety of those who walk below in any city.

The sill and window frame must be in good condition. Any weight attached to a rotting wooden frame is a hazard.

The window must not be a means of egress, that is, it cannot lead to or block a fire escape or other exit from the building.

In some cities, the window must be no more than five stories above the street level (about 50 feet) and must be set back slightly

A rooftop container garden can be much more than a bunch of pots set in a row. In this garden, herbs and flowers flourish in a box clamped to the outer wall, cucumber vines in boxes climb trellises to surround and hide an exhaust pipe, an arbor of potted grapevines provides a shady retreat for a hot afternoon and pots of lettuce dress up a shelf right outside the window.

from public walkways (so you don't water a passing pedestrian's head).

The box must be securely fastened to the window frame. The best materials for window boxes themselves are wood or fiberglass. Metal boxes rust out quickly and tend to absorb heat that can burn plant roots. To fasten the boxes in place with noncorroding materials, string several strands of rust-

proof piano or picture wire between brass screw eyes that have been sunk into the window frame. If the box is made of wood, it can be attached to the window frame with a pair of long latch hooks or brackets.

Few things look more desolate in fall than a once gaily colored window box sporting the brown, frost-wilted remains of summer's bounty. To spruce up the box and add some seasonal

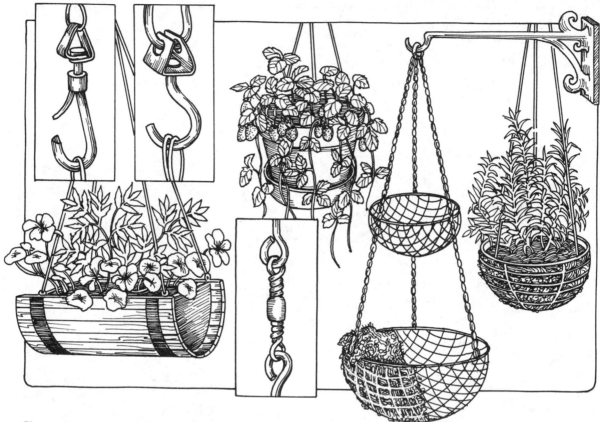

Shown here are a wire basket, a two-tiered wire basket (line with sphagnum moss before planting), a round-bottomed wood planter and a plastic pot with built-in saucer. Hardware options for attaching pots to hangers include (from front) a swivel from a set of fishing tackle, a lock spring from a dog leash and a hook made from a bent nail and plumber's tape.

cheer, first remove the dead plants, including roots. Then add a layer of peat moss and dried cow manure to enrich the soil for next year's plantings. Finally, arrange and fasten down boughs of evergreens to spill over the edge of the box.

Hanging Baskets

These airborne containers have a very special advantage besides their mobility: they can serve as a screen, thus assuring privacy in a most friendly way. Their immediate effect can range from quiet, dignified charm while hanging under the eaves of a front porch, to the unexpected and spectacular, when grouped

and hung at different heights. What's more, they give a lot of pleasure for their size. Before planting a hanging basket with crops from the charts at the end of Chapter 6, there are a few things you'll need to know.

Baskets: Your choice of hanging containers should be made on the basis of durability, capacity and lightness of weight. Lightweight plastic pots or wire domes lined with sheet sphagnum moss are best to use for the largest sizes. Take into account the fact that the weight will increase as the plant grows. The extra weight of soil and water also has to be considered.

Supporting Hardware: The hardware, of

course, must be strong enough and well-secured to support the full weight of the water-saturated basket. For example, a filled 12-inch basket weighing about 12 pounds when dry will have 5 or 6 pounds of additional weight when wet. A swivel attachment permits complete rotation of a hanging basket for all-around sun exposure and easier access for watering, feeding and grooming.

Watering and Feeding: Moisture loss is always more rapid for totally exposed hanging planters, but the extent of drying depends upon the size and material of the basket and its location. A basket hung in hot sun or constant, drying winds will naturally dry out more quickly than a basket hung on a tree limb in dappled shade. Daily watering may be needed in warm weather or windy locations, but the loss of moisture can be reduced in moss-lined baskets by lining them with a perforated plastic sheet before adding soil. A weekly addition of a diluted liquid fertilizer such as fish emulsion will keep things growing well.

Planting an Open Wire Basket

Hanging containers made of plastic or pottery can be planted in much the same way you plant pots or tubs that will sit on the ground. But open wire, wire mesh and open wood baskets need special treatment. Here's how to plant an open basket:

First soak several sheets of green moss in water. Squeeze out the water and form the moss into a pad ¾ inch thick and the size of the basket's bottom.

Push the pad into the bottom of the basket, working some of the moss through the wire mesh to hide it somewhat. Cover the sides of the basket in the same way, overlapping the moss pads and mounding them up about 1½ inches over the top rim. To plant strawberries, leaf lettuce or herb seedlings, poke several evenly spaced holes around the sides of the basket and push the top of

each plant gently through the hole from the inside of the basket. The roots remain inside the basket. Then fill the basket with a lightweight soil mix, and plant the top surface with one or two additional plants. Small cucumbers and tiny tomatoes also do well in these baskets but they should be planted only in the top of the basket (the same holds true for baskets made of plastic, clay or wood).

Strawberry Jars or Barrels

These tall containers have pockets or pouches cut out all over them, and a plant is put in each pocket instead of just in the top of the jar. Thus, more plants grow in the same space. Although they work so well for strawberries, which normally sprawl out horizontally and take up lots of room, strawberry jars adapt elegantly as a visual accent to display a number of shallow-rooted herbs or vegetables.

Strawberry jars can be frustrating to plant if you don't know the little tricks that keep water from gushing out of the many pockets,

The classic strawberry jar is a traditional way to get plants off the ground.

but they are easy to plant if you know how. Both jars and larger barrels are planted in the same way. Here's how to do it easily:

Cover the bottom drainage hole or holes with a piece of broken clay pot.

Cut pieces of old nylon hose or burlap, equal to the number of pockets, and slightly larger than their openings.

Poke a hole in the center of each piece of fabric and push the roots of the plant through, forming a sort of "collar" on each plant. The fabric keeps the soil from running out of the pouches each time the whole container is watered.

Prepare a central drainage core; a cardboard tube from a roll of paper towels or a taller paper mailing tube for larger barrels will do nicely.

Stand the tube upright in the middle of the jar and fill around it with a lightweight soil mixture until you reach the first openings on the lowest part of the jar.

Pour sand, gravel or lighter weight perlite into the hollow center of the tube to the same soil level in order to keep the pressure even, so the tube won't cave in.

Starting from the bottom of the jar, pop a plant out of each hole, working from the inside of the jar, filling with plants and soil until you almost reach the top. At this point, slip a coffee can or other can with the top and bottom cut off, over the tube so it extends to the top.

Top with more soil around the can and place several plants on the top of the container. The cardboard tube will disintegrate in time so there's no need to remove it.

To water, pour water into the central column, using the can as a guide, so that moisture will filter out and reach all the plants in the pockets.

Pyramid Plantings

Vertical and versatile, a three-tiered pyramid will accommodate a given number of plants in only a third as much ground space as they'd otherwise require, in an appealing and decorative manner. Pyramid gardens combine the advantages of raised bed gardening with a

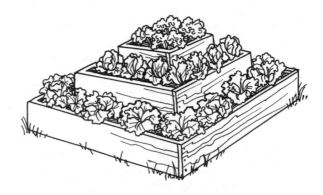

A pyramid made of three wood frames set atop one another is a good way to get more plants in a small space, top. A similar tiered bed in a circular shape can be made of metal lawn-edging strips.

contained structure that reaches up instead of out. They can be designed with square, circular, oval or rectangular bases, with each tier providing a growing space about 1 foot wide all around. Add tiers to achieve the height you wish. Here's how to do it:

Design the size and shape structure you want to fit the space you have.

First make a base frame and place it directly on the soil. Inside the frame, place a large plastic bag or sheet of plastic on the bottom to prevent the soil from washing out, or build a bottom as you would for a container. Pierce the bag with a few drainage holes and put a layer of perlite in the bag. Fill the rest of the bag with soil and trim off the plastic at the frame level.

Next, make a frame 1 foot smaller than the base frame, center it on the base, and fill that one with soil. Top that second tier with a third frame that's 1 foot smaller, and fill the third frame with soil.

Plant shallow-rooted plants such as lettuce, radishes, or cabbage on the base level. Then plant carrots, peppers or beets on the next level, and put your deepest-rooted plants (like tomatoes) in the top level.

There is another type of vertical pyramid garden called a Patio Tower Garden, which you can buy. Made of redwood slats, this four-sided planter tapers up from a 2-foot-square base to a narrower top, forming eleven planting levels. The tower contains a vertical tube in its center, which acts as a water reservoir; you fill it from the top and the water and soluble fertilizer seep down through each planting level, much like the strawberry barrel principle. Food crops such as herbs, lettuce, nasturtiums and strawberries grow easily and attractively in this minimum amount of space. A 2 by 4-foot-high tower is available through mail order from W. Atlee Burpee Company, and can be easily assembled with a screwdriver.

Growing Walls

You can squeeze more garden produce from less space than you ever thought possible with a growing wall. With the construction of two closely parallel wire fences lined with moss or plastic and filled in the center with soil, you can create a vertical garden that takes up as little as 1 or 2 feet of ground space, and goes as high as you like. A growing wall is perfect for the landless who live in small or cramped quarters; the garden can be placed hard up against the side of a mobile home, under the windows, or even on the roof of a houseboat. It can be used on a city balcony, or garage roof in the suburbs. In short, a growing wall is just a rectangular garden bed standing on its end, its height and size determined by your particular needs.

If you are handy you can build your own growing wall, but if you are all thumbs when it comes to constructing anything, a commercially available vertical growing system that includes various sizes of walls and tubs can be purchased from the Living Wall Garden Co. For further details write to them at: 2044 Chili Ave., Rochester, NY 14624, or phone: (716) 247-0070. Naturally, it is always less costly to design and build your own, and it's really not that difficult if you'd like to try to adapt some of these wall garden ideas to your own space. Incidentally, this is a marvelous device to hide

A stair-step platform is a space-saving way to accommodate a garden of potted herbs.

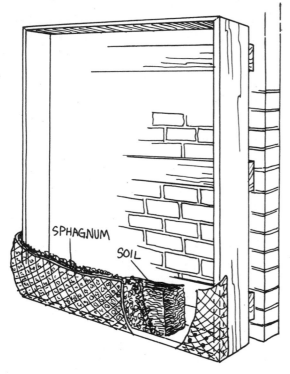

SPHAGNUM

SOIL

When there's no place to go but up, create a living wall. Plant roots grow in the inner layer of soil, and the sphagnum moss and chicken wire keep the plants from pulling out of the ground. As the plants grow they will cascade downward and eventually cover the chicken wire, to create the illusion of a living wall.

an ugly wall. Here's how to make one:

Make a wooden bottomless box, the size you need, just as you would if it were to be placed on the ground. Be sure to drill drainage holes in the bottom.

Turn the box on one end, with the "bottom" against the wall. If it is to be attached to the side of a house, it is best first to attach a wooden grid or grill to the house surface to allow for air circulation.

Next, hang the box and staple 1-inch mesh chicken wire in 1-foot-wide strips horizontally across the box so the wire bellies out into a curve.

Place overlapping pads of wet long-fiber sphagnum moss against the chicken wire surface, and fill behind it with soil. Repeat this process until you get to the top, working 1 foot at a time, stapling the top of the chicken wire to enclose the surface.

Plant seedlings are poked through the chicken wire and moss into the soil. Gravity will pull some of them down, so they will hang and create a wall of herbs and vegetables as they grow, eventually covering the moss surface entirely.

Watering and feeding are done through the top of the wall.

For a variation on this theme you can also make a long, narrow hanging plank garden by stapling chicken wire to a board and hanging it from a screw eye. You can take down the plank garden and lay it flat to water it easily. A growing wall is an exciting gardening adventure—one that you may want to try, perhaps on a small scale, even if you already have a large garden. A hanging plank garden of parsley, for example, alongside a doorway leading into the kitchen, lets you snip that last minute garnish without having to go out to the garden.

Designing Your Garden— The Add-a-Garden Plan

If you have ever had the pleasure of strolling through a formal garden, you may have found that you were at once awed and charmed by the carefully massed patterns of color and greenery. In a formally laid out garden, you sense and enjoy the strong axial layouts and the overall drama of the surroundings. During the Middle Ages, European formal gardens planted in patterns utilized basic geometric shapes in their designs. They usually featured pathways running in patterns among the garden beds leading to a spectacular center focal point—a bird bath, sundial, fountain or perhaps a garden sculpture accented with ornate, urns planted with flowers. Later, Elizabethan gardens incorporated plantings in the shape of interwoven knots and ribbons in their geometrically shaped beds. Still later, a more informal, freeform style became popular, and gardens took on a more natural, rambling look.

When I began to study the designs of these old formal gardens I began to see the practicality of translating this traditional concept into contemporary terms. And upon further examination, I realized that a geometric design would work quite well in my garden, since everything was already growing in small manageable areas. With so many garden spaces today having shrunk from gargantuan to lilliputian proportions, the idea of small gardens based on geometric shapes is one whose time has come again.

A garden that's attractively designed doesn't have to be hidden away "out back," but can instead become an integral part of the home landscape. In fact, an herb, fruit and vegetable garden can be handsome enough to do double duty as a source of both food and visual pleasure. A simple, well-thought-out garden design will add an all-year-round decorative touch to your yard. Good design enhances the landscape and gives pleasure to passers-by, but best of all, *you* get to eat the goodies. Long before the first seeds begin to sprout, growing beds in the shape of circles, triangles, squares and rectangles look attractive especially when they are grouped into a pleasing overall design—a total master plan.

In the pages that follow I will offer some ideas for designing your own geometric gardens, and I will also give you some sample plans to follow directly if you like. The idea is to start with one small bed and add more beds as you have time, working toward an overall pattern in several simple and attractive stages. I call it The Add-a-Garden Plan, and I hope the following ideas revived from the formal gardens of yore, with an overlay of Euclid's basic geometry, will be inspirational enough for you

Here's an example of how a geometrically shaped garden can dress up a lawn. In this garden, wood edging keeps the borders neat and bed shapes apparent even when plants are at peak growth.

to want to proudly display your vegetable beds grouped into neat designs and tucked into whatever space you have available, no matter how tiny it is.

If what you wish to achieve eventually is a large, unified garden, then you should work with ideas for the total space. Start with the central core, or nucleus, of the overall pattern, and transfer this first phase of the design from a graph paper plan to your actual garden space. A bit more of the pattern can be added each year if you wish, and you can watch your garden grow and develop as additional beds are prepared and added to complete the total design a few years hence. It's an orderly and efficient way to create productive garden space that always looks attractive.

If your space is tiny, the marvel of any symmetrical design is that it can be halved or

quartered and still look correct. Take a piece of paper and cover up half or one quarter of any of the three design plans on pages 79, 80 and 81, and you will have created several more design possibilities. These little shapes can be broken up and placed in several separate locations, but they will still present a unified look.

The Add-a-Garden Plan will never bore you, since it's not the same old vegetables growing in the same old rows in the same old rectangular space that's become such a habit for so many of us. This design concept will grab and hold your interest, and may well fascinate you and your neighbors for years as you watch it change and grow a little bit more each season.

You may choose to use as few or as many beds as your time allows—or assign a bed or two to other family members for their own special project. These design plans are flexible enough to adapt to almost any terrain and they suit changing contemporary needs to a T. Geometric shapes lend themselves nicely to containers, too (roof gardeners, please note). A clay pot or a wooden half-barrel is, after all, just a circle. A square is a square, whether it's dug in the ground or takes the form of a square box on a rooftop.

Scaling the size of only part of a design up or down for your site is yet another possibility. The central core of the gardens shown in Designs 1 and 2 can be enlarged and used as a guide, since each is a self-contained element. A series of triangles looks lovely for a long, narrow plot or next to a path. The idea is simply to be conscious enough to design the elements of your garden so that your vegetables, fruits and herbs are planted in attractive patterns. The crops are planted intensively, according to the methods outlined in Chapters 8 and 9.

Putting the Add-a-Garden Plan into Practice

Your first step in designing your garden is to plan a "graph paper garden." Mistakes are much easier to erase on paper, and a carefully detailed plan is one that you can (and will) keep and refer to year after year. Here is a list of supplies you will need:

Graph paper ruled into ¼-inch blocks (each block can represent 1 square foot of garden space)

A ruler

A pencil

A few templates of the type used by architects and draftsmen to use in playing with design possibilities, and to help you depict the size and amount of vegetables you can grow in each garden bed (see Chapter 6 for further details).

Tracing paper and five different colored pencils or pens for color-coding the vegetable plot to depict succession plantings (discussed in Chapter 5).

On pages 75 through 79 you will find three sample garden designs. These designs may be copied in their entirety or merely serve as a point of inspiration and departure. Page 79 shows two additional garden designs which, when scaled down to a miniature size, make especially lovely herb gardens. Included also are some additional "serendipity" samples, which you will find on page 73. These are design possibilities that I arrived at while playing with a template and some graph paper. Consider these designs as rough, easy-to-do doodles. After you have come up with some of your own design doodles that you like, transfer them in detail and to scale onto your graph paper. Don't be afraid to play with your ideas. Pencil and paper help you to clarify them.

The first step of any design, however, is to go outside and study the site, even before you work out your preliminary master plan on paper. This first step is crucial—it can mean success or failure. So take into account the suggestions below.

Step One: Assess the Site

Carefully study and measure the space to be used. Take notes—it's easy to forget from garden to house. Then, while standing in the future garden space and looking around you, ask yourself as many of the following questions as are applicable:

How does the sun travel?

Which parts of the space are partly shaded? Which ones are in full sun? Or total shade? Which have sun throughout the entire day?

Are there ugly views—towers, traffic, blank walls, exposed pipes, chimneys on roofs—that your garden should conceal?

Is there a great deal of wind or smoke?

Will you solve these problems by building structural screens or fences, or by plantings—or both?

If your garden will be on a rooftop, what about the floor? You must decide on an easily maintained flooring if none is in place now, and also consider whether there are adequate drains, a source of water, and lighting for evening use.

Should you consult someone with engineering experience and get some advice on weight loads for rooftop gardens?

Did you remember to get permission from your landlord if your apartment building is not a co-op?

When planning your design, consider the style of your surroundings and try to relate what you will put outside with what you have inside. Finally, throughout the whole planning process, consider realistically how much time you can devote to your garden. Starting small with bigger ideas for the future gives you something to look forward to and will not overwhelm you. Don't be overly ambitious or your beautiful garden may never get finished. You don't want to plot and plan more than you can take care of. Creating a garden design in phases in an easy way to go. Therefore, each separate phase of the total plan must be a unit that is complete unto itself.

Step Two: Draw the Plan

Now you're ready to put a design on paper. Don't expect to get it looking exactly like you want it to on the first try. Let yourself play a little, and try different shapes in different places. Placing a sheet of tracing paper over your graph paper and securing it with masking tape allows the graph paper to show through. You will then be able to make as many scaled, rough experimental drawings as you wish. When you decide on a final design, draw it more carefully, directly onto the graph paper.

Step Three: Put It All Together

The design looks beautiful on paper, but how do you transfer it to the garden? Simple. First, you walk through your ideas in the actual space, making changes as you go—much like the way you would a room from a floor plan. Then, along with your graph paper design, take with you a roll of strong kite string, a package of bamboo chopsticks or wooden stakes of the same size, and a length of garden hose. Mark off the outer boundaries of the garden by tying the kite string to the chopsticks, sticking them into the ground at intervals of the same depth, and keeping the string taut.

After that you must find the central core, or nucleus, of the design. This will be the first complete phase, or unit, of your total design plan. To find the center, make an X by running strings diagonally between the points of the shape which you have already marked off. The point at which the strings cross over one another is the center of your garden. From this point, laying out the beds is "a piece of cake," as they say. Working from the core and consulting your graph paper plan, just continue to measure and mark the design on the ground with string and chopsticks, allowing for pathways between the geometric beds within this first unit of your garden.

Next, using another chopstick as a tool and the strings as a guide, trace the shape of this first unit into the earth. If the garden-to-be is a lawn at the moment, forget the tracings and just use the strings as your guide for digging into the sod and preparing the soil beds. If you want to test an idea quickly, or if you are using a freeform bed design, then stretch the garden hose until it forms the curved shape you're after. Just as the eraser is your friend on graph paper, so are your garden hose, string and chopsticks all effort savers in the actual garden. It's easy to alter the shape of the garden before you dig it.

At this point, stop. Don't be in a hurry.

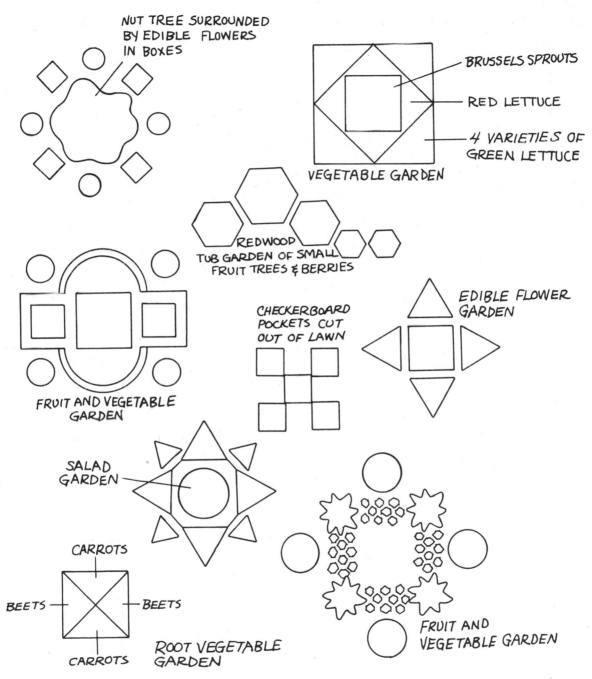

NUT TREE SURROUNDED BY EDIBLE FLOWERS IN BOXES

BRUSSELS SPROUTS

RED LETTUCE

4 VARIETIES OF GREEN LETTUCE

VEGETABLE GARDEN

REDWOOD TUB GARDEN OF SMALL FRUIT TREES & BERRIES

CHECKERBOARD POCKETS CUT OUT OF LAWN

EDIBLE FLOWER GARDEN

FRUIT AND VEGETABLE GARDEN

SALAD GARDEN

CARROTS

BEETS

BEETS

CARROTS

ROOT VEGETABLE GARDEN

FRUIT AND VEGETABLE GARDEN

Some examples of garden designs made with an architect's template.

Wait a day. Then study your marked-off design again for changes before you pick up a shovel.

Adding the Plants to the Design

Like any flat floor plan, the two elements that are missing in your garden design are height (the third dimension) and grouping or arrangement of the plants. Here are some design tips for special effects to consider as you begin to figure out what to plant where within the design:

One of anything, whether it is a plant or a garden ornament, gives a very special emphasis and creates a focal point or accent. If you wish to create a scene stealer, place it above eye level and its importance will be further spotlighted.

Two of something also has impact; the effect is a bit more formal when the objects are obviously paired. The uniqueness of an effect is sometimes diminished and sometimes punched up. This is a tricky factor to handle.

Three plants or three growing beds grouped together (remember this for containers, too) is a universally pleasing and restful number. Even in a vase with cut flowers, one or three stems always look better than two.

Four plants or shapes grouped together, unless they are in a block, are strangely less effective than three or five. Somehow, odd numbers have more appeal.

Five plants, beds, or containers massed together create a very strong, bold group.

To place vegetables in a plot effectively, you must know what height the mature plants will be. Usually taller plants are placed on the north side of the garden and also where they can support each other visually and physically. Smaller plants are positioned to the south, so they will not be shaded by the taller plants.

Grouping vegetable plants (or any plants for that matter) of like kind is always more effective than spreading them out in a line, or dotting them here and there. Grouping solves other problems as well. Not every plant grows best in the same soil. Some need alkaline soil while others prefer acid soil; some like it moist, some like it dry; some like it warm, some like it cool. Having several small growing beds solves these problems since you can easily group vegetables with like needs together.

Multiple units also make it easier to practice crop rotation and companion planting; a geometric bed used for lettuce and other leafy vegetables one year might be planted with root crops the next year. Confining a planting area to a set space allows you to concentrate all your efforts on creating the very best growing environment for each vegetable. Having it all look beautiful while the plants grow is only a matter of designing the geometric forms into a pleasing arrangement fitting whatever shape and size space you have. By all means try growing your food plants in a more attractive, less conventional way than the standard rectangle filled with rows, even if you are an experienced gardener. The chances are that adding a new element of design to your vegetable plots will challenge your creativity and add a new joy to one of the oldest occupations in the world: creating a garden out of the wilderness.

Design 1: Add-a-Garden

Unit A

The central unit of this garden consists of a 6 by 14-foot rectangle divided into seven growing beds. The entire garden design will cover approximately 24 by 30 feet of space. The area marked 7 in the illustration is a 4-foot square placed at an angle in the center of the garden. You can add numbers 2, 3, 5 and 6, which are 3 by 4-foot triangles, and later add numbers 1 and 4, which are also 3 by 4-foot triangles. All paths in this garden are

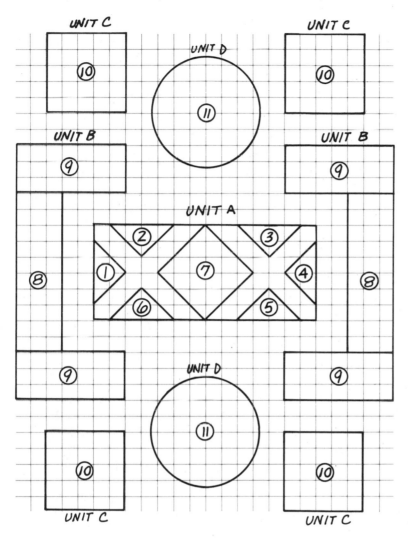

Design 1.

approximately 18 inches wide.

The central 6 by 14-foot rectangle can be carved out and planted as a small self-contained

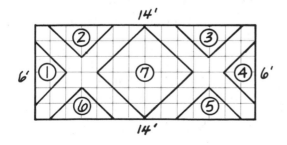

unit, and each year additional shapes can be added until the overall design is complete. Additional units can be cut directly into the earth, or contained with low walls of wood, brick or any other sturdy material. The pathways can be of straw, gravel, marble chips, brick or any material you like, with an underlayer of black plastic sheeting to keep down weeds.

Unit A can be planted with various kinds of leaf lettuce to create a colorful, leafy ornamental tapestry. For example, area 7 can contain alternating rows of red-tinged Ruby and ice green Salad Bowl lettuce to create a striped effect. Areas 1 and 4 can alternate carrots and radishes, whose foliage looks well together. Area 7 can also hold several Brussels sprouts plants, or a teepee of beans and then a cage of tomatoes—all plants that will create height and a central focus.

Unit B

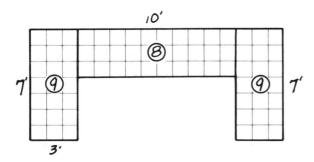

Unit B is used twice in this garden, to either side of Unit A. Area 8 is a 3 by 10-foot rectangle. The areas labeled 9 are 3 by 7-foot rectangles. The smaller rectangles are placed at either end of the large one. Allow approximately 24 inches for a wide path between Unit A and the two Unit B designs. (Refer back to the overall design on page 75.)

The 3 by 10-foot bed, area 8, has room for two fruit trees on either side. The trees can be espaliered if the garden is next to a wall or fence, or you could grow grapes trained to a fence. Strawberry plants can serve as a ground cover.

The 3 by 7-foot rectangles, area 9, can be used for bush fruits such as blueberries, currants or gooseberries.

Unit C

Unit C is used four times in this garden. It consists of four squares (area 10), each one 5 by 5 feet. These are placed to line up with area 9 of Unit B, on the outer edges. (See overall design on page 75.) The path between

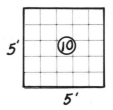

the two is about 24 inches wide.

These squares can hold raspberries in containers (so they don't overrun the garden) or dwarf fruit trees, either in the ground or planted in square containers.

Unit D

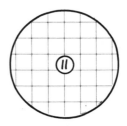

Unit D, which is used twice in this design, consists of two circular beds. Area 11 is a circle 7 feet in diameter. Each circle can be divided into smaller geometric-shaped beds to grow herbs, or can hold two small nut or fruit trees. For more information on planning circular beds, see Design 2 on page 77.

Each unit of Design 1 has great possibilities for change as your plot dictates. These beds can accommodate both ornamentals and down-home vegetable favorites with equal ease.

Possible Themes for Design 1

The Suburban Alternative to a Front Lawn: This Add-a-Garden is an attractive way to grow vegetables right out front for the same investment in money and time that you would otherwise apply to wasteful grass.

The Edible Poolside Garden: What could be more luxurious than picking fresh vegetables or fruit for a salad, just after a swim?

Design 2: In Circles

Design 2 can be used in its entirety, or you can try variations using Unit A (areas labeled 1) with areas 4, 5, 8 and 9. Another variation would be to use half of Unit A (only one area 1 semicircle) with areas 7, 8, 9 and 2. Use the following instructions according to the design in which you are interested.

To make a circle garden like Design 2, you must first establish a center point. In Design 2, the total space is a 20-foot square. Divide the square into four equal parts (as shown in illustration 1) and again from the four corners (illustration 2). The point where the four lines intersect is the center point.

From this center point, measure a circle approximately 8 feet in diameter (illustration 3). This is simple to do if you make yourself an outdoor compass from a chopstick, a funnel and a length of string. The string should be half as long (plus a few inches for tying) as the diameter of the circle you want to make. Tie one end of the string to the chopstick and anchor it in the ground at the center point. Tie the other end of the string to the funnel and fill the funnel with lime. Keep your finger over the end of the funnel. Pull the string taut and walk in a circle. Release your finger from the funnel as you walk so the lime traces the circle on the ground. Bisect the circle with an 18-inch access path (illustration 4), forming two semicircular beds. These beds, both of which are labeled 1, make up Unit A. Unit A is the core of Design 2, as well as a self-contained garden with other add-on possibilities.

How to lay out a circle. The numbered illustrations follow the text above.

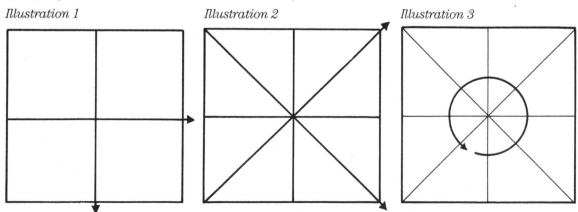

Illustration 1   Illustration 2   Illustration 3

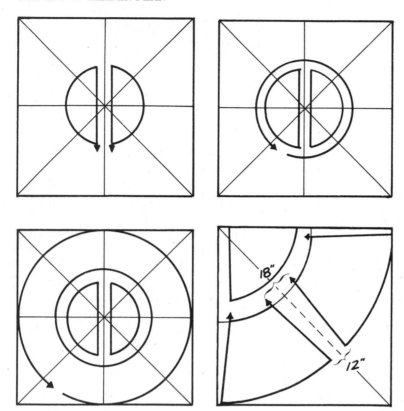

Illustration 4, top left; illustration 5, top right; illustration 6, bottom left and illustration 7, bottom right.

To complete Design 2, start from the center point and measure a second circle 9½ feet in diameter around Unit A (illustration 5). This circle marks an 18-inch access path around the core.

From the center point again, measure a circle 20 feet in diameter (see illustration 6). Use the lines dividing the original square (illustration 3) to mark off eight access paths, which will automatically form the eight wedge-shaped beds (areas 2 through 9 on the illustration of Design 2 shown on page 77). The paths will create a spoked wheel pattern around the beds, with Unit A as the hub or core.

The paths are formed by measuring an 18-inch opening at every intersecting line on the inside circle, and a 12-inch opening at the same point on the outside circle (see illustration 7 for an enlarged view). In the four cor-ners outside the circles there is enough room for tubs, barrels or boxes that you could use to grow some dwarf fruit trees or berry bushes.

There are many advantages and great flexibility with a circular garden. The garden can be easily watered by a revolving sprinkler set in the center. Each bed can be prepared for plants of different soil requirements, and crop rotation is easily achieved by shifting to the next or the opposite bed. The paths here may be planted as lawn (but they will have to be hand trimmed since a lawn mower may not fit), or fieldstone, slate, wood or marble chips.

Possible Themes for Design 2

To Each His Own—A Family Garden: Each member of the family can be assigned his or her own wedge or two as an individual project. Dividing the garden like this always

78

spurs a friendly competitive spirit, and also insures that one family member won't get stuck doing all the garden work.

Weekend Escape Garden: For a country house or seashore retreat where a low maintenance garden is needed, the separate wedges are more manageable.

Design 3:
The Circle in the Square

Design 3 is garden that can measure 14 by 14 feet, or the space can be doubled to 28 by 28 feet to fit nicely into city or suburban back or front yards. The garden is composed of thirteen separate growing beds. Unit A, area 13, is the central core which is the nucleus of the design. Unit B consists of four center beds in an angled square, areas 9, 10, 11 and 12. Unit C is made up of eight triangles, areas 1, 2, 3, 4, 5, 6, 7 and 8.

Unit A consists of an inner circle 3 feet in diameter with a 1-foot-wide path around it (area 13). This bed is small enough to let you reach the middle from all sides. It could easily accommodate tomatoes in a tower cage, or

serve as a sanctuary for birds, with a bird bath surrounded by dwarf sunflowers. Or the circle could be tiered, for height, to grow flowers, herbs or strawberries.

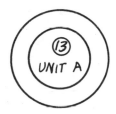

Unit B is achieved by marking off a 9-foot square and placing it on an angle within the 14 by 14-foot space. Areas 9 through 12 are about 3½ by 3½ feet and could easily grow anything that goes with salad. It is possible to add areas 9 through 12 as a second phase, and then add the remaining eight triangular beds in phase three.

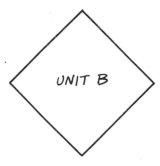

Paths (a) and (b) are 2 feet wide, path (c) is 1 foot wide. Bricks can be laid for the pathways, or you can use any other suitable material you have available. The advantage to using bricks is that there is virtually nothing to maintain. The garden paths can easily be swept or even vacuumed, and two of the paths are wide enough for an evening stroll.

The triangular beds, areas 1 through 8, measure approximately 2 by 4 feet each. They could accommodate a selection of culinary herbs nicely.

Paths for Design 3. Paths a and b are 2 feet wide; path c is 1 foot wide.

Eventually a 3-foot-wide border of bricks could frame this garden, and it could then become a patio with seating or dining space.

Possible Themes for Design 3

A Small Garden for Small People: For children, the separate beds encourage neatness and are small enough to sustain interest.

A Vest Pocket Salad Garden: Good for those who don't have much time for garden maintenance. A great deal of pleasure can be derived from a garden that people can cope with easily.

A Garden for a Chinese Chef: Everything needed for cooking in a wok could grow in areas where Oriental vegetables and herbs are hard to come by.

Designs 4-8

The following five garden designs offer additional possibilities for your own space, be it square or rectangular. The geometric beds within break up the overall space symmetrically and are achieved in the same way as those in Designs 1, 2 and 3. Just follow the numbered beds in sequence to add on to your garden plan a bit at a time.

Some additional design possibilities, below, designs 4 and 5.

In designs 4 and 5 shown at left and 6, 7 and 8, above, textured areas indicate pathways, white areas are growing beds. Numbers indicate the sequence in which the beds should be laid out. Each of these designs can be cut in half vertically or horizontally, or divided into quarters, to create smaller gardens that are still symmetrical.

81

CHAPTER 5

The Plot Thickens— Planning the Plantings

When you're dealing with small garden beds in a variety of shapes and sizes, careful planning is the prime ingredient for maximum production. Essentially what you want to do is make practical use of every available inch, but in an attractive, orderly manner. Ideal planting plans call for the continuous ripening of small quantities of many different crops over the longest possible period of time. That's your goal. But to achieve it, or come as close to it as possible, you must skillfully plan on paper how to take the best advantage of the grab bag of intensive gardening techniques.

When selecting vegetables, fruits and herbs for my garden, I consider a number of things. I try to choose crops that produce well in my climate. I grow those that are either difficult to find in markets or expensive to buy. I select those that we enjoy eating, knowing that their nutrition, flavor, texture and crispness will be greatly enhanced because they are freshly picked. Every year I experiment with either a few new vegetables or some different varieties of the same ones. I like to experiment, mostly to increase my know-how, but also because it's always fun to see something new growing. I try not to go overboard by planting too much, since I'm not trying to feed the whole neighborhood. It's best, I have found, to take good care of fewer vegetables rather than plant too many and neglect them all.

Even the most experienced gardeners usually plan their plantings on paper first, although after years of experience the plan may be pared down to a simple list of what crops to grow and how much of each to plant. For less experienced gardeners, a detailed planting plan is a valuable learning aid and should be used. First, remember that a paper plan should only be a working document—not a work of art. But if you do not invest a little time in paperwork first, to plot your growing beds, you may waste a lot of the precious growing season, along with your time and effort later. A paper plan organizes the decision-making process and so allows you to make the most efficient use of space and to use the techniques of companion and succession planting. You will be able to see at a glance from your paper plans the best combination of growing conditions, proper planting dates and the best placement for plants. Just standing in the garden with a packet of seeds and tossing them in the ground haphazardly will *insure* poorer results. Since you've already designed your garden beds on paper (in the last chapter), you'll now just basically be filling in that plan.

When you begin to plan, these are the

things you must consider:

What vegetables, fruits and herbs (and flowers!) to grow

The best varieties for your space and climate

The quantity you need

Where you will position them in the plot

The spacing between plants, and which ones will need support as they grow

The approximate planting and harvest dates

Companion plants and where to place them

You can see that a preliminary paper plan will save you lots of hard work, money and confusion. Thinking it all out beforehand will help you avoid mistakes and disappointments in the end.

The vegetable selection chart on page 101 can be used as a guide for your own planning. Take a look at it now. Here's an example of how it can help you plan. Suppose you want to grow cabbage. The chart tells you that cabbage is a cool season (CS) vegetable that needs full sun ☼ and is very hardy (VH), which means that it can go into the ground several weeks before the first frost-free date in spring. The chart gives you a choice of four varieties, all of which are suited for small spaces or containers. The chart also gives information on maturity dates, to help guide you in planning for succession crops. In addition, there are suggestions on equidistant spacing based on the size of the mature plant. The chart also offers information on the characteristics of

each plant and which seed companies sell the varieties recommended. You will find similar information for fruits and herbs in the charts on pages 122 and 131, respectively.

In Chapter 4, where I showed you several geometric beds and garden designs, the scale for the graph paper was ¼ inch on paper to 1 foot of actual garden space. That scale allows you to sketch out the garden on a smaller piece of paper. But when you are plotting which vegetables to grow in those beds, I suggest that you enlarge your scale to let 1 inch on paper equal 1 foot in the garden. This will allow you more space on your graph paper to indicate placement of the plants in the beds (see the illustration on page 85).

You may also want to tuck in some extra vegetables or herbs in more scattered areas that are not part of the main garden beds. These extra pocket gardens increase limited space and may offer better growing conditions— more sun, perhaps, or support along a fence, or some dappled shade for midsummer lettuce. To make your own graph paper plans, just measure the spot where you want to plant (it might be along a path or fence, for example), transfer the measurements to scaled graph paper and draw the geometric shapes to represent the extra places you have found. Then decide if the plants you'd like to grow will fit in these spaces. If the match can be made, cut out the shapes and arrange them on a large sheet of paper to make your own permanent master plan of all the growing spaces on your property.

When plotting my plantings, I use tracing paper overlays on top of my original graph paper design. The value of tracing paper is that by counting the squares underneath, I can plan equidistant or squared or row spacings between plants in better scale to the allotted space. The graph paper original can then be used over and over again while the tracing paper is used only to indicate seasonal changes.

Another method I used when I planned my own garden plots was to devise color-coded seasonal references, using a separate sheet of tracing paper and a different color for each planting season. Since my vegetable and herb garden started out only as a weekend affair, there was no time to waste, and the color coding gave me at-a-glance information. Each sheet quickly showed me what to plant during each part of my growing season. The plan also gave me an indication of the amount and spacing of each crop, and showed me which ones were perennials that would remain in the garden beds every year.

You might want to try my color-keyed system, so I've explained it below. First, you should be aware that the seasonal categories are keyed to the growing season in New York City, where I live. You will have to determine your own categories to make your plan correspond to your growing season. (Your county extension agent can give you information.) Second, because this book is not printed in color, I've devised texture symbols to substitute for colors. Different colors will be much easier to tell apart when you sketch out your own plan. For each vegetable, note the planting date, crop variety, and whether you will set out seeds or transplants. You can also color-code your plant labels in the garden to match your paper plan.

⊙ **Green:** Early spring crops. First planting as soon as ground can be prepared. These are the cold-tolerant, very hardy vegetables which can be planted four to six weeks before the frost-free date. Examples include broccoli, peas, Brussels sprouts and spinach (see the vegetable selection chart at the end of Chapter 6 for more).

◉ **Purple:** Later spring crops. These are hardy, cold-tolerant vegetables which can be planted frequently in small amounts from two weeks before the frost-free date until the heat of the summer sets in. Vegetables in this category include beets, radishes, carrots and lettuce.

⊜ **Orange:** Early summer. This group makes up the third planting, and consists of vegetables that are tender, warm-weather crops that cannot tolerate frost. They should be planted out between two and four weeks after the first frost-free date, or before, with protection. Most are heat tolerant and need lots of sun. This group includes tomatoes and cucumbers. I usually grow my own transplants for most of these vegetables, except for corn and snap beans, which are seeded directly. Many of these vegetables now grow in spaces where the purple-keyed vegetables had grown. I plant a few more purple-keyed varieties along with them, since they mature quickly and can grow in the shade that is cast by the taller-growing warm season vegetables.

○ **Blue:** Summer planting. For very tender vegetables such as transplants of eggplant and peppers. Most of the vegetables planted earlier are still in the garden. At the time these vegetables are planted, you can also make a second planting of green-keyed vegetables to mature for harvest in fall. Homegrown transplants of blue-coded vegetables are planted in the sunniest spots available, near vegetables to be harvested soon, to allow the blue-coded vegetables the additional room they will need to grow. New transplants of vegetables that can withstand some frost or that mature quickly before frost sets in are also planted in late summer. Broccoli, lettuce and Chinese cabbage are examples.

◍ **Brown:** Companion plants. They are grown nearby, usually as borders or in separate containers to help deter pests. Companions include various herbs, particularly chives and garlic, as well as flowers such as marigolds and nasturtiums.

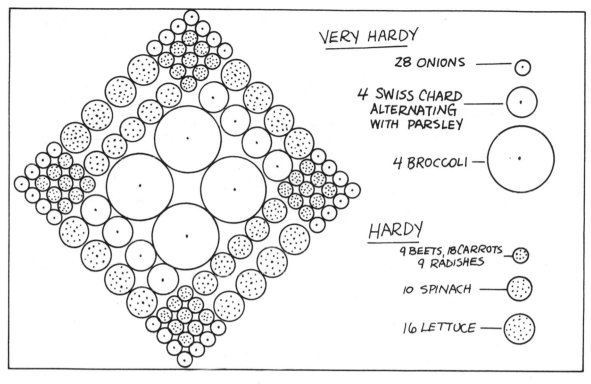

VERY HARDY

28 ONIONS ⎯⎯⎯⎯ ⊙

4 SWISS CHARD
ALTERNATING ⎯⎯⎯⎯
WITH PARSLEY

4 BROCCOLI ⎯

HARDY

9 BEETS, 18 CARROTS
9 RADISHES

10 SPINACH ⎯⎯⎯⎯

16 LETTUCE ⎯⎯⎯⎯

This diagram shows the first planting of hardy spring crops for bed 7 in the center of unit A of Design 1 (see page 75).

⊕ Red: Perennials, such as asparagus and rhubarb, which occupy the same space at all times.

I suggest that you work in pencil first, on tracing paper, and when you have indicated all the plants and their spacings with circles in an arrangement that pleases you, then go over the pencil marks with color. Indicate the variety as well as the type of vegetable on an accompanying piece of paper. The next crop that is to follow in the same space or be interplanted with the main crop is drawn in the same manner on a fresh sheet of tracing paper, using another color to indicate the next planting. Take a look at the accompanying illustration to see how a plan might look. Remember that when you draw your own plan you will be able to use different colors instead of symbols for the various plantings.

Some Advice on Deciding What To Grow

Here is a quick rundown of the criteria you can use to decide what you want to grow in your garden. At this point, don't worry about specific varieties—that will come later. It's enough now to concentrate on the crops. Here are some points to consider:

Vegetable, fruit or herb is difficult (or impossible) to find in the market.

Can't find it as fresh as it should be.

Can't find vegetables as young as you'd like them (baby eggplant or new potatoes, for example).

Vegetable, fruit or herb is available but prices are unreasonable (raspberries, for example).

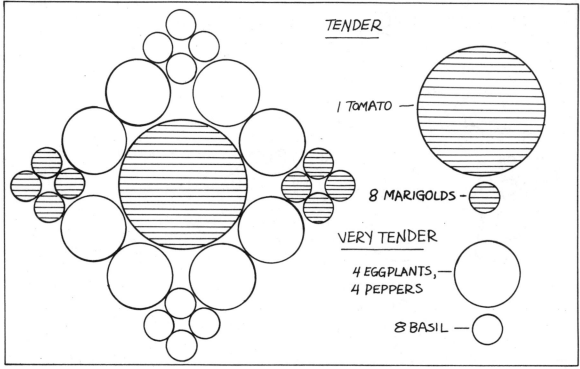

This plan indicates location and spacing of a summer planting of tender crops for bed 7. These seasonal planting plans can be done on tracing paper overlays on your basic garden design, so you don't have to redraw it for every new planting.

Finally, ask yourself if this vegetable, herb or fruit will give you a good return for the amount of space and time you will invest in growing it.

If you are considering putting some fruit trees in your garden, there are some special points to take into account when you start narrowing your list of choices:

Fruit trees need space. In a limited space, choose a dwarf or semidwarf tree. A dwarf tree needs 8 to 10 square feet; a semidwarf needs about 15 square feet.

Get in touch with your local Cooperative Extension agent for specific information about tree fruits that are hardy in your climate zone. The agent can also give you pruning and thinning information. Remember to check on hardiness before ordering from a nursery.

The most important ingredients in good fruit production are a sunny site, even and abundant moisture, and the most disease-resistant varieties.

When you're ready to buy trees, get the oldest you can afford. Burlap-covered roots are better than bare roots.

If you buy any grafted trees (and many dwarfs are grafted onto special rootstocks), remember when you plant them that the graft union must be at least an inch *above* the surface of the soil.

Remember that tree fruits need time—it takes at least two years before you can harvest from a dwarf tree, depending on the age of the tree when you bought it. Full-size trees take even longer.

Succeeding with Succession Planting

There are several ways to make successive plantings in order to have a nonstop garden. The idea is simply to keep all your small garden spaces working from very early spring through the summer and well into fall. Here are some suggestions for successsion planting; you can try some or all of these techniques in your own garden:

Don't plant everything all at once, but don't let your garden space stand empty, either. Repeated sowings of the same vegetable keep the harvest coming for longer time. For example, put in a new lettuce transplant in the same place where you have harvested a fully grown lettuce. Or, try staggered sowings or "relays," which work well for short season vegetables that reach maturity quickly, such as radishes. Just plant a few at a time in the same row or space so they all don't need to be harvested at once.

Plant several different varieties of the same vegetable with differing maturation times. This method also allows you to pick ripe produce over a longer period of time, and instead of staggering your plantings, you can do it all at once.

Plan seasonal plantings. Early spring plantings of hardy cool-weather vegetables can be followed by a planting of warmth lovers, which are in turn followed by a fall crop of cool-weather plants.

Timing is crucial. For warm-weather crops like corn, cucumbers and squash, the soil must be at least 60°F or warmer or the seed could rot. To keep plants growing fast, don't put in the summer crops too early. How can you tell when the time is right? Legend has it that the Indians waited until oak leaves were the size of a mouse's ear before planting their corn. If there are no mice around to compare oak leaves with, a soil thermometer will help.

Interplant. In the same space sow two or more crops that differ in maturation time. You can alternate the plants in the same growing bed and space them very close together. Fast-growing vegetables such as radishes, lettuce or spinach can be planted along with a slower-growing crop such as corn. The fast growers will be harvested by the time the slower crops need the additional space. You can also interplant vegeta-

Interplanting three crops with different maturation times is a great space saver. An early crop of lettuce and radishes will be harvested by the time the corn is large enough to need the extra growing room.

bles of different sizes and growing habits, such as carrots and lettuce, or corn and squash, to make more efficient use of available space.

Interplant vegetables with similar cultural needs, like peppers and eggplant. It's easier to care for plants when they need similar amounts of sun and water, and the soil can be specially prepared for their needs (in the case of flowering and fruiting plants like peppers and eggplant, you'd probably put more bone meal in the soil). Besides, the plants look decorative growing close to one another, with their varying colors and leaf shapes.

To keep the garden working as hard as it should, start your successive plantings either in flats indoors or in a separate small outdoor growing bed designated as a supply garden or holding area, which acts as a continuous nursery. When garden space becomes available you can replace the spent crops with new transplants, instead of starting again from seed. This obviously saves growing time in the main garden beds.

Toward the season's end, extend the harvest by several weeks and protect tender vegetables from early frosts with the same protective devices you have used to get an early spring start. (These protective devices are discussed in Chapter 13.)

Cool-weather vegetables that are transplanted out in late summer to mature in fall usually do better than when they are planted in the spring. These are mostly the cole crops: kale, Brussels sprouts, broccoli, cauliflower, Chinese cabbage. In a small garden filled to the brim with summer crops it is difficult to find space for these fall crops until the tender vegetables have been harvested. But the young transplants grow slowly at first, taking up very little space, and they will grow faster as the weather turns cooler. Plant them wherever space exists after the tender vegetables are harvested, or as a replacement for faded summer flowers.

Planning for Powerful Partners

Companion plants have been used by gardeners for a long, long time. But as with most gardening principles, gardeners dispute the success of the attraction and protection that companion planting tries to achieve. Some people call companion planting a questionable combination of fact and fancy. But I know many gardeners who have witnessed the desired results of planting with companion plants, and I feel strongly that they are indeed the helpmates so many gardeners believe them to be. One thing that may cause companion planting to fail for some gardeners is not planting the companions in sufficient quantity. One marigold plant sitting alone in a tomato patch will do little more than be a spot of yellow in a field of green. When you garden in small, scattered Euclidean beds, as I have suggested here, planting sufficient amounts of companion plants can become a problem when you're looking for extra space to include them. But the problem is not an insurmountable one if you follow these two suggestions for companions:

First, select easy-care companions that don't interfere with the time you can give to your first priority—growing vegetables.

Second, use only companion plants that are capable of serving you in more than one way.

The two easiest-to-grow insect-repellent flowers I use in my own garden are dwarf marigolds in several shades of yellow and the jewellike, multi-colored nasturtiums. They practically grow themselves. In addition to repelling nematodes in the soil, the marigolds also provide bouquets for the table. The nasturtium flowers and leaves have a peppery flavor;

Good and Bad Companions

Good Relationships (Marry)

Beans - marigolds - potatoes

Beets - carrots - onions

Beets - kohlrabi - carrots - onions — any of the brassicas (cabbage family)

Any brassicas - onions - beets - radishes - lettuce - carrots

Carrots - onions - peas - beets

Corn - beans - squash

Cucumbers - radishes

Marigolds (planted throughout the garden to cut nematode population) - cucumbers - brassicas

Nasturtiums - squash - potatoes - brassicas

Onions - lettuce - carrots - beets - radishes

Peas - carrots - corn - beans - turnips - parsnips

Peppers - Swiss chard

Potatoes - beans - peas - eggplants - corn

Radishes - squash - lettuce - tomatoes - cucumbers

Squash - corn - radishes - beans

Tomatoes - marigolds - radishes - carrots - spinach

Bad Relationships (Divorce)

Bush beans - onions

Pole beans - onions - beets - kohlrabi - sunflowers

Carrots - dill

Chives - peas - beans

Cucumbers - potatoes

Onions - peas - beans

Peas - onions - garlic - potatoes

Squash - potatoes

Tomatoes - kohlrabi

they can be used in salads and sandwiches and as edible garnishes, as well as for repelling insects. I also rely heavily on the alliums—onions of all kinds, leeks, garlic, chives and other onion relatives—as another proven, double-duty companion. Finally, I plant lots of culinary herbs, which also make useful companion plants. (See the herb chart in Chapter 6 for companion recommendations.)

Since my garden space is at a premium, I find that the most effective and practical way for me to practice companion planting is to use a narrow band or border no more than 4 inches wide of these flowers, herbs or vegetables from the onion family around each of the garden beds. This practice also defines the shapes of the beds and enhances them either with the brilliant color of flowers, with the strong, spiky foliage of the onion family or with fragrant herbs for cooking. There are so few dishes that are prepared without some kind of allium or herb that these plants never go to waste. Basil repels insects that bother cucumbers, squash and tomatoes, so I plant lots of basil near these vegetables. When I needed to choose between thyme or hyssop as a plant to repel the cabbage worm, I decided not to use hyssop because it's not edible. Instead, I chose a low, creeping border of delicate, silvery-leaved thyme to surround my cabbage patch.

Another way I use companions is to plant companion herbs in movable containers which are situated near the vegetable the herbs are intended to protect. For example, rosemary and sage are said to repel carrot fly, bean beetle and cabbage moth, so pots of them are kept near my carrots, beans and cabbage.

One more way to companion plant effectively would be to place several small herb gardens close by your vegetable beds and have the herb beds serve as a collection of many different kinds of companion plants.

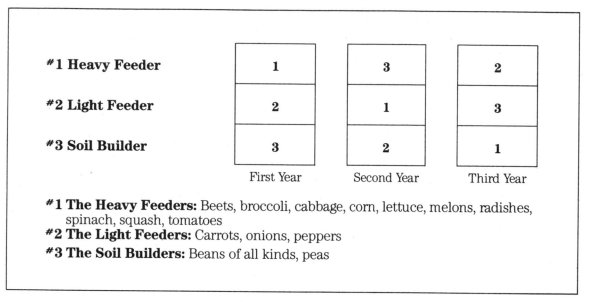

	First Year	Second Year	Third Year
#1 Heavy Feeder	1	3	2
#2 Light Feeder	2	1	3
#3 Soil Builder	3	2	1

#1 The Heavy Feeders: Beets, broccoli, cabbage, corn, lettuce, melons, radishes, spinach, squash, tomatoes
#2 The Light Feeders: Carrots, onions, peppers
#3 The Soil Builders: Beans of all kinds, peas

This diagram shows a three-year plan for rotating crops among three garden beds.

When we refer to certain plants as companions, we are talking not only about plants which repel destructive insects and attract pollinators but also about those which have positive influences over one another, which seem to help each other grow in a symbiotic relationship. Just as a good marriage is one in which both partners contribute to and benefit from the relationship, so it is with the plant world. Some plants like each other while others do not and will inhibit each other's growth. The chart titled Good and Bad Companions lists plant pairs that have a good relationship and should marry, and pairs that are better off divorced and kept at opposite ends of the garden.

When companion plants are intercropped together, the resulting vegetable tapestry can help to defeat bugs whose reproduction rates depend on an unlimited food supply. The bugs are kept to a minimum because no *one* crop predominates in the garden. When you do plant large amounts of one crop, staggering the planting times can also help make the insects' food scarce and thus aid in keeping down their populations.

Crop Rotation Made Easy

The last technique we will consider in relation to planning what to plant where is rotation of crops throughout the various garden beds. Here are two important reasons for rotating your vegetables, followed by some easy ways you can do it on a small scale:

First, many insects and some soilborne disease organisms can build up and remain in the soil if the same crop is planted in the same place year after year.

Second, some vegetables take enormous quantities of nutrients from the soil and deplete it severely. They are the heavy feeders. Although it is possible to replace some nutrients with supplemental organic fertilizers during the growing season, vegetable quality and quantity will eventually decline if the same nutrients are always taken from the soil in one spot.

The vegetables which are heavy feeders, and which deplete the soil in one bed, should be replaced the following year by those which are light feeders. Legumes such as peas and beans are blessed with the ability to take nitrogen from the air and fix it into the soil in a form that is readily used by other plants. They are the soil builders. It's only logical to rotate heavy feeders with soil builders, and then follow with the lighter feeders, to outsmart bugs and diseases as well as to keep the soil in good nutrient balance. The illustration shows how you might plan your garden rotations for the first three years. Then the entire sequence can be repeated again.

On a small scale, as when you're growing vegetables in containers, you simply have to remember never to plant the same vegetable in the same container two seasons in a row. Assign each of your vegetables to a numbered group according to their nutrient needs. Put a numbered label (written in waterproof ink) on each container as a quick reference to what grew where the year before. Then change labels each year and plant a vegetable from the next group.

Another helpful guide to planning crop rotations, besides knowing vegetables' feeding habits, is knowing which botanical family the vegetables come from. Members of the same botanical family, whether they are vegetables, flowers or even weeds, are usually susceptible to many of the same types of insect pests and diseases. They also tend to absorb the same nutrients from the soil as they grow.

For me it was love at first sound, botanically speaking. The Latin family names are endowed with the most mellifluous sounds, which have the delightful ring of grand opera to my ears. Of course, when you rotate your vegetables it's not necessary to know related vegetables by their Latin family names, or even their genus names. But it doesn't hurt, and it can be fun to learn them. The following list includes family groups of some of the more familiar vegetables.

Cruciferae: also referred to as cole crops or the Cabbage family, this family includes broccoli, Brussels sprouts, cabbage, cauliflower, Chinese cabbage, collards, cresses, horseradish, kale, kohlrabi, mustard greens, radishes, rutabagas and turnips.

Chenopodiaceae: the Goosefoot family, includes beets, spinach and Swiss chard.

Leguminosae: the legumes, includes all beans and peas.

Umbelliferae: includes carrots, celery, Florence fennel and some herbs, such as dill, parsley and caraway.

Cucurbitaceae: includes cucumbers, melons, pumpkins and squash.

Solanaceae: eggplant, peppers, potatoes and tomatoes.

Some day all of this information may come in handy. You may hear a botanically astute mother issue a command to her child to "Eat your Chenopodiaceae!" and you will be the only one at the table who can translate for others that she is admonishing her child to eat his spinach. Or you may just have an easier time figuring out your crop rotations.

Summing Up: A Checklist of Tips to Help You Plot a Vegetable Garden

Here is a checklist you can use at garden-planning time, when you're figuring out what to plant where:

First, group your list of crops into leafy vegetables, root crops, and flowering/fruiting plants. Next you can take note of some important characteristics.

Check the preferred soil conditions of each.

Root crops need the most friable soil since their edible parts are formed underground.

Note their NPK demands: leafy greens require more nitrogen (N), flowering crops need more phosphorus (P), root crops need more potassium (K) for good growth.

Next, note the space each plant takes and the height to which each grows. Also consider what type of support, if any, is required.

Most leafy crops and root crops grow to a fairly limited height and provide the greatest yields in the smallest space. You will want to position them to the south of taller-growing plants.

Plants that flower and produce fruit generally grow taller and take up lots of space when allowed to sprawl. When tied to a vertical support, they will occupy only a fraction of the space. They will also cast some shade on leafy crops during the time of year when you may just want to shield them from strong sunlight. Plant them on the north side of the garden.

Grouping plants together according to their harvest time will allow you to replant a whole small bed at once. For example, eggplants and peppers take about the same amount of time to mature and have compatible growth habits. They would make natural bedmates. Beets, kohlrabi, radishes and carrots, which share the same needs and can be picked about 60 days after planting, would be another likely group to plant together.

When planning, remember the "two-timers"; which can be planted twice during the growing season, to produce a crop in spring and fall. This group includes most of the cole crops.

Also, don't overlook the "cut-and-come-again" vegetables; these may remain in the garden for a longer period, but if you cut individual outer leaves, the plants continue to produce new leaves from the center. Many leaf crops are cut-and-come-again plants, including collards, Swiss chard, mustard greens, and leaf lettuce.

How to Plan a Vacation Garden

Garden season is also the traditional vacation time, and if you plan a vacation, you may also want to plan your garden with this in mind. You may rent or own a summer place and want to be a minimal weekend or summer farmer. If so, consider these four options:

1. An early spring and early summer garden, with fast-maturing root and leaf crops.

2. A three-month summer garden concentrating on the heat-loving vegetables—tomatoes, beans, cucumbers, squash and eggplant.

3. A late summer and fall garden to be started from transplants for an "instant" garden of frost-tolerant vegetables. Start your own seeds indoors a month before setting out transplants, or buy them already started from a nursery.

4. A garden of delightful herbs to use in cooking.

One final note about planning your garden: when planning how many plants of each vegetable to grow, don't plant more than you can use. It still amazes me that one tiny seed weighing a fraction of an ounce eventually turns into a food plant that gives and gives and gives. In one week one tomato plant could yield three tomatoes, one squash plant could yield three squash and one cucumber plant could yield two cucumbers. A single Brussels sprout plant could hold up to 100 tiny sprouts on its stem and provide two to three pounds of them in a season. So keep this in mind as you plan, or you may find yourself overwhelmed at harvest time. You don't need lots of space, just a lot of ingenuity to make your paper plans work in the garden.

Deciphering the Catalogs— Choosing Vegetable, Fruit and Herb Varieties

January is always an appropriate month to get a head start on the next growing season and to plan what you are going to plant and where you will put it. And just in time to feed this rousing, awakening garden fever is when the seed catalogs arrive. When they do, I caution you to practice a most rigid exercise in self-control. Seed catalogs are specifically designed to seduce you with fantasies of color and word pictures tempting enough to make you desire just about everything (and in a weak moment, order everything). But hold back! Most gardeners have a tendency to go overboard when ordering by mail from seed catalogs.

We flip through the beckoning pages lost in a trance, gazing upon offerings of perfectly shaped, totally blemish-free vegetables portrayed in all their colorful glory.

And I must confess that even though I know better, I weaken and join the gardeners who always order too many seeds. In another category there are last minute gardeners who wait to buy transplants—a six pack of instant gratification—young vegetable seedlings, nursery grown and ready to be set out into the garden. But personally I think that seedling varieties are usually boring and of limited variety, and prefer to start my own seeds.

However, gardeners who are content to buy the same old seeds or transplants year after year are missing out on new or better vegetable varieties. In addition, seed catalogs are a good source of information about the characteristics of vegetables, fruit trees, berries, nut trees, herbs and flowers, and the many varieties of each that are available. Along with planting and cultural instructions, recommendations of varieties for different climates and growing zones, there is garden lore, recipes and advice on freezing the surplus, plus a dizzying array of the latest available garden tools and gadgets. Once you learn to decipher the adjectives, terms and symbols, and as long as you bear in mind that the information is naturally promotional in nature, seed catalogs can become an ongoing educational tool to increase your garden savvy. Don't overlook the catalogs of small, regional seed companies, either. Many of these small firms specialize in varieties adapted to the region, or in hard-to-get, imported, or exotic seed varieties. Often, these companies also are first to offer a private stock, exclusive to them, of seed varieties that their own nurserymen have developed: a special hybrid or disease-resistant variety that they have improved along the way. The wildly popular Sugar Snap pea, for example, was developed by a breeder at the small Gallatin Valley Seed Company in Idaho.

Seed Catalog Hieroglyphics

So, before your eyes begin to glaze over and your head begins to swim when you leaf through the annual crop of catalogs (see the list at the back of this chapter for my favorites), and particularly if you are a novice gardener, take a look at the following guide to comprehending what I call "seed catalog hieroglyphics."

All-America Selections

An award given by the organization of the same name to new varieties that have been judged after trial growing in carefully monitored test plots to be adaptable to a wide climate range and possessed of a high degree of plant vigor. The awards are given each year. The All-America Selection designation in a catalog can reassure you that the variety is recognized as an advance in the seed breeder's art.

Times to Maturity

These are the numbers following the name of the variety, and they indicate the average number of days needed from planting to harvest. These numbers can be a valuable aid in planning succession plantings and intercropping early and late vegetables. But the numbers in the catalogs are only averages, and will vary with geographic location and the weather in a given year. Also, be sure to note whether the time to maturity is based on planting seeds or setting out transplants.

Early, Midseason or Late

Different varieties of the same crops mature at various times in the growing season, and these terms indicate their relative maturation times. Planting early, midseason and late varieties of some of your crops is another way to stretch your harvest over a longer time.

Hybrid

A hybrid is produced when parent plants of genetically different strains of the same species are cross-pollinated to develop a plant that possesses special desirable characteristics such as disease resistance, early maturity or sweeter flavor. Hybrids are more expensive because of these characteristics. Seed from a hybrid variety will not produce a plant just like its parent, because although hybrid plants all look alike, they are not genetically identical. Planting their seeds would produce plants with different combinations of genetic traits. Thus, you cannot collect seed from a hybrid plant to sow next year.

Open-Pollinated

This word refers to plants that haven't been hybridized. The plants have similar characteristics to those of the parent plants for many generations. You can collect and save the seeds of these vegetables when they have ripened.

Resistance

This term describes the ability of a plant to withstand the stresses of insect attack or disease, without interruption of its normal growth and production. Even a resistant plant can eventually succumb to a particular disease; the word resistant only means that the plant can withstand the attack for a longer time and to a greater degree than one that is not resistant.

Tolerance

A tolerant plant is less able than a resistant plant to withstand pests or disease, however, it can tolerate a certain level of disease or pest injury.

Traits for both tolerance and resistance appear after the variety name, sometimes as a set of initials designating the pathogen(s) to which the plant is resistant or tolerant. For example, the Beefmaster tomato carries the letters VFN after its name. The V indicates resistance to verticillium wilt, F indicates resistance to fusarium wilt, and N indicates resistance to nematodes. Seed catalogs usually explain these abbreviations; seed packets list them but don't explain them.

Slow-to-Bolt

Leafy plants like spinach and lettuce slow down on leaf production and send up seed stalks when temperatures get hotter and days get longer. Slow-to-bolt varieties are a better choice if you want to keep these leafy plants producing longer in summer.

Gynoecious

This word is a tip-off to plants which bear more fruit because they have all female flowers. Seed packets also include seeds for "male" plants, which have to be planted along with the females in order for pollination to occur. Some European varieties of cucumbers and squash are gynoecious..

Vegetable Characteristics

This is usually the "purple prose" part of the catalog, and the most promotional. However, catalog descriptions of a variety's characteristics will give you basic information, on the color of corn, for example, or whether peppers are hot or sweet or if a type of string bean will freeze well.

Vegetables— Spacemakers and Space Takers

When shopping through seed catalogs on your sofa, you have the advantage of comparing and considering different seedmen's recommendations. You have the leisure of learning about new available vegetable varieties and time to sort through the abundance of offerings. However, variety names differ from catalog to catalog and there is other confusing information to wade through when selecting what you want to grow. Take beets, for example. They produce a lot of food in a small space, with the bonus that both the roots and the

leaves are edible. Although beets are slow to germinate, once up they grow rapidly and are comparatively disease-free. In short, beets are a perfect choice for a small garden or an early crop in any garden. But there are round beets, beets with flat tops (called semiglobe), long cylindrical beets, dark red and golden beets, even white beets, and each seedsman has a different name for them. It's a lot like nail polish colors—they're all basically red and they're still nail polish but the changes in color range are subtle. So it is with beets (and all other vegetables as well).

What to do? How do you choose if you are a busy person with limited garden time? To help make your choice easier, I've put together a chart of vegetable varieties that are well suited to small spaces and containers, and that will work nicely in the garden designs in Chapter 4. For all of the varieties you can grow from seed I have listed by number some seed or nursery companies that carry them. The names and addresses of the companies are given (by number) at the back of this chapter.

Pick the correct vegetable and fruit varieties and put them into the proper size container, and you're two steps closer to gardening success. These varieties can also be used in spot pocket gardens and for food among the flowers. The selections were culled from my own favorite seed catalogs, and I chose them with their large yields and good taste in mind, as well as their compact size. I have stressed easy-to-grow varieties, and have also included vegetables that are not always available in the market and some that are too expensive or too unusual or too fragile to be shipped to market.

Tom Thumb lettuce, yellow sweet peppers and white eggplants are some examples of vegetable varieties which you may only be able to taste if you grow them yourself. In cases where standard-size varieties will fit into small spaces or containers I have included some. But some regular-size vegetables are simply out of bounds; a pumpkin or watermelon vine can blanket 50 square feet of a garden with their umbrella-size leaves and massive fruit. For these vegetables you should definitely seek out dwarf and miniature varieties.

Finally, the chart includes a few selections just for the fun of having them. Corn, for example, is not a practical choice for a small garden. It must be planted in groups for pollination to occur. On balconies and rooftops the tall stalks can easily blow over. And you must also remember that each corn stalk generally produces only two ears of corn. If you feel that the taste of sweet corn, freshly picked and rushed into the pot, is something you can't live without, then by all means do try some. But try one of the smaller varieties listed in the chart; they might be a bit more practical to grow.

If you decide to branch out on your own and do some seed catalog shopping, look for compact plants and varieties. They may be called bantam, midget, dwarf, patio and bush types. But basically there are three kinds of plants to look for:

Dwarf Plants: Also called bush, midget, patio and bantam types, these are heavy, stocky plants with short stems that produce *normal-size* fruit. Examples include Early White Bush squash, Bush Whopper cucumber and White Beauty eggplant.

Normal-size Plants: Some standard varieties have compact growth or produce small fruits. Examples include Bush Table Queen squash and Ichiban eggplant.

Small Plants: These are the true miniatures—little plants that produce small fruit (or leaves). This group includes Tiny Tim tomatoes, Tom Thumb lettuce, Mincu cucumbers and Minnesota Midget muskmelon.

The vegetable variety chart can be found on page 101. For your convenience in using them, all the variety selection charts are at the back of this chapter.

Advice for Selecting and Planting Fruit

Fruit trees and bushes can provide lots of pleasure both visually and with the gift of their luscious, sun-ripened fruit. Fruit trees come in a range of sizes, from the genetic dwarfs that make excellent container plants, to dwarfs that grow 8 to 10 feet tall, to the standards that grow 15 or more feet tall. Where space is limited, a dwarf or genetic dwarf variety is your best bet. Semidwarf varieties, at 12 to 15 feet tall, are also space savers, and will give you the most fruit per tree.

Dwarf varieties are actually full-size trees grafted onto a dwarfing rootstock that limits their growth. The result is a compact tree that bears full-size fruit. Genetic dwarf varieties have been specially bred so the entire tree is small, and the fruit is also somewhat smaller.

Bush fruits such as blueberries (also called small fruits) are nice additions to the landscape. They can be trained to grow as a hedge, and will help attract birds to your garden. Bush fruits also do well in containers—I have blueberry bushes in my rooftop garden in the city.

Here are some tips to keep in mind when selecting fruit varieties:

Many fruit trees are self-pollinating or self-fruitful, meaning they will produce fruit without pollination from another tree. Many of the genetic dwarf varieties that are so well suited to container growing are self-fruitful. But some fruit trees require pollination from a tree of another variety. To make your life easier, try to select self-fruitful varieties wherever possible. If you have room for only one tree, it will *have* to be self-fruitful. The chart on fruit varieties at the back of this chapter emphasizes self-pollinating varieties.

Don't be disappointed when your tree doesn't bear any fruit a year later; most standard fruit trees take from five to ten years to produce full crops. Dwarf trees mature faster and will begin to yield in two to three years; check your source for exact information.

Dwarf varieties tend to be shallow-rooted and are easily uprooted by wind storms. Try planting them near a fence, in a hedgerow, alongside a trellis or espaliered against a wall for extra support. (Also, it's very important when planting grafted trees to make sure the graft is at least 1 inch above the soil surface.)

No matter what variety you buy, always buy the oldest tree you can afford; balled and burlapped is better than bare-rooted.

Think about how you'd like to use the fruit you grow. Some varieties are outstanding for canning or freezing, or for jams and jellies. Others are good winter keepers, and will let you enjoy fresh fruit out of season. Check catalog descriptions for pointers on which varieties are best suited for which purposes. These characteristics are also noted in the chart Fruits for Containers and Small Spaces, on page 122.

Know your climate. That means knowing the climatic traits of your general region as well as the idiosyncrasies of your particular microclimate. Then choose varieties that are suited to your area. Your county extension agent can give you information on which varieties grow well in your region. You can also look for nurseries that cater to fruit growers in particular areas. For example, J. E. Miller Nurseries (see page 100 for their address) and Green Tech Nurseries (53 Four Mile Rd. S, Traverse City, MI 49684) offer hardy varieties for the North; Raintree Nurseries (265 Butts Rd., Morton, WA 98356) specializes in varieties for the Pacific Northwest.

Pay particular attention to varieties described as having disease resistance or tolerance.

If you have enough room for several fruit trees or bushes, try to stagger maturity dates. Choose early, midseason and late-bearing varieties to get a continuous harvest instead of an all-at-once glut.

Be cautious about the claims made for trees that have several varieties grafted onto one rootstock. These trees may solve cross-pollination and small space dilemmas, but caring for them can sometimes be tricky. The different varieties may exhibit differing levels of vigor, and the stronger ones will dominate and shade the weaker ones.

Your local Cooperative Extension agent is a good source of information on which fruit varieties generally do well in your area. It would be wise to consult him before buying any fruit trees or bushes.

Herbs—Double Pleasure Double-Duty Plants

A medieval scholar once proclaimed that since time began, herbs have been the "friends of physicians and the praise of cooks." Consuming passions often inspire other passions. Cooking and gardening are just such handmaidens, in which an interest in one provokes an attraction to the other. It is common for herb gardening to lead the cook into the inspiration and invention necessary for transformation into a passionate chef. In truth, he or she becomes totally involved with the flavor, character and distinction that freshly grown herbs add to the simplest of hurry-up meals. It is no wonder, then, that there are so many gardeners who are committed to growing herbs, for these charming "friends of the cook," lead a double life and pay off with the double dividend of edible, aromatic foliage (some of which repel insects) as well as an explosive burst of colorful flowers.

Since herbs are so very adaptable to any one of the growing methods outlined in this book: raised beds, pockets directly in the earth, food among the flowers and containers of all sorts, it seems only fitting to include a guide to some favorite culinary herbs. If you have only cooked with dried herbs until now, you are in for an adventure your palate will salute, for fresh herbs have a delicacy and true flavor range that cannot be achieved when dried and placed on a shelf. Dried herbs are stronger so you need to use less, but their flavors are sometimes "off" depending upon brands, the amount of light passing through the jars and the length of time they have been on the shelf. And the flavors of most herbs change significantly during drying, even when you carefully dry them yourself. Another strong argument for growing your own herbs is that so many fresh cooking herbs are never seen in the marketplace. And when you *can* buy fresh herbs, they are tremendously expensive. There is a whole new world of taste and fragrance waiting for you which will change your reputation from that of an ordinary cook to chef *extraordinaire*.

The chart 23 Herbs to Grow, at the back of this chapter, is a guide to 23 personal favorites that I have grown in bottomless containers of square flue tiles sunk into the sand at my seashore house. The tiles are placed at an angle, outlining a long narrow raised bed that is 2 feet wide and split into two sections. You can find the plan for my herb garden and directions for planting it on page 55.

If you are new to growing herbs, make an identification tag for each herb in your garden, noting the variety, its soil and sunlight needs, basic culture and uses. If you want to experiment with two or more closely related herbs, such as common thyme and lemon thyme, for example, look up the Latin name in *The Rodale Herb Book* or another reliable source, and use it when ordering seeds or plants to make sure you get what you want.

Gardening By Mail: A Gardener's Crop of Catalogs

Here's a list of my favorite sources of seeds and plants. The numbers in this list correspond with those given in the sources column in the preceding charts titled Vegetables for Containers and Small Spaces, and Fruits for Containers and Small Spaces. I compiled this list for your convenience; it should save you the time of having to plow through scores of catalogs in search of varieties for small spaces.

1. Vernon Barnes & Son Nursery
   P.O. Box 250L
   McMinnville, TN 37110
Fruit trees, grapes, and berries, varieties for gardens in the South.

2. Bountiful Ridge Nurseries, Inc.
   Box 250
   Princess Anne, MD 21853
Large growers of dwarf fruit trees, berries, and grapes.

3. Brittingham Plant Farms
   Salisbury, MD 21801-2538
Features good selection of strawberry plants as well as other berries and grapes.

4. Burgess Seed & Plant Co.
   905 Four Seasons Rd.
   Bloomington, IL 61701
Catalog features some unusual varieties and their own exclusives for vegetables. They also carry fruit trees, berries and herbs.

5. W. Atlee Burpee Co.
   Clinton, IA 52732
   Riverside, CA 92590
   Warminster, PA 18947
Few gardeners will want to be without this catalog from one of the oldest mail order seed companies. A very comprehensive catalog offering a wide range of things to grow, including vegetables, fruit, herbs and ornamentals.

6. Desert Seeds Company, Inc.
   P.O. Box 181
   El Centro, CA 92244
Beautifully and elegantly designed full color catalog. Clear, nonconfusing information on seed varieties. They offer only vegetables,

have eleven pages on onions alone.

7. Epicure Seeds
   Box 23568
   Rochester, NY 14692

Many European varieties of herbs and vegetables, not usually available in this country. Including small-leaf French basil, and the famous Italian red radicchio of Treviso.

8. Farmer Seed and Nursery
   Faribault, MN 55021

Very complete catalog—vegetables, fruit, berries, flowers and garden aids. Special attention is paid to early-maturing varieties for northern states and midget vegetables for small space container gardening.

9. Henry Field Seed & Nursery
   Shenandoah, IA 51602

Large, complete catalog over 100 pages—good range of various vegetable, fruit tree, berry, grape and herb varieties. Contains hard-to-come-by bush-type sugar snap peas, elephant garlic, the tropical winged bean, and some organic gardening aids such as fish meal fertilizer and predator insects. Includes good tips for gardeners.

10. Dean Foster Nurseries
    Hartford, MI 49057

Large selection of berries, including hard-to-find varieties such as boysenberries, mulberries, loganberries, the new tayberry from Scotland and the Japanese wineberry. They also feature fruit trees and grapes.

11. Gurney Seed & Nursery Co.
    Yankton, SD 57079

Very complete with many extras; large selection of garden aids in addition to vegetables, berries, grapes, fruit trees and herbs. Some good varieties for short season northern gardens.

12. Joseph Harris Co.
    Moreton Farm
    Rochester, NY 14624

Another old and reputable seed company with a clean and clearly designed catalog featuring selected and excellent performers.

13. Hastings
    P.O. Box 4274
    Atlanta, GA 30302

Nicely designed catalog with good code symbols for special varieties that are space savers. Specializes in varieties for the South—fruit trees, berries, grapes, as well as vegetables.

14. Fred P. Herbst Seedsmen, Inc.
    1000 N. Main St.
    Brewster, NY 10509

Orderly, well designed variety charts with good descriptive information. Specializes in good varieties of hot chili pepper. Garden aids and some organic pest control supplies.

15. Jackson & Perkins Co.
    Medford, OR 97501

Although Jackson and Perkins is synonymous with roses of every kind, their catalog also contains several hard-to-find excellent dwarf fruit tree varieties.

16. Johnny's Selected Seeds
    Albion, ME 04910

Fine catalog with a lovely personal touch—and very informative. Concentrates on vegetables for northern short season gardens. A source for grain amaranth and the alpine strawberry Baron Solemacher. Also carries several herbs.

17. J. W. Jung Seed Co.
    Randolf, WI 53956

Features good selection of vegetables for gardeners in the North as well as berries, grapes, flowers and fruit trees.

18. Kelly Brothers Nurseries, Inc.
    Dansville, NY 14437

A generous list of dwarf fruit trees, grapes, and berries with lots of helpful tips. No vegetables.

19. Le Jardin du Gourmet
    West Danville, VT 05873

A shopping center for European seeds, mostly

with a French accent. They offer a marvelous assortment of miniseed packets containing about 30 seeds for around 20¢ each. Ideal for small gardens, containers, and those who want to experiment with such unusual goodies as rocambole, cornichon and Egyptian onion. They also supply herb seeds.

20. Henry Leuthardt Nurseries, Inc.
    Box 666
    East Moriches, NY 11940

Specialists in dwarf and espalier fruit trees. Offer some rare, old choice varieties, e.g. French Mirabelle plum.

21. Earl May Seed & Nursery Co.
    Shenandoah, IA 51603

A large choice of vegetables, herbs, fruit trees, berries and flowers, including a collection of midget vegetables.

22. Mellinger Seed, Nursery & Garden Supply
    North Lima, OH 44452-9731

One of the best catalogs with emphasis on a generous assortment of garden supplies. Also runs the gamut for things to grow in the garden.

23. J. E. Miller Nurseries, Inc.
    Canandaigua, NY 14424

Features a good selection of fruit trees including several antique apple varieties.

24. Geo. W. Park Seed Co.
    S.C. Highway, 254 N.
    Greenwood, SC 29647

Beautifully illustrated, a real tempter of a catalog. Has the new, delicate, hybrid Kuta squash, a tiny Japanese melon (Golden Crispy) completely edible, including the thin skin, and an incendiary hot pepper variety from Thailand. They also feature all kinds of fruit, berries, and herbs. A good selection of varieties for southern gardens, too.

25. R. H. Shumway Seedsman, Inc.
    P.O. Box 777
    628 Cedar St.

Rockford, IL 61105

Old-fashioned looking catalog with great charm, featuring only vegetables.

26. Spring Hill Nurseries
    110 W. Elm St.
    Tipp City, OH 45371

Fruit trees, grapes and berries, are the specialties for this catalog. Includes a collection of miniature citrus for containers.

27. Stark Brothers, Nurseries and Orchards
    Louisiana, MO 63356

Concentrates mostly on fruit trees, and new improved items from the highly reputable Zaiger breeding stations, which specialize in premium quality stock.

28. Stokes Seeds, Inc.
    Box 548
    Buffalo, NY 14240

A thick, authoritative catalog in small size format, mostly of vegetables and flowers.

29. Thompson & Morgan
    P.O. Box 100
    Farmingdale, NJ 07727

Colorful catalog features vegetable and flower varieties from all over the world, including the Ogen minimelon from Israel, a particularly aromatic sweet small fruit for small space gardens.

30. The Urban Farmer
    22000 Halburton Rd.
    Beachwood, OH 44122

Multinational seeds, from Germany, France, Australia, Japan, etc. Unusual miniature varieties, and good selection of Oriental vegetable seed. A catalog for those who like to experiment with the unusual.

31. White Flower Farm
    Litchfield, CT 06759-0050

Although this catalog is for high-quality flowers only, they are one of the very few suppliers of the costly French wild strawberry plants, Charles V, *fraises des bois.*

A List of Herb Specialists

Here is a list of my favorite sources of herb seeds and plants. In addition to the sources given here, some of the companies listed in the previous pages also sell herbs. Burpee, Johnny's Selected Seeds, Le Jardin du Gourmet and Geo. W. Park all offer nice selections of herbs.

1. Capriland's Herb Farm
    534 Silver St.
    Coventry, CT 06328

2. Merry Gardens
    Camden, ME 04834

3. The Naturalist
    P.O. Box 435
    Yorktown Heights, NY 10598

4. Nichols Garden Nursery
    1190 N. Pacific Hwy.
    Albany, OR 97321

5. Taylor's Garden
    1535 Lone Oak Rd.
    Vista, CA 92083

Vegetables for Containers & Small Spaces

The following codes are designed to help you identify at a glance the growing conditions and sizes of various vegetables to help you in your selections.

WS - Warm season

CS - Cool season

◑ - Partial shade

☼ - Full sun

VH - Very hardy: very cold tolerant; can withstand subfreezing temperatures; grows best at 60-65°F.

H - Hardy: can withstand light frost somewhat; grows best at 60-65°F.

T - Tender: susceptible to frost; grows best at 60-70°F.

VT - Very tender: extremely susceptible to frost; grows best at temperatures above 70°F.

On the chart, plant and container sizes and spacings are noted at the beginning of each vegetable. This information pertains to all cultivars listed for that vegetable, unless otherwise noted.

Vegetable	Recommended Varieties	When to Plant/ Days to Maturity	Equidistant Spacing	Mature Plant Size
BEANS, SNAP WS ☼ T	Bush type	Sow seeds after last spring frost; succession plant every week for steady supply.	4 in. apart	24 in. tall
	Gold Crop	45-52	. . . .	. . . .
	Tender Crop	50-60	. . . .	. . . .
	Tenderette	55	. . . .	. . . .
	Pole type	Sow seeds after last spring frost.	4 in. apart	5-8 ft. tall
	Blue Lake	55-66	. . . .	. . . .
	Kentucky Wonder	58-74	. . . .	. . . .
	Purple Pod	50-65	. . . .	. . . .
BEETS CS ☾ H		Start sowing seeds after last spring frost until midsummer; sow again in fall up until 8 weeks before first frost.	3 in. apart	Given for height of leafy growth
	Baby Canning	48-56	. . . .	10-12 in.
	Detroit Dark Red	55-60	. . . .	10-12 in.
	Early Wonder	48-55	. . . .	16-18 in.
	Little Ball	56	. . . .	10-12 in.
	Ruby Queen	52-55	. . . .	10-12
BROCCOLI CS ☾ VH		Start transplants 6-8 weeks before setting out; plant spring crop 4 weeks before last frost; plant fall crop 8 weeks before first frost.	12 in. apart	. . . .
	De Rapa (Raab)	40	. . . .	10 in. tall
	Green Dwarf	50-60	. . . .	8 in. tall
BRUSSELS SPROUTS CS ☾ VH		Start transplants 4-6 weeks before setting out; best as fall crop planted 6-8 weeks before first frost.	16 in. apart	. . . .
	Improved Extra Dwarf	70	. . . .	. . . .

Approx. Fruit Size	Container Size	Remarks	Sources
Given for length of pods	Per plant: 8 in. wide, 8-10 in. deep	Easy to grow; quick to mature; short harvest period per plant.	
5-6 in.	. . . .	Yellow wax type; stringless; good fresh, frozen, canned.	5, 11, 14, 24, 28
5 in.	. . . .	Stringless; disease resistant; freezes well.	5, 24, 28
6 in.	. . . .	Stringless; good fresh, frozen, canned.	5, 9, 24, 25
Given for length of pods	Per plant: 12 in. wide, 8 in. deep; 2 gal. soil	Requires trellis or some sort of vertical structure for support; matures later than bush beans but bears for longer period.	
5-6 in.	. . . .	Stringless.	5, 9, 13, 14, 24
7-9 in.	. . . .	Stringless; very meaty texture.	5, 9, 11, 13, 14, 24
. . . .	. . . .	Stringless; pods turn green when cooked.	9, 11, 14
Given for diameter of root	Per plant: 6-12 in. deep	Leaves taste best when harvested 5-8 in. tall; roots taste best when harvested at 2-3 in. diameter.	
Golf ball size	. . . .	Perfect size for pickling.	11, 21
2½-3 in.	. . . .	Glossy, attractive leaves; sweet-flavored roots; good for canning, freezing.	4, 5
3 in.	. . . .	Quick to mature; very tasty greens; good for canning.	4, 5
1½ in.	. . . .	Stays tender and smooth; ideal for pickling; adds gourmet touch when served whole.	5
2-3 in.	. . . .	Excellent greens.	4, 8, 21
Given for diameter of head	Per plant: 12 in. wide, 12 in. deep; 5 gal. soil	Don't pull plants after harvesting main head; cutting head stimulates secondary crop of sideshoots; long harvest season.	
Nonheading	. . . .	Rapidly produces many sideshoots; no central head.	14
5½ in.	. . . .	Resists downy mildew; very compact plant.	28
Given for sprouts	Per plant: 12 in. wide, 12 in. deep; 5 gal. soil	Requires long growing season; sprouts maturing in heat of summer have loose texture, poor flavor; flavor greatly enhanced by frost.	
1 in.	. . . .		12

Vegetable	Recommended Varieties	When to Plant/ Days to Maturity	Equidistant Spacing	Mature Plant Size
	Jade Cross Hybrid	80-95	. . . .	28 in. tall
	Long Island Improved	85-90	. . . .	20 in. tall
CABBAGE CS ☼ VH		Start transplants 6-8 weeks before setting out; plant twice, first in spring, 4 weeks before last frost; plant again in fall, 8 weeks before first frost.	12 in. apart	. . . .
	Babyhead	70-72	. . . .	Compact
	Earliana	60	. . . .	Compact
	Early Greenball	63	. . . .	Compact
	Morden Dwarf	55-60	. . . .	Compact
CARROTS CS ¢ H		Sow seeds starting 4 weeks before last spring frost; succession plant every 2 weeks for continuous supply.	3 in. apart	Topgrowth averages 10 in. tall
	Gold Nugget	71	. . . .	. . . .
	Little Finger	65	. . . .	. . . .
	Oxheart	70-75	. . . .	. . . .
	Short 'N Sweet	68	. . . .	. . . .
CAULI- FLOWER CS ¢ H		Start transplants 6-8 weeks before setting out; in spring, plant 4 weeks before last frost; in fall, plant 12 weeks before first frost.	12 in. apart (unless noted otherwise)	. . . .
	Garant	82-86	6 in. apart	Dwarf
	Predominant	90-94	6 in. apart	Dwarf
CORN WS ☼ T		Sow seeds after last spring frost.	12 in. apart	Given for plant height
	Faribo Golden Midget	60	. . . .	30 in.
	Golden Midget	58	. . . .	36 in.

Approx. Fruit Size	Container Size	Remarks	Sources
1½-2 in.	. . . .	Very heavy yielder; sprouts freeze well.	5, 6, 13, 24, 28
1 in.	. . . .	Sprouts freeze well.	5, 9, 11, 22, 24
Given as diameter, weight of single head	Per plant: 10 in. wide, 12 in. deep; 3-5 gal. soil	Cut main heads off spring-planted cabbage to stimulate smaller, secondary heads to form.	
4 in., 1 lb.	. . . .	Miniature head; more white than green; resists splitting.	11
4 in., 2½ lb.	. . . .	One of the earliest to mature.	5, 24
4 in., 2½ lb.	. . . .	English variety; globe-shaped heads have small cores.	28
4 in., 1 lb.	. . . .	Miniature head, firm texture; resists splitting.	24, 25
Given as length × width of root	8-10 in. deep; allow 3 in. spacing between plants	Seeds are slow to germinate; soak overnight before planting and cover with sand, peat moss or sawdust to prevent crusting.	
2-3 in. x 2 in.	. . . .	Golf ball shaped.	8, 11
3½ in. x ⅝ in.	. . . .	Perfect for cooking whole as gourmet delicacy.	5
4-6 in. x 4 in.	. . . .	Easy to pull out of soil; tender; stores well.	11, 14, 25
3½ in. x 2 in.	. . . .	Good choice for heavy, less-than-ideal soils.	5
Given for diameter of head	Per plant: 12 in. wide, 12 in deep; 5 gal. soil	Requires long growing season; matures best in cool temperatures; needs constant, even supply moisture; leaves must be gathered loosely around head to blanch.	
1½-3½ in.	. . . .	Quick growing and vigorous. Early.	29
1½-3½ in.	. . . .	Good choice for fall crop. Late.	29
Given for length of ears	Plant 3 plants per 21 in. wide, 8 in. deep container	Must plant in groups of 3 or more to ensure good pollination; choose varieties with different maturity rates to stagger harvest.	
4 in.	. . . .	Sweet and tender; freezes well.	8
5 in.	. . . .	Each plant produces 2 ears with 8 rows each; has highest sugar content among miniature varieties.	5, 9, 11, 21

Vegetable	Recommended Varieties	When to Plant/ Days to Maturity	Equidistant Spacing	Mature Plant Size
	Golden Miniature	54	. . . .	. . . .
	Midget Sweet Corn	63	. . . .	30 in.
CUCUMBER WS ☼ T	Bush type	Sow seeds 1 week after last spring frost; or, start transplants 2-3 weeks before setting out after last frost.	36 in. apart	Compact plants require only 3 sq. ft. of space; grow approx. 2 ft. tall
	Burpless Bush	42	. . . .	. . . .
	Bush Whopper	55	. . . .	. . . .
	Little Minnie	52	. . . .	. . . .
	Patio Pik Hybrid	51-58	. . . .	. . . .
	Spacemaster	60	. . . .	. . . .
	Vine type	See Bush type.	6 in. apart (when grown vertically)	Vines can reach 8-10 ft. long
	Gemini	65	. . . .	. . . .
	Mincu	50	. . . .	. . . .
	Sweet Slice	58-62	. . . .	. . . .
EGGPLANT WS ☼ T	. . . .	Start transplants 8-10 weeks before setting out; plant 2-4 weeks after last spring frost.	12 in. apart	2-3 ft. tall
	Early Beauty Hybrid	62	. . . .	. . . .
	Ichiban	65	. . . .	. . . .
	Morden Midget	65	. . . .	. . . .
	Slim Jim	65	. . . .	. . . .

Approx. Fruit Size	Container Size	Remarks	Sources
5 in.	. . . .	Slender cobs are well filled; freezes well.	28
4 in.	. . . .	Ears sweet, tender; freezes well.	11
Given as length of fruit	Per plant: 8 in. wide, 12 in. deep pot; 1-2 gal. soil	Prolific plants; pick continuously to keep new fruit forming.	
9-11 in.	. . . .	First bush variety with "burpless" feature, early harvest; very productive.	24
6-8 in.	. . . .	Thick cucumbers with nice crisp texture.	24
4 in.	8 in. deep basket	Good for hanging basket.	11
4-6 in.	. . . .	Produces early and heavily; tolerant of mildew	8, 13, 24
7½-8 in.	. . . .	Nice crisp texture; suited to wide range climates; mosaic resistant.	5, 25
Given as length of fruit	Per plant: 8 in. wide, 12 in. deep; 2 plants: 5 gal. soil. 3-5 plants: 10 gal. soil or half-barrel	Requires trellis or some other type of vertical support.	
7½-8 in.	. . . .	Great degree disease resistance.	6, 14, 24, 28
4 in.	. . . .	Pickling type; early and very productive.	8
12-14 in.	. . . .	Burpless type; tolerates hot weather well; disease resistant.	5, 24
. . . .	Per plant: 10-12 in. wide, 10-12 in. deep	Very tender plant that doesn't tolerate cold weather well.	
Small, oval	. . . .	Very prolific plant.	5
Up to 12 in. long, slender.	. . . .	One of the highest yielding eggplants.	9, 11, 25
Small, oval	. . . .	Very bushy, compact plant.	8
4 in. long	. . . .	Can grow in 6 in. pot. Fruits grow in clusters.	4

Vegetable	Recom- mended Varieties	When to Plant/ Days to Maturity	Equi- distant Spacing	Mature Plant Size
GREEN ONIONS (also called bunching onions, scallions)		Sow seeds 4-5 weeks before last spring frost; make succession plantings until 2 weeks after late frost.	2 in. apart	10-12 in. tall
CS ⟡ VH	Beltsville Bunching	65	. . . .	. . . .
	Evergreen Bunching	65-120	. . . .	. . . .
KALE CS ⟡ VH		Sow seeds 4-6 weeks before last spring frost for early crop; sow seeds 10 weeks before first fall frost for second crop.	15 in. apart	12 in. tall
	Dwarf Blue Curled Vates	55	. . . .	. . . .
	Dwarf Green Curled Scotch	50-65	. . . .	. . . .
LETTUCE CS ⟡ H	Butterhead type	Sow seeds and set out transplants starting 3-6 weeks before last spring frost; plant small amounts every 3 weeks until mid-summer to assure steady supply; plant again 8 weeks before first fall frost.	6-12 in. apart	6-10 in. tall
	Butter- crunch	65-70	. . . .	. . . .
	Summer Bibb	60-70	. . . .	. . . .
	Tom Thumb	65	. . . .	. . . .
	Leaf type	See Butterhead type.	6 in. apart	8-9 in. tall
	Black Seeded Simpson	45	. . . .	. . . .
	Grand Rapids	40-45	. . . .	. . . .
	Oak Leaf	38-50	. . . .	. . . .

Approx. Fruit Size	Container Size	Remarks	Sources
. . . .	10-12 in. deep allow 2-3 in. spacing between plants	Nonbulbing type; long, slender stems are parts used; unlike bulbing onions, not finicky about climate or daylength; easy to grow.	
. . . .	. . . .	Hardy plants.	13, 28
. . . .	. . . .	Silvery white stems; will divide continuously at base.	5, 25
. . . .	Per plant: 8 in. wide, 8 in. deep	Pick outside leaves gradually for cut-and-come again harvest; withstands extremes of both hot and cold; flavor enhanced by frost.	
. . . .	. . . .	Low compact plants with tightly curled blue green leaves.	5, 12, 13, 14, 25
. . . .	. . . .	Low compact plant with gray green curled leaves.	5, 8, 11, 12, 13, 14, 25
. . . .	Per plant: 8 in. wide, 6-8 in. deep	Savored for its soft, buttery texture and delicate flavor; loosely folded leaves form semihead; best to harvest head all at once. Good choice for window boxes, hanging baskets.	
. . . .	. . . .	Tolerates heat, slow to bolt.	4, 5
. . . .	. . . .	Vigorous grower; resists bolting.	6, 13
4-5 in. head	. . . .	Tennis ball size, perfect for windowboxes, other tiny spaces.	5, 8, 24, 25
. . . .	Per plant: 8 in. wide, 6-8 in. deep.	Harvest a few outside leaves from each plant at a time for cut-and-come again harvest; be sure to plant small amounts at staggered intervals to avoid sudden glut; choose heat-resistant varieties for hot-weather planting.	
. . . .	. . . .	Crisp leaves are broad, slightly crinkled, medium green color.	5, 8, 11, 13, 14, 21, 22, 28
. . . .	. . . .	Slow to bolt; light green leaves have delicately frilled edges.	5, 8, 9, 11, 13, 21, 24, 28
. . . .	. . . .	Heat resistant; doesn't turn bitter; leaves resemble those of oak trees.	5, 8, 11, 24, 25

Vegetable	Recommended Varieties	When to Plant/ Days to Maturity	Equidistant Spacing	Mature Plant Size
	Ruby	47	. . . .	. . . .
	Salad Bowl	45	. . . .	. . . .
	Slo-Bolt	45	. . . .	. . . .
	Romaine/ Cos type	Sow seeds 3-6 weeks before last spring frost; sow again in midsummer for fall crops.	12 in. apart	10 in. tall
	Crisp Mint	65-80	. . . .	. . . .
	Dark Green Cos	55-70	. . . .	. . . .
	Parris Island Cos	70-75	. . . .	. . . .
	Sweet Midget Cos	. . . .	. . . .	5 in. tall
	Corn Salad (also called mache, lamb's tongue, fetticus)	See Butterhead type.	3 in. apart	. . . .
	A Grosse Graine	45-50	. . . .	. . . .
	Rocket (also called roquette, rochetta, arugula)	Sow seeds in early spring and again in midsummer for fall crop.	3 in. apart	. . . .
	Roquette	35	. . . .	. . . .
	Rucola cultivata	65	. . . .	. . . .
MELONS WS ☼ VT	Cantaloupe or Muskmelon	Sow seeds outdoors 2 weeks after last spring frost; in short-season areas start transplants 10-30 days before setting out; set out after last spring frost.	12 in. apart (when grown vertically)	2-3 ft. across
	Minnesota Midget	60	. . . .	3 ft. across
	Musketeer	90	. . . .	2-3 ft. across

Approx. Fruit Size	Container Size	Remarks	Sources
. . . .	. . . .	Crinkled leaves have pleasing bright red color.	5, 6, 8, 13, 24
. . . .	. . . .	Heat resistant; very tender and sweet; plant produces abundance of bright green leaves.	5, 6, 8, 11, 14
. . . .	. . . .	Resists bolting; produces good quality leaves throughout summer; leaves are slightly crinkled with frilly edges.	8, 14, 24
. . . .	Per plant: 8 in. wide, 6-8 in. deep	*The* lettuce to grow for Caesar salad; crispy leaves have crunchy, juicy midribs; upright, elongated heads.	
. . . .	. . . .	Resists mildew and virus.	29
. . . .	. . . .	Early to mature; very crisp texture; does well in summer.	6, 16
. . . .	. . . .	Large plant with mild-flavored leaves.	5, 6, 11, 13, 14, 25, 28
. . . .	. . . .	Compact heads are sweet and crisp; good for tiny spaces.	8
. . . .	Per plant: 8 in. wide, 6-8 in. deep	Does not tolerate heat well; small, spoon-shaped leaves have tangy, cresslike flavor. Light frost improves flavor; good fall crop.	7, 19, 25
. . . .	. . . .	Compact, dark green leaves.	7, 19, 25
. . . .	Per plant: 8 in. wide, 6-8 in. deep	Doesn't do well in heat of the summer; flavor akin to mustard greens; light frost enhances flavor.	5, 7
. . . .	. . . .	Leaves have peppery flavor.	5
. . . .	. . . .	Leaves have peppery flavor.	7
Given as diameter of melons	Per plant: 24 in. wide, 24 in. deep; 5 gal. soil	Needs long, warm growing season; train errant vines along trellis to conserve space; place fruit growing on vertical vines in slings for support.	
4 in.	. . . .	Bush type. One of the earliest to ripen; melons have high sugar content; half-melon is just right for individual serving.	5, 25
5-6 in.	. . . .	Bush type. Heavy netting prevents splitting; very sweet and juicy.	24

Vegetable	Recom- mended Varieties	When to Plant/ Days to Maturity	Equi- distant Spacing	Mature Plant Size
	Watermelons	See Cantaloupe.	12 in. apart (when grown vertically)	2-3 ft. across
	Golden Midget	75	. . . .	. . . .
	Market Midget	69	. . . .	. . . .
	Sugar Baby	70-90	. . . .	. . . .
OKRA WS ☼ VT		Sow seeds outdoors once soil has warmed to 60°F; start transplants 3-4 weeks after last spring frost; set out 6-8 weeks after frost.	18 in. apart	Given for plant height
	Dwarf Green Long Pod	50	. . . .	2-2½ ft.
	Lee	50	. . . .	2½-3 ft.
PEAS CS ✤ VH	Garden type	Sow seeds 4-6 weeks before last spring frost, as soon as soil is workable.	3 in. apart	Given for vine length
	Freezonian	63	. . . .	2½ ft.
	Little Marvel	63	. . . .	18 in.
	Wando	68	. . . .	2½ ft.
	Snap Pea type	See Garden type.	3 in. apart	Given for vine length
	Sugar Bon	56	. . . .	18-24 in.
	Sugar Rae	70	. . . .	24-28 in.
	Snow Pea type	See Garden type.	3 in. apart	Given for vine length

Approx. Fruit Size	Container Size	Remarks	Sources
Given as diameter or weight	Per plant: 24 in. wide, 24 in. deep; 5 gal. soil	See Cantaloupe.	
8 in.	. . . .	Skin turns yellow when ripe; extra-sweet red flesh.	8, 11, 21, 25
3-5 lbs.	. . . .	Oval fruit with very sweet flavor.	11, 25, 28
8-10 lbs.	. . . .	Excellent sweet, dark red flesh; fewer seeds than other varieties.	4, 5, 6, 9, 11, 14, 19, 21, 24, 25, 28
Given for length of pods	Per plant: 12 in. wide, 12 in. deep	Warm temperatures critical for good growth; good succession crop to follow early spring crop; soak seeds overnight for good germination; harvest pods continuously; best at 2-3 inches long.	
7 in.	. . . .	Dwarf. Ribbed pods are fleshy, dark green.	4, 5, 6, 8, 13, 14
6-7 in.	. . . .	One of the smallest varieties; spineless pods easy to harvest.	13, 24
Given for length of pod	Per plant: 4 in. wide, 12 in. deep. Rectangular boxes with string trellis work best	Shelled peas are edible part; need to plant considerable number of vines to get adequate harvest; some sources say 37 vines needed for one person.	
3 in.	. . . .	Wilt-resistant plants; peas freeze well.	4, 5, 11, 12, 14
3 in.	. . . .	Heavy yielder; good for freezing.	4, 5, 11, 12, 13, 21, 24, 25, 28
3 in.	. . . .	Heat and cold tolerant; good for canning and freezing.	4, 5, 12, 13, 14, 21, 28
Given for length of pod	See Garden type	Both sweet, juicy pods and full-size peas are edible; plants give higher yield than garden type peas; vigorous vining variety grows to unwieldy 8 ft.; low-growing varieties may need some support.	
2-3 in.	. . . .	Low-growing variety.	5, 24
2-3 in.	. . . .	Low-growing variety; plant along with Sugar Bon for staggered harvest.	5, 11, 13
Given for length of pod	See Garden type	Pods are edible quality best when peas are just starting to form in pod. Can also shell and use mature peas.	

Vegetable	Recommended Varieties	When to Plant/ Days to Maturity	Equidistant Spacing	Mature Plant Size
	Dwarf Gray Sugar	65	. . . .	2½ ft.
	Snowbird	58	. . . .	16-18 in.
PEPPERS WS ☼ VT	Hot type	Start transplants 6-8 weeks before planting outdoors; set out 2-4 weeks after last spring frost.	12 in. apart	Given for plant height
	Hungarian Wax	60-65 (from transplanting).	. . . .	14-22 in.
	Jalapeño	72-80 (from transplanting).	. . . .	26-36 in.
	Long Red Cayenne	70-75 (from transplanting).	. . . .	18 in.
	Pepper Thai Hot	65 (from transplanting).	. . . .	8 in.
	Sweet type	See Hot type	12 in. apart	Given for plant height
	Sweet Pickle	65 (from transplanting).	. . . .	12-15 in.
	Sweet Banana	58-70 (from transplanting).	. . . .	12-15 in.
	Sweet Cherry	78 (from transplanting).	. . . .	10-12 in.
	Yolo Wonder	78 (from transplanting).	. . . .	12-15 in.
RADISHES CS ✿ H		Sow seeds 2-4 weeks before last spring frost; succession plant small areas every other week until temperatures warm up; plant again in late summer for fall harvest.	3 in. apart	Tops grow 6-8 in. tall
	Cherry Belle	22	. . . .	. . . .
	Early Scarlett Globe	24	. . . .	. . . .
	French Breakfast	23	. . . .	. . . .
	Sparkler	25	. . . .	. . . .

Approx. Fruit Size	Container Size	Remarks	Sources
2½-3 in.	. . . .	Produces plump, tasty pods in abundance.	5, 6, 8, 9, 11, 13, 16, 19, 24, 25
3 in.	. . . .	One of earliest to mature; plants need no support.	5
Given for length of fruit	Per plant: 24 in. wide, 12 in. deep; suitable for hanging baskets and small containers	Attractive plants with compact shape, glossy leaves and bright-colored fruit.	
5 in.	. . . .	Yellow fruit, turns glossy red when ripe; fairly hot.	5, 6, 22, 24, 28
3 in.	. . . .	Green, maturing to red fruit; very hot; good for pickling.	6, 9, 11, 13, 21
5 in.	. . . .	Red fruit; often curled or twisted; taste buds beware—fiery hot.	4, 5, 11, 13, 19, 25, 28
1 in.	8 in.	Fiery hot, green and red peppers blanket mound-shaped plant.	24
Given for length of fruit	See Hot type	See Hot type.	
2 in.	. . . .	Yellow fruit turns red then purple as it matures.	24
6 in.	. . . .	Yellow fruit gets orange red blush as it ripens; long, tapering fruit.	5, 13, 14, 21, 22, 24, 25, 28
Small, round	. . . .	Bright green fruit ripens to scarlet; good for pickling.	5, 13, 24
4¼ in.	. . . .	Resists tobacco mosaic virus; large, blocky green fruit changes to red as it matures.	6
. . . .	12 plants per 1 gal. pot; 36 plants per 10 gal. container	Very quick to mature; needs cool weather for best growth and best flavor; too much heat causes them to be hot tasting and pithy.	
¾ in. globe	. . . .	Red with white flesh; stays well in garden.	4, 5, 6, 9, 11, 13, 14, 22, 24, 25, 28, 29
1 in. globe	. . . .	Bright red roots with crisp white flesh.	6, 8, 9, 13, 16, 19
Oblong, 1¾ in. long	. . . .	Scarlet root with white top; pleasantly tangy, crisp flesh.	5, 6, 11, 13, 25, 28
1¼ in. globe	. . . .	Red root with white tip; crisp and pungent.	5, 6, 11, 14, 25

Vegetable	Recom-mended Varieties	When to Plant/ Days to Maturity	Equi-distant Spacing	Mature Plant Size
	White Icicle	28	. . . .	. . . .
RHUBARB Perennial CS ☾		Plant crowns in early fall or spring; stalks of established plants mature in 30 days.	24 in. apart	30 in. tall
	Canadian Red	. . . .	. . . .	. . . .
	Valentine	. . . .	. . . .	. . . .
	Victoria	. . . .	. . . .	. . . .
SPINACH CS ☾ H		Sow seeds 4-6 weeks before last spring frost; plant second crop 4-6 weeks before fall frost.	4 in. apart	Under 12 in. tall
	America	50	. . . .	. . . .
	Bloomsdale	40-50	. . . .	. . . .
	Malabar	70	. . . .	. . . .
	Melody	42	. . . .	. . . .
SQUASH WS ☼ VT	Summer type	Sow seeds 2 weeks after last spring frost.	Bush: 36 in. apart. Vining: 16 in. apart (grown vertically).	Bush squash needs 3 sq. ft. of space; vining type takes up twice as much unless grown vertically
	Aristocrat	48	. . . .	Vining
	Early Golden Summer Crookneck	48-53	. . . .	Bush

Approx. Fruit Size	Container Size	Remarks	Sources
Oblong, 5 in. long	. . . .	White-skinned, slender root; mild-flavored white flesh.	5, 6, 8, 9, 11, 13, 21, 22, 24, 25, 28
. . . .	Per plant: 24 in. wide, 8-10 in. deep	Don't harvest first year; second year, harvest only a few stalks; wait until third year for full harvest; plant in landscape where it can remain for many years. Note: Do not eat leaves; they can be toxic.	
. . . .	. . . .	Thick, deep red stalks; heavy yielder.	4, 5, 8, 13
18-22 in. long, 1-in.-thick stalks	. . . .	Attractive, dark red stalks; very good cooking quality.	5, 21
. . . .	. . . .	Pleasant tart flavor; heavy yielder, reliably hardy; green stalks tinged with red.	5, 13, 21, 22
. . . .	2 plants: 8-10 in. wide, 6 in. deep. 3 plants: 2 gal., soil. 7 plants: 10 gal. soil.	Quick to mature; frost tolerant but not heat tolerant at all; only Malabar spinach grows well in warm temperatures; harvest few outside leaves at a time for cut-and-come again harvest.	
. . . .	. . . .	Glossy, heavily crinkled leaves, slow to bolt; heavy yielder.	5, 6, 11, 13, 14, 21, 24
. . . .	. . . .	Glossy, heavily crinkled leaves, slow to bolt. Upright growth habit.	9, 14, 19, 21
. . . .	. . . .	Warm-weather spinach substitute; large, glossy green leaves grow on climbing vines; requires trellis or fence	5
. . . .	. . . .	Semicrinkled leaves; resists downy mildew, mosaic; heavy yielder.	5, 8, 21, 24, 28
. . . .	Per plant. Bush: 24 in. wide, 24 in. deep; 10 gal. soil. Vining: 24 in. wide, 24 in. deep, 10 gal. soil; provide vertical support.	In order to manage rangy vining types in small spaces, train vertically along a support; harvest all throughout season, the younger the better.	
. . . .	. . . .	Green straightneck type; very heavy yielding; adapts to wide range climates.	5, 24
3-10 in. long, 3 lb.	. . . .	Yellow crookneck type; very tender when harvested young.	5, 6, 14, 21

Vegetable	Recom- mended Varieties	When to Plant/ Days to Maturity	Equi- distant Spacing	Mature Plant Size
	Early White Bush	54	. . . .	Bush
	Gold Rush	45-50	. . . .	Bush
	Kuta Hybrid	42	. . . .	. . . .
	Park's Creamy	55	. . . .	Bush
	Winter type	Sow seeds 2 weeks after last spring frost.	Bush: 36 in. apart; vining: 24 in. apart (grown vertically)	See Summer type
	Burpee Butterbush	75	. . . .	Bush
	Bush Table King	75	. . . .	Bush
	Gold Nugget	95	. . . .	Bush
	Table Ace	70	. . . .	Semibush
SWISS CHARD CS ✡ H		Sow seeds 2-4 weeks before last spring frost.	12 in. apart	12-14 in. tall
	Fordhook Giant	60	. . . .	. . . .
	Lucullus	55	. . . .	. . . .
	Rhubarb chard	55-60	. . . .	. . . .
TOMATOES WS ☼ T	Determinate type	Start transplants 6-8 weeks before last spring frost; set out after last spring frost.	24 in. apart	. . . .

Approx. Fruit Size	Container Size	Remarks	Sources
7 in. across	. . . .	Round, scallop-type fruit, greenish white skin; white flesh.	5, 9, 13, 14, 25
4-8 in. long	. . . .	Yellow straightneck type; open plant habit makes harvesting easy.	24
6 in. long	. . . .	Young fruit light green, crisp with smooth flavor. Mature fruit dark green, eggplantlike consistency.	
6-8 in. long	. . . .	Yellow straightneck type; withstands temperature extremes well.	24
. . . .	See Summer type	Slow to mature than summer type; thick shells make them good keepers; harvest in fall before first hard frost when shells are hard; cure and store in warm, dry location.	
3-4 ft. long., 1-2 lb.	. . . .	Butternut type; each plant yields 4-5 squash; takes ¼ space of usual vine type; excellent winter keeper.	5
6 in. long, 5 in. wide, 1¼ lb.	. . . .	Acorn type; doesn't need curing before storage.	5, 8, 14, 21, 24, 28
5 lb. each	. . . .	Turban shaped.	9, 11, 13, 24, 25
. . . .	. . . .	Acorn type; doesn't need curing before storage; high disease resistance.	24
. . . .	Per plant: 12 in. wide, 8-12 in. deep; 2 gal. soil	Reliable high yielder; tolerates heat and light frosts; provides long season harvest; harvest a few outside leaves at a time for cut-and-come again harvest.	
. . . .	. . . .	Dark green, crinkled leaves with white stalks.	5
. . . .	. . . .	Light green, heavily crinkled leaves with white stalks.	8, 11, 13, 14, 22, 24, 25
. . . .	. . . .	Dark green, lightly crinkled leaves with ruby red stalks and veins.	5, 6, 11, 25, 28
. . . .	Per dwarf plant: 8 in. hanging basket or pot 8-10 in. wide 8-10 in. deep. Per regular determinate plant: 12-18 in. wide, 12-18 in. deep, 1-2 gal. soil.	Determinate tomatoes stop growing at certain point; growth is more contained, bushlike; pruning cuts down on harvest; occasionally may need staking; shorter harvest period than indeterminate type.	

Vegetable	Recommended Varieties	When to Plant/ Days to Maturity	Equidistant Spacing	Mature Plant Size
	Burgess Early	45	. . . .	6-8 in. tall
	Pixie Hybrid	52	. . . .	14-18 in. tall
	Small Fry	60-65	. . . .	. . . .
	Tiny Tim	45-55	. . . .	15 in. tall
	Indeterminate type	See Determinate type	12 in. apart (trained vertically)	varies
	Early Girl	54-62	. . . .	. . . .
	Better Boy	70-72	. . . .	. . . .
	Sugar Lump (also called Gardener's Delight)	65-70	. . . .	30 in. tall
	Sweet 100	60-65	. . . .	. . . .
TURNIPS CS ✿ H		Sow seeds 4-6 weeks before last spring frost; sow second crop 6 weeks before first frost.	4 in. apart	18-20 in. tall
	Purple Top	55	. . . .	. . . .
	Tokyo Cross Hybrid	35	. . . .	. . . .

Approx. Fruit Size	Container Size	Remarks	Sources
1½ in. across	. . . .	Each plant can produce up to 300 tomatoes.	4, 24
1¾ in. across	. . . .	Small enough to grow in windowboxes.	
1 in. across	. . . .	Resists verticillium, fusarium wilts and nematodes; very good producer.	5, 8, 9, 11, 21
¾ in. across	. . . .	Suited for hanging baskets.	5, 9, 13, 21, 24, 28
. . . .	Per plant: 24 in. wide, 24 in. deep; 4-5 gal. soil	Plants keep on growing and producing fruit until frost; pruning and some sort of support necessary to keep plant growth under control.	
4-5 oz.	. . . .	Early harvest; tart and juicy fruits.	5
12-16 oz.	. . . .	Resistant to verticillium, fusarium wilts and nematodes; solid fruit with minimum of seeds.	5, 11, 13, 14, 24, 28
1 in. across ⅓-½ oz.	. . . .	Very sweet fruit; vines need tidy staking; can grow in hanging baskets.	5, 24
1 in. across	. . . .	Disease resistant; sweet fruit grows in clusters; high yielder—single plant can produce over 200 tomatoes; does well trained along trellis.	24, 28
. . . .	Per plant: 6 in. wide, 10-12 in. deep	Quick to mature; prefers cool temperatures during growth but does not withstand frost well; leaves are edible, best when small; roots are best when 2 in. across; larger roots are woody.	
. . . .	. . . .	Roots are purple on top with white lower portion; good keeper.	5, 8, 11, 13, 25
. . . .	. . . .	Creamy white root.	5, 9, 13, 14, 19

Fruits for Containers & Small Spaces

Variety	Tree/Plant Characteristics	Fruit Characteristics	Sources
APPLES			
Bisbee Red Delicious	Available as semidwarf; spur-type Red Delicious. Produces heavy crops season after season; requires another variety for cross-pollination.	Rich red fruit has 5 distinctive bumps on blossom end. Juicy and sweet; excellent dessert and fresh eating apple. Mid- to late-season harvest.	2
Bountiful Improved Winesap	Available as dwarf, semidwarf; hardy in all but southernmost and northernmost regions. Needs companion pollinator variety; grows best in zones 5-8.	Red-skinned with yellowish flesh that's coarse, juicy, tends to be slightly acidic; good dessert and cider apple. Good keeper; late-season harvest.	2
Empire	Available as dwarf, semidwarf. Moderately vigorous tree does well in zones 5-7.	Dark red fruit has creamy white flesh; firm, crisp, juicy, a bit tart; good for fresh eating, not recommended for cooking. Long keeping; mid- to late-season harvest.	2, 23
Granny Smith	Available as dwarf, semidwarf. Vigorous tree bears annually; moderately hardy; needs long growing season (180-200 days from blooming to maturity); grows best in zones 7-9.	Bright green, shiny fruit has excellent tart flavor and hard, crisp texture; medium- to large-size fruit; use as dessert, cooking and fresh-eating apple. Very good keeper; late-season harvest.	2, 13, 18, 23, 5
Jonagold	Result of cross between Golden Delicious and Jonathan; more vigorous than Jonathan. Very productive; does well in all but most northern and southern regions.	Yellow green fruit streaked with red; crisp and juicy with slightly coarse texture; good for cooking, fresh eating. Good keeper; late-season harvest.	2, 18, 23, 27 5
Jonamac	Result of cross between McIntosh and Jonathan; more vigorous than Jonathan. Available as semidwarf; good annual producer; does well in zones 4-6.	Bright red fruit is crisp, juicy, on the tart side; outstanding for fresh eating, but can also be used for cooking. Good keeper; midseason harvest.	2, 18, 23, 27 5
Macoun	Available as semidwarf; very hardy; does well in all areas except warm regions; suited to zones 4-6. Thinning promotes better fruit size and annual crops.	Red-skinned McIntosh type with blue blush; flesh is white, crisp with rich flavor; excellent for fresh eating; not recommended for cooking. Good keeper; late-season harvest.	2, 18, 23
Mutsu	Available as dwarf, semidwarf; resists frost injury; vigorous tree bears excellent crops each year. Needs another variety for polli-	Large green fruit turns slightly yellow when mature; fruit resists russeting; coarse flesh is crisp, firm with slightly spicy flavor; good	2, 18, 23

Variety	Tree/Plant Characteristics	Fruit Characteristics	Sources
	nation; grows best in zones 5-8.	for fresh eating, baking. Stores well; mid- to late-season harvest.	
Starkspur Compact Mac	Genetic dwarf; full-size fruit produced on tree growing 6-8 ft. tall; suited for container culture.	Full-size fruit with all characteristics of McIntosh apples. Midseason harvest.	27
Supergold	Available as dwarf, semidwarf; spur-type Golden Delicious. Vigorous tree bears early crop; withstands cold temperatures better than standard Golden Delicious. Self-fertile; use as pollinator for other varieties; grows best in zones 5-8.	Large to extra-large fruit is golden with red blush; crisp, sweet flesh. Mid- to late-season harvest.	2
Yellow Delicious	Available as dwarf, semidwarf; very productive; bears large crops while still young. Excellent pollinator; does best in zones 5-8.	Fruit has golden yellow skin with firm, crisp, juicy flesh. Good keeper; late-season harvest.	2, 18

APRICOTS

Variety	Tree/Plant Characteristics	Fruit Characteristics	Sources
Bush Apricot	Attractive bush with glossy green leaves; grows to 10 ft. tall; blanketed with fragrant white blossoms in spring. Bears while still young.	Large, juicy, golden fruit with very sweet flavor.	2, 13
Dwarf Moorpark	Very productive; needs another variety for cross-pollination. Does well in all but most extreme climates.	Deep yellow fruit with red blush; large and juicy with rich flavor; good fresh or frozen. Midseason harvest.	18
Garden Annie	Dwarf tree; recommended for southern growers.	Firm, semifreestone fruit.	13, 27
GoldenGlo	Genetic dwarf; tree starts bearing while still young. Good choice for containers; grows best in zones 5-8.	Medium-size fruit has mild, sweet flavor; good for fresh eating, drying, jams and jellies. Midseason harvest.	27
Stark Earli-Orange	Available as semidwarf; grows best in zones 5-8.	Largest of all apricots; rich, juicy fruit with slight orange flavor; best used fresh, but suitable for drying, freezing, canning. Early-season harvest.	27
Wilson Delicious	Available as semidwarf; among the hardiest and heaviest bearing. Very reliable; grows best in zones 5-8.	Large, golden orange fruit; very good for canning and freezing. Midseason harvest.	27

SOUR CHERRIES

Variety	Tree/Plant Characteristics	Fruit Characteristics	Sources
Meteor	Available as dwarf; extra hardy; grows even in northernmost parts of zone 4. Grows best in zones 4-7.	Light red fruit has pleasant tart flavor. Early-season harvest.	2, 11, 27
North Star	Genetic dwarf; hardiest and smallest growing of the sour	Medium to large fruit is wine red, juicy, with pleasant tart flavor that	1, 2, 8, 10, 11,

Variety	Tree/Plant Characteristics	Fruit Characteristics	Sources
	cherries; bears at very young age. Self-fruitful; grows best in zones 4-8.	holds up well in cooking, freezing. Easy-to-remove stones; early to midseason harvest.	13, 18, 22, 23, 25, 26 27
Starkspur Montmorency	Available as semidwarf; self-pollinating. Grows best in zones 5-7.	Biggest fruit of sour varieties; bright red with yellow flesh; pleasant tangy flavor; resists cracking in wet weather. Good for cooking, freezing; midseason harvest.	27
Suda Hardy	Available as semidwarf; bears at early age; self-pollinating; extra hardy. Grows best in zones 4-7.	Dark red, extra-tart fruit excellent for cooking, canning, freezing. Midseason harvest.	27

SWEET CHERRIES

Variety	Tree/Plant Characteristics	Fruit Characteristics	Sources
Black Tartarian	Available as semidwarf; exceptionally heavy bearer; can produce 2 lbs. fruit per branch. Grows best in zones 5-7.	Fruit purple black to cherry red, depending on where grown; meaty, sweet fruit, excellent for canning. Early-season harvest.	1, 2, 10, 11, 13, 18 20, 21 22, 23, 25
Compact Stella	Available as dwarf; good choice for areas with wet springs. Self-pollinating; best in zones 6-7.	Juicy, deep red fruit. Midseason harvest.	27
Hedelfingen	Available as dwarf; very hardy, good for growers in cool, humid regions. Grows best in zones 5-7.	Glossy, ruby red fruit is crack resistant; good for fresh eating, freezing, canning. Early-season harvest.	27
Star Stella	Compact growing but not dwarf; self-pollinating. Bears at younger age than other sweet cherries that require pollination.	Large, wine red cherries are firm and juicy.	11, 18, 23, 27
Starkrimson Dwarf Sweet Cherry	Bears heavy crops every year; self-pollinating. Suited for areas with rainy spring weather; grows best in zones 5-8.	Dark red, deep-flavored cherries; good for fresh use, cooking, freezing. Early-season harvest.	27

BUSH CHERRIES

Variety	Tree/Plant Characteristics	Fruit Characteristics	Sources
Black Velvet (also called Improved Hansen's)	Grows 4-5 ft. tall; very adaptable to soil and climate conditions; bears first year after planting.	Single bush produces buckets of black cherries; good for fresh use or cooking.	2
Hansen's Bush	Grows 4-5 ft. tall; rapid grower, bears large harvest; starts bearing first year after planting. Covered with white blossoms in spring; silvery green leaves turn red in fall; very hardy.	Semisweet, large, dark glossy fruit; use fresh or in pies, jams and jellies.	2, 9, 11, 18 23

Variety	Tree/Plant Characteristics	Fruit Characteristics	Sources
FIGS			
Brown Turkey	Dwarf-type growth; very prolific; produces two crops in June and August. Very hardy but needs winter protection; grows best in zones 7-10.	Medium- to large-size fruit has coppery skin with white to pink flesh; good quality fruit. Good both fresh and preserved.	2, 10, 11, 13, 22, 23
Celeste	Grows from 6-10 ft. tall; widely grown in Southeast. Very hardy, grows where less hardy figs fail; grows best in zones 7-10.	Medium-size fruit has violet skin and white to pink flesh; firm, juicy and exceptionally sweet. Excellent for drying; ripens late June.	2, 10 13, 23, 27
Everbearing	Very attractive bush form; one of hardiest varieties; starts to bear early in season through to late fall; grows well in tubs that can be taken in over winter. Grows best in zones 7-10, but can tolerate up to zone 5; self-fruitful.	Fruit is sweet, firm, meaty; suited for fresh use, canning, drying, jam.	2, 13, 18, 25
Gurney's Dwarf Fig	Grows 3-4 ft. tall; does well in containers indoors; attractive gray green foliage.	Can produce edible fruit in 6 months; fruit larger than plums; good fresh or dried.	11
NECTARINES			
Flavortop	Available as dwarf; vigorous and productive; self-fruitful. Moderate chilling requirement; grows best in zones 5-8.	Large-size, reddish fruit of excellent quality. Early-season harvest.	2
Garden State	Available as dwarf, semidwarf; vigorous and productive; grows best in zones 5-8.	Large freestone fruit with yellow flesh; good for canning, freezing. Midseason harvest.	2, 18
HoneyGlo	Dwarf that grows 6-7 ft. tall; does well in containers; self-pollinating. Grows well in zones 6-8; northern growers in zones 4-5 can plant in containers and provide winter protection.	Medium-size, freestone fruit. Midseason harvest.	27
SunGlo	Dwarf that grows 8-10 ft. tall. Grows anywhere peaches can be grown; grows best in zones 5-8.	Large fruit can weigh up to 1 lb. each; golden yellow, juicy flesh has mild, sweet flavor; good for freezing, canning. Midseason harvest.	2, 27
Sweet Melody	Genetic dwarf; grows 6-8 ft. tall; can grow in 18-24 in. container. Grows best in zones 6-8; northern growers in zones 4-5 can plant in containers and provide winter protection.	Red freestone-type fruit with delicious yellow flesh; good for fresh eating, canning, freezing. Midseason harvest.	27

Variety	Tree/Plant Characteristics	Fruit Characteristics	Sources
PEACHES			
Bonanza	Genetic dwarf; grows 4-5 ft. tall; needs only 5 sq. ft. of space; good choice for containers. Self-fruiting; hardy wherever most peaches grow; does best in zones 5-7.	Large-size, yellow freestone fruit. Midseason harvest.	10, 18 23
Candor	Available as dwarf; very productive vigorous. Has some degree resistance to bacterial spot; buds somewhat tolerant to spring frosts. Grows best in zones 5-8.	Yellow, semifreestone fruit has sweet, mild flavor; good texture; resists browning. Very good for canning; early-season harvest.	2
Compact Redhaven	Natural dwarf, grows 8-10 ft. tall; very cold resistant and disease resistant. Good producer; grows best in zones 5-8.	Large crops of yellow freestone fruit, nearly free of fuzz. Midseason harvest.	1, 2, 18, 27
EarliGlo	Available as dwarf; hardy and productive; reliable in cold areas where other varieties fail. Vigorous and heavy bearing; grows best in zones 5-8.	Yellow freestone type; good for fresh eating, freezing, canning. Early-season harvest.	27
Erly-Red-Fre	Available as dwarf; vigorous and hardy tree bears annual crops; resists bacterial spot. Grows best in zones 5-8.	Large (2½ in.) white fruit; can harvest 95 days after blooming. Good keeper; early-season harvest.	2
Madison	Available as dwarf; extra hardy, will produce even in areas with subzero winter temperatures; does best in zones 5-8.	Golden freestone fruit with juicy flesh and rich flavor; excellent for cooking, canning. Mid- to late-season harvest.	2, 27
Sensation Miniature	Grows 6-8 ft. tall; does well in containers. Grows best in zones 5-8.	Yellow flesh, freestone type fruit; juicy but with firm texture. Early-season harvest.	27
PEARS			
Bartlett	Available as dwarf, semidwarf; very productive and vigorous; moderately susceptible to fireblight. Requires pollinator; Seckel won't cross-pollinate; Moonglow is good pollinator. Medium hardiness; grows best in zones 5-7.	Large, golden yellow pears with buttery smooth, sweet, aromatic flesh; excellent for fresh use and canning. Early-season harvest.	2, 5, 18, 20, 23, 27
Duchess	Dwarf available; hardy tree that bears extra young; cross-pollinates with any variety. Grows best in zones 5-7.	Large fruit with golden russeting; smooth, crisp flesh has slightly spicy flavor; keeps well under refrigeration. Mid- to late-season harvest.	2, 9, 11, 18 20, 22, 27
Magness	Cross between Seckel and Comice;	Medum-size, lightly russeted fruit	1, 2,

Variety	Tree/Plant Characteristics	Fruit Characteristics	Sources
	available as dwarf; vigorous tree, sometimes grows thorns; very resistant to fireblight; requires pollinator variety. Good choice for southern growers; does best in zones 5-7.	with virtually grit-free, soft, juicy flesh; tough skin resists insect injury; stores well under cool conditions. Midseason harvest.	10, 13
Moonglow	Available as dwarf, semidwarf; very vigorous and resistant to fireblight; bears large annual crops. Requires pollination; a good pollinator for other varieties, with abundant pollen. Grows best in zones 5-8.	Large yellow fruit with pink blush; mild, sweet flavor; no gritty texture; excellent for fresh use, cooking, canning. Early to midseason harvest.	2, 10, 13, 20, 22, 23, 27
Seckel	Available as dwarf; very hardy and productive; requires pollinator, any variety but Bartlett. Some resistance to fireblight. Grows best in zones 5-8.	Golden brown fruit with red blush spicy, sweet flavor; good for fresh use and canning. Midseason harvest.	2, 18, 27

PLUMS

Variety	Tree/Plant Characteristics	Fruit Characteristics	Sources
Green Gage (also called Reine Claude)	Available as dwarf; European type; very productive; self-pollinating. Hardy, suited to any region.	Greenish yellow, freestone fruit with amber flesh; buttery smooth texture, extra sweet, aromatic; good for fresh use, freezing, canning, preserves. Midseason harvest.	18, 20, 22, 23
Ozark Premier	Available as semidwarf; Japanese type; productive; hardy; use Methley as pollinator. Does well for growers in South and Southwest; grows best in zones 5-9.	Large, semiclingstone fruit; bright red skin with juicy yellow flesh; sweet, mild flavor; good for fresh use, cooking, canning. Midseason harvest.	2, 10, 27
Santa Rosa	Available as dwarf; Japanese type; very prolific; cross-pollinates with any other Japanese variety; also self-fruitful. Grows best in zones 5-7.	Large fruit has crimson skin, purple flesh; clingstone. Early to midseason harvest.	1, 2, 10, 18, 20, 22, 23
Stanley	Available as dwarf; European prune plum type; widely grown; self-fertile; hardy. Grows best in zones 5-7.	Large, dark blue fruit with firm, rich-flavored yellow flesh; freestone type; excellent for fresh use, canning and drying. Midseason harvest.	2, 4, 8, 18, 20, 22, 23, 27

QUINCE

Variety	Tree/Plant Characteristics	Fruit Characteristics	Sources
Champion	Very hardy; heavy producer; no pollinators required.	Large, pear-shaped fruit; flesh is yellow with tinge of green; good for preserves; high in pectin. Late October to November harvest.	11
Dwarf Orange	Self-pollinating; yields are heavy each year; can grow as bush or tree in large container.	Large, round fruit with orange yellow flesh; good for preserves, cooking. Early October harvest.	18, 22, 23, 27

Variety	Tree/Plant Characteristics	Fruit Characteristics	Sources
BLACKBERRIES			
Darrow	Best erect type; very productive; ripens over long period. Very hardy; can withstand subzero temperatures.	Firm black berries often over 1 in. long; slightly tart; 2-3 week harvest period; good for fresh use, jams and jellies. Early to midseason harvest.	2, 4, 18, 23, 24
Thornfree	Trailing plant that becomes semi-erect as it matures; thornless; produces no suckers; semihardy. Grows best in zones 6-8.	Large, glossy black fruit is firm, nearly seedless; good for fresh use, jams and jellies, syrups. Late-season harvest.	2, 4, 10, 18, 23, 27
BLUEBERRIES			
(Highbush— good for northern growers)			
Bluecrop	Medium hardy, vigorous; bears consistently heavy crops; grows best in zones 6-7.	Large clusters of light blue, firm, somewhat tart berries; keep well. Midseason harvest.	2, 3, 10, 18, 23, 27
Earliblue	Relatively hardy and vigorous; grows best in zones 5-8.	Medium clusters of large, light blue berries; slightly tart; keep well and crack resistant. Extra early season harvest.	2, 3, 5, 10, 18, 27, 5
Jersey	Vigorous, spreading bush; grows best in zones 4-7.	Very large berries hang in long, loose clusters; crack resistant; excellent flavor. Early to midseason harvest.	2, 4, 10, 11, 18, 22, 23
Northland	Very productive; grows 4 ft. tall; hardiest of all; grows in zones 4-7.	Very firm, sweet berries. Early-season harvest.	23
(Rabbiteye—good for southern growers)			
Delite	Vigorous bush with upright canes; grows best in zones 7-9.	Medium to large berries with good flavor. Late-season harvest.	2
Tifblue	Vigorous, heavy producer; tolerates heat and drought well; grows best in zones 7-9.	Large, light blue berries are firm, sweet.	2, 27
Woodard	Medium-size plant; grows best in zones 7-9.	Large, light blue berries are firm, sweet; considered to have best flavor of all rabbiteye varieties. Midseason harvest.	2, 27
CURRANTS			
Redlake	Upright, vigorous plant; hardy and disease resistant; grows best in zones 4-6.	Glossy red fruit in grapelike clusters; easy to pick; long harvest period; good for jams and jellies. Midsummer harvest.	4, 10, 11, 21, 24, 27
GOOSEBERRIES			
Pixwell	Heavy yielder; canes have few or no thorns; very hardy; grows well	Large green berries turn pinkish purple when ripe; easy to pick;	2, 4, 10, 11,

Variety	Tree/Plant Characteristics	Fruit Characteristics	Sources
	in zones 4-6.	good for pies and preserves. Midseason harvest.	18, 21, 24, 27
GRAPES			
Buffalo	Ripens 3 weeks before Concord; disease-free. Hardy to 15°F; needs wind protection.	Blue/black; high dessert quality; good for wine and juice.	10, 18, 23
Concord (seedless types as well)	Midseason to late bearing; most common eastern grape. Disease resistant, productive. Hardy to -15°F.	Deep purple to black; large clusters. Fine dessert quality, also makes good jelly.	1, 4, 10, 11, 13, 18, 21, 22, 23, 26
Dearing	Muscadine type; good choice for southern growers; heavy producer; self-fruitful; will also pollinate Scuppernong. Grows best in zones 7-9.	Bronze, medium-size fruit. Midseason harvest.	2
Fredonia	Ripens 2-3 weeks before Concord. Hardy to -15°F. Vigorous, productive.	Black; large clusters; medium size. Makes good jelly.	1, 2, 10, 11, 13, 18, 20, 21, 23, 28
Golden Muscat	Robust vines; late bearing, ripen mid-October.	Yellow with distinctive flavor. Unusually large berries.	4, 18, 22, 23, 27
Himrod	Hybrid of Ontario and Thompson seedless; ripens four weeks before Concord. Hardy to -5°F; disease-free.	Early; yellow; large, loose clusters. Fine dessert quality. Seedless, not slipskin.	8, 10, 11, 18, 20, 21, 23, 27
Scupper-nong	Muscadine type; self-unfruitful; needs pollinator variety. Grows best in zones 7-9.	Medium to large-size fruit has sweet-tart flavor. Early season harvest.	2, 13
Suffolk red	Ripens 3 weeks before Concord. Good hardiness.	Red; loose, medium clusters, large berries. Best eastern table grape; seedless.	2, 10, 18, 20, 23, 26, 27
RASPBERRIES			
Dormanred	Very productive canes; suitable for southern growers.	Late summer crop of dark red berries; good fresh or in preserves.	13
Heritage	Erect and sturdy bush form; canes need no support; produces one summer crop and one fall crop. Hardy; grows best in zones 4-8.	Firm and sweet red berries; good for fresh use, canning, freezing. Moderate summer crop in July, larger fall crop from September to frost.	2, 3, 8, 10, 11, 13, 21, 23
Latham	Extremely productive; very hardy;	Large, firm berries with rich red	3, 8,

129

Variety	Tree/Plant Characteristics	Fruit Characteristics	Sources
	susceptible to disease; virus-free stock critical. Grows best in zones 3-8.	color; good for fresh use, canning. One long summer harvest period.	18

STRAWBERRIES

(Ever-bearing)

Variety	Tree/Plant Characteristics	Fruit Characteristics	Sources
Ogallala	Vigorous and hardy; good for cold climates.	Large, dark red, aromatic berries; freeze well.	5, 8, 10, 18
Ozark Beauty	Very productive; grows well in zones 4-8.	Large, sweet berries with good flavor; very good for freezing.	2, 4, 5, 8, 10, 13, 18, 22, 23
Superfection	Very dependable; tolerates drought and hot weather; grows best in 4-8.	Tart, medium-size berries; ready to harvest 90 days after planting; produces heavy crops late summer to early fall.	2, 5, 10
Sweetheart	Cross between alpine and ever-bearing types; started from seed, which assures virus-free plants. Takes 120 days to mature from seed; sends out runners.	Large, 1½ in. berries have pleasing, extra sweet flavor.	5, 24

(June-bearing)

Variety	Tree/Plant Characteristics	Fruit Characteristics	Sources
Florida 90	Heavy yielder; tolerates sandy soil; suited to Deep South, Gulf Coast areas.	Medium to large, cone-shaped fruit; early-season harvest.	10, 13
Pocahontas	Exceptionally high yielding; virus-free; foliage resistant to most leaf problems. Tolerates hot summer weather; suited to areas from Northeast to mid-South, zones 6-8.	Large, glossy red berries; great flavor; ship well; excellent for freezing. Midseason harvest.	2, 3, 5, 22
Sparkle	Heavy yielder; sends out runners energetically; good disease resistance. Grows well in zones 5-8.	Medium-size, bright red berries; one of the best for freezing and preserving. Mid- to late-season harvest.	2, 3, 10, 18, 22, 23
Surecrop	Makes runners freely; drought resistant; foliage resists most leaf problems. Suited to zones 4-8.	Medium-size, firm, bright red fruit; good fresh or preserved; recommended for freezing. Midseason harvest.	2, 3, 4, 10, 18, 22, 27

(Alpine)

Variety	Tree/Plant Characteristics	Fruit Characteristics	Sources
Baron Solemacher	Perennial plant; sends out a few runners; plant seeds or plants.	Flavorful, bright red berries twice the size of wild strawberries.	16
Catherine the Great	Hardy perennial; runnerless, compact plant; good for borders or containers; start from seed.	Thimble-size fruit.	31

23 Herbs to Grow

The following codes are designed to help you identify at a glance the basic growing conditions and habits of the plants.

⊙ Annual. Will not winter over; must be seeded yearly.

☐ Perennial. Lasts many years; can be started from seeds or transplants. As plants mature, cuttings may be taken and rooted for new plants.

⊡ Tender perennial. Not hardy outdoors below 20°F, but will winter over in warm areas. In the North, plants may be moved indoors over winter and brought back outdoors in spring.

☒ Biennial. First year plant will produce leaves; blooms second year. Sow seeds early in season for maximum growth.

☼ Full sun.

☽ Part sun.

☻ Shade.

Herb	Description and Growth Habit	Cultural Tips	Use in Garden
BASIL ☉ ☽ or ☼	Light green, crinkly leaves are strongly aromatic and clovelike in flavor. Depending on variety, will grow from 6-24 in. tall. Will grow in container 6 in. or more deep.	Start from seed indoors 4-5 weeks before transplanting. Set out around same time as tomatoes. Keep moderately rich soil slightly moist. Pinch tops to encourage bushiness and to keep flowers from forming.	Grow in ground as border plant; dark opal variety makes a very decorative border. Or use as container plant.
BORAGE ☉ ☽ or ☼	Blue green, hairy leaves have cucumberlike flavor. Plant blooms profusely with blue star-shaped flowers. A sprawling plant that needs space to grow. Reaches 1-3 ft. tall. Can grow in container at least 8 in. deep, 12 in. wide.	Sow seeds after last spring frost. Once established, plant often reseeds itself. Provide well-drained, moderately rich soil; mulch to keep soil moist.	Grow as accent plant in landscape. Will also grow in containers.
CHAMOMILE ☐ ☽ or ☼	Plant has fernlike foliage with tiny daisylike flowers. Has strong apple fragrance and flavor. Spreads rampantly with matlike, creeping growth.	Sow seed after last spring frost; will self-sow once plant is established. Needs well-drained, sandy soil; mulch to keep moist.	Grows well in containers and looks lovely in hanging baskets.
CHERVIL ☉ ☽ or ☼	Leaves resemble flat leaf Italian parsley, but flavor and scent are blend of of licorice and tarragon. Leaves turn pink as tiny white flowers appear, then plants go to seed. Spreading growth reaches from 1-2 ft. tall. Will grow in container 6 in. or more deep.	Sow seed in spring and again in late summer. Seed needs light for germination; press into soil, don't cover. Chervil doesn't transplant well. Grows best in cool weather. Established plants may reseed themselves. Provide rich soil and mulch to keep it moist and cool. Cut top leaves just as they begin to yellow to encourage more growth.	Good border or container plant.
CHIVES ☐ ☽ or ☼	Hollow, grasslike leaves have mild onion flavor. Also produce lavender blossoms that are edible. Grows to 10 in. tall. Clumps grow larger each season as bulbous roots multiply. Can grow in container at least 8 in. deep.	Start transplants 6-8 weeks before last frost; set out after last frost. Or, sow seeds in garden as soon as soil can be worked. Divide old clumps every 4-5 years. Provide well-drained, rich soil; mulch to retain moisture. For lush growth pinch flower heads before blooming.	Compact plants can be used as a border accent with flowers or vegetables. Grow well in containers.

Culinary Use	Harvest and Preservation	Companion Planting	Varieties to Try
Use leaves, fresh or dried, in all tomato and onion dishes. Makes rich, flavorful pesto sauce. Also flavors vinegar.	Cut 2-3 in. from top of central stem every 2-3 weeks for continuous fresh supply until first frost. Preserve by pureeing leaves and freezing in ice cube trays.	Enhances growth and flavor of tomatoes. Attracts bees, repels gnats, flies, mosquitoes. Doesn't like to be planted near rue.	French Leaf: small leaves, compact size, mild flavor. Dark Opal: purple bronze leaves, edible and ornamental Green Bouquet: dwarf, bushy plants with ¼-¾ in. long leaves; good for borders, containers.
Use young leaves raw in salads or steam as vegetable. Steep leaves to make tea. Use as accent for chicken and fish. Flowers can be candied or used fresh as garnish.	Best used fresh; clip a few leaves as needed from each plant. Don't strip all leaves from single plant until it's time to make final harvest.	Enhances growth and flavor of tomatoes and squash. Said to deter tomato hornworm; helps and is helped by strawberries. Flowers powerful attractant for bees.	. . . .
Use dried flower heads for tea.	Harvest flower heads when white petals droop and yellow centers form cones. Dry flowers on screen placed in 150°F oven with door ajar. When dry, store in airtight container.	Said to improve flavor of cabbage and onions when grown nearby.	German chamomile: very similar except has rather scraggly upright growth up to 2½ ft. tall, and is an annual.
Use fresh leaves with fish, poultry, vegetables and in omelets, soups. Prime ingredient in classic *fines herbes* mix.	Use leaves only; harvest by cutting leaves with 1 in. of stem. Does not preserve well, best eaten fresh.	Said to improve flavor and growth of radishes.	. . . .
Use both leaves and flowers in salads, salad dressings; use leaves with meat, poultry, fish, eggs, cheese and sour cream. Try flowers as accent in fresh spinach salad.	To harvest leaves, clip with scissors close to ground. Don't cut entire plant down during season; that reduces vigor. To preserve, snip leaves and freeze flat on cookie sheet. Place in plastic container, store in freezer.	Helps growth and improves flavor of carrots.	Chinese or garlic chives: mild garlicky flavor; white blooms in fall, flat leaves.

Herb	Description and Growth Habit	Cultural Tips	Use in Garden
CILANTRO (also called Chinese parsley and leaf coriander) ⊙ ☼	Slender, erect stems bear finely divided leaves. Pale mauve flowers appear, then plants set seed. Distinctive taste and smell is very strong. Can grow to 2½ ft. tall. Will grow in container at least 8 in. deep.	Sow seed in late spring in successions every 3 weeks to assure ample supply of leaves before seeds form. Needs darkness to germinate. Established plants may reseed themselves. Doesn't transplant well. Provide light, fertile, well-drained soil. Grows well in arid climates.	Large plant useful as accent in landscape. Grows well in containers.
DILL ⊙ ☼	Delicate, feathery foliage resembles fennel. Broad, flat yellow flower heads form, then go to seed. Can reach 3 ft. tall. Will grow in container at least 8 in. deep.	Sow seeds in late spring. Plant succession each month to ensure steady supply. Doesn't transplant well. Will reseed itself if flower heads left on plant. Needs rich, sandy, well-drained soil.	Creates lovely feathery backdrop for flowers. Can soften fenceline or foundation. Grows well in containers.
FENNEL ⊡ ☼	Feathery leaves taste like licorice, stems are crisp like celery. Plant can grow 3-5 ft. tall. Dwarf variety available, nice in container at least 8 in. deep.	Sow seed in early spring. Doesn't transplant well. Needs light, well-drained, fertile soil.	Creates decorative, wispy backdrop for flowers. Dwarf variety best in containers.
GARDEN CRESS (also called curly cress and mustard cress) ⊙ ❁	Tiny, pungent, peppery leaves and edible stems form low-growing carpet. Grows to maturity in 10 days. Can grow in shallow flats 2 in. deep.	Start from seed pressed gently into soil. Plant weekly for continuous harvest. Needs very moist soil or vermiculite that's kept moist at all times.	Grow in shallow pots or flats. Great favorite in childrens' gardens.
LEMON BALM ☐ ❁ or ☼	Heart-shaped leaves with evenly scalloped edges have lemony scent and flavor. Plant spreads like mint. Can reach 3-4 ft. tall in the garden; in container (8 in. deep) reaches only 1 ft.	Sow seed as soon as ground is workable in spring. Or, start from rooted cuttings. Established plants can be divided in early spring. Provide well-drained soil and keep it slightly on dry side.	Makes good border plant when cut back to keep foliage compact. Will also grow in containers.

Culinary Use	Harvest and Preservation	Companion Planting	Varieties to Try
Leaves used in Oriental, Indian and Mexican cuisines. Use sparingly with fish, poultry, bean dishes. Coriander seed used primarily as pickling spice and as ingredient in curry powder.	Harvest leaves as needed throughout season. Leaves don't preserve well—use fresh. Select one plant to let go to seed and dry for use.	Strong smell attracts pollinating insects. Helps anise set seed. Doesn't like to grow near fennel.	. . . .
Use fresh or dried leaves with fish and fish sauces, cucumbers, soups, cottage cheese, vinegars, poultry. Can add to butter for seasoned spread. Use dill seed in breads and for pickling.	Clip leaves from main stem and use fresh or dry. To dry, spread out on fine mesh screen in shade; store in airtight jar. Harvest seeds when flowers have turned light brown. Cut off flower heads, dry in sun for several days, then shake out seeds.	Flowers attract honey bees. Improves health and vigor of cabbage. Don't plant near carrots which are said to suppress dill growth.	Dill Bouquet: small, compact plant, suited to container growing.
Use leaves in soups, salads, sauce for pasta, as fish garnish. Blanch stalks and eat with oil and vinegar or grill with fish. Use seeds in pork sausage, sauerkraut, beets, cakes, cookies.	Leaves and stems used fresh or dry. Clip hollow stems with feathery leaves as needed. Let some plants go to seed. To dry, see Dill.	Fennel can inhibit growth of certain vegetables. Particularly bush beans, kohlrabi, tomatoes. Coriander planted nearby will prevent fennel seed from forming. Flowers attract pollinating insects.	Look for dwarf variety.
Use fresh with cottage cheese, for garnish in soups, salads, sandwiches, grain dishes and vegetables. Gives bite to bland foods.	Harvest with scissors; snip off leaves with 1 in. of stem. Doesn't preserve well, best used fresh.	. . . .	. . . .
Use leaves, fresh or dried, in fruit salads, punches, soups, herb butters or with vegetables, poultry, fish. Also brew for tea.	Harvest before plant blooms for best quality leaves. Can make up to 3 harvests a season. Cut off entire plant 2 in. above ground. Strip leaves and use fresh, or dry on fine mesh screen in shade or in oven with pilot light on and door propped open. Store in airtight container.	Attracts pollinating bees.	. . . .

Herb	Description and Growth Habit	Cultural Tips	Use in Garden
LOVAGE (also called Chinese celery) ☐ ❄ or ☼	Dark green leaves look, taste, smell like celery; hollow stems are also edible. Vigorous, abundant grower. Reaches 3-5 ft. tall. Will grow in container at least 8 in. deep.	Sow seed in late summer for following spring crop. Take root divisions from established plants in spring. Difficult to grow in hot climates, prefers winter freeze. Needs fertile soil; use mulch to keep soil evenly moist and cool.	Grow in out-of-the-way corners of garden where large plant won't interfere with other plantings.
MARJORAM, SWEET ⊡ ☼	Gray green, oval leaves borne on short stems. Have sweet and pungent flavor. In garden, can reach 12 in. tall. Will grow in container at least 6 in. deep.	Treat as annual and start new plants each spring. Soak tiny, slow-to-germinate seed 24 hours before planting; sow indoors 4-6 weeks before setting out. Transplant after last frost. Can also start from rooted cuttings. Does not tolerate cold climates well and usually can't survive even mildest winter. Provide rich, alkaline, well-drained soil.	Nice container plant.
MINT ☐ ❄ or ⊜	Shallow rooted, sends out vigorous runners. Spreads rampantly and grows to various heights depending on variety. Will grow in container at least 8 in. deep.	Root stem cuttings or divide roots of established plants in spring. Needs fertile soil kept evenly moist.	Must be confined or it will take over garden. In ground, confine by planting in large clay pot and sink entire pot into the soil. Will also grow well in aboveground containers.
OREGANO ⊡ ☼	Erect plant covered with oval, gray green leaves. Very similar to marjoram in appearance, but flavor is different. Grows to 2 ft. tall. Trailing varieties also available, do well in containers at least 6 in. deep.	Start transplants indoors and set out after last frost. Or, take root divisions from established plant in spring. Needs average, well-drained garden soil; doesn't require heavy doses of water. Trim plant back to 1 in. 6 weeks after planting to stimulate bushy growth.	Does well in containers and hanging baskets when trailing variety used.
PARSLEY ⊠ ❄	Mounding plant that puts out profusion of crinkled or flat leaves, depending on variety. Plant develops taproot that may reach	Technically a biennial, usually treated as annual. Start from seed in early spring; speed germination by soaking 24 hours before planting. Provide rich,	Curly parsley makes marvelous border plant. Both types can be grown in containers.

Culinary Use	Harvest and Preservation	Companion Planting	Varieties to Try
Use fresh leaves in soups, salads, stews, stuffings as you would celery. Can also peel and cook stems in chicken stock and enjoy as vegetable.	Pick fresh leaves in small amounts as needed. Harvest stems by cutting close to ground. Stems and leaves best used fresh since they don't preserve well.	Said to improve health and flavor of many vegetables when grown throughout garden.	. . . .
Use leaves, fresh or dried, with all meat dishes, seafoods, vegetables, eggs.	Harvest frequently to prevent flowering. Cut back to 2 in. from ground to spur second flush of growth. To preserve, cut stems with with leaves, spread on fine mesh screen in dry, shaded area. When dry, sift powdered leaves through screen, leaving stems behind. Store in airtight container.	Said to improve health and flavor of vegetables of vegetables when grown throughout garden.	There are many varieties to choose from.
Use fresh or dried in teas, jellies, sauces, salads salad dressings, or with meat, fish, poultry, sugar snap and other green peas. An integral part of Middle Eastern tabouleh salad.	Cut mint at base of plant before it flowers or when bottom leaves begin to yellow. Several cuttings may be taken during growing season. Use fresh or preserve by stripping leaves from stems and drying in warm, shady spot on screen. Store in airtight container.	Enhances growth of tomatoes and cole crops. Said to repel cabbage moth.	Wide range of varieties with distinctive flavors available: apple mint, orange mint, pennyroyal, pepper- mint, pineapple mint, spearmint.
Use fresh or dried with meat and tomato dishes. Use in tomato-based pasta sauces, herb mixtures, soups, stews.	Pick fresh leaves as needed. To preserve, strip leaves and dry on screen in sun. Rub dry leaves through screen and store in airtight containers.	Plant around cole crops; said to repel cabbage moth. Some varieties attract butterflies.	Greek: small leaved, trailing plant with white flowers.
Curly parsley preferred as attractive garnish but is also edible. Flat parsley, fresh or dried, used with all foods except	Cut stems from base of plant, along outside only so center of plant can continue to grow. Best when used fresh.	Enhances asparagus growth.	Extra Triple Curled: compact plant with very finely curled leaves. Flat Italian: flat

Herb	Description and Growth Habit	Cultural Tips	Use in Garden
	12 in. long. Can grow in container at least 8 in. deep.	humusy soil; keep fairly moist with mulch. Plant is quite hardy and can stay in garden, well mulched, well into winter.	
ROSEMARY ⊡ ☾ or ☼	Spiky, needlelike dark green leaves with grayish undersides grow on woody branches. Leaves have strong piney flavor. In warm dry climate may grow into 2-6 ft. tall bush in ground. When grows in container, reaches 12-15 in. tall.	Seeds have very poor germination rate, best to use cuttings or transplants. In late summer, take 6 in. cuttings from established plants and root 4 in. of base in damp sand or vermiculite. Prefers well-drained sandy, alkaline soil. Let soil dry between thorough waterings; be careful not to overwater.	In cold climates, best to grow in movable container so plant can be wintered over in frost-free place.
SAGE ☐ ☼	Oblong, silvery-green leaves with pebbly surface borne on woody branches. In ground, will grow 1-2 ft. tall. Can grow in containers at least 8 in. deep.	Sow seeds in early spring or propagate in spring or early fall by dividing established plants. Needs well-drained fertile soil. Use compost, but avoid manure; it produces undesirable flavor in herb. Cut back woody parts of established plants in spring to encourage new growth.	Does well in rock gardens. Variegated varieties are very showy. Will grow well in containers.
SAVORY, SUMMER ☉ ☼	Large, fast growing plant with more delicate flavor than winter savory. More erect growth than winter savory, with stronger stems. Grows to 1½ ft. tall in ground. Also grows in container at least 6 in. deep.	Start from seed or cuttings in early spring. Provide well-drained sandy soil, not too rich, not too moist. Pinch off flowers as they appear.	Grows well in containers.
SAVORY, WINTER ☐ ☼	Small, narrow leaves grow in pairs along delicate stems. In ground, grows 6-12 in. tall. Will also grow in container at least 6 in. deep.	Start from seed in spring. Or, divide roots of established plants every few years in spring. Provide well-drained, sandy soil, not too rich, not too moist.	Good border plant. Low, spreading growth also good for containers.
SCENTED GERANIUM ⊡ ☼	Each type has distinctive leaf shape and scent. Strong scent is released by touch or warmth. In ground, in warm climates, may grow 2-4 ft. tall. Or grow in container at least 6 in. deep.	Grows best from stem cuttings rooted in moist sand. Provide friable, fertile, well-drained soil. Don't keep too moist. In cold climates, winter indoors in sunny spot.	Charming in hanging baskets and containers.

Culinary Use	Harvest and Preservation	Companion Planting	Varieties to Try
sweets. Stems tied together in bundle add flavor to soups, stews, sauces.			leaves with pungent almost spicy flavor.
Whether fresh or dry use sparingly with poultry, lamb; in stews, soups, jellies, salad dressings. Also good as flavoring for vinegar.	Harvest tender tips by cutting 3 to 4 in. from end of branch. Use fresh as needed. To preserve, dry quickly in oven with pilot light on and door propped open. Store in airtight container.	Grow near cabbage, beans, carrots; said to deter cabbage moth, bean beetle, carrot fly.	. . . .
Use sparingly, fresh or dried, with cheese, pork, veal, poultry, sausages and in stuffings.	Cut fresh leaves as needed. At end of season, snip off stems, tie together and hang upside down to dry in shaded area. For best flavor, enclose dried stems in plastic bag and tie; hang to store.	Plant with cabbage, carrots; said to deter cabbage moth and carrot fly. Grows well near rosemary. Flowers attract pollinating bees. Keep away from cucumbers; said to stunt their growth.	Many varieties available including a dwarf.
Acts as antiflatulant when added to bean dishes. Also useful as salt substitute. Use leaves fresh or dried with vegetables, soups, sauces, rice, game, egg dishes.	For fresh use, cut off ends of branches as needed. To dry, strip leaves and spread on screen in sunny place. Store in airtight jar.	Grow with beans; said to deter bean beetle.	. . . .
Use fresh for best flavor. See above.	See above.	See above.	. . . .
Use leaves fresh or dried in puddings, drinks, cakes, cookies and with fruits and berries. Also flavors apple jelly.	Harvest fresh leaves as needed. To dry, spread on tray and set in oven with pilot light on and door propped open. Store in airtight containers.	Scent attracts pollinating bees and repels harmful insects. Grow interspersed throughout vegetable garden.	Available in a wide array of scents: apple, apricot, lemon, rose, strawberry, to name a few.

Herb	Description and Growth Habit	Cultural Tips	Use in Garden
SORREL, FRENCH ☐ ☾ or ☼	Light green, succulent leaves have tart acidic flavor. Nearly indestruct-ible plant grows 1-2 ft. tall and produces lavishly over many years. Can grow in container at least 6 in. deep.	Sow seed in early spring, as soon as soil is workable. Can also divide roots of established plants in spring. Needs rich, well-drained soil; mulch to retain moisture. Don't allow flowers to form or leaves will be of inferior quality.	Grows well in containers.
TARRAGON, FRENCH ☐ ☾ or ☼	Slender, aromatic leaves have scent of new-mown hay, with hint of licorice when fresh. In ground, can reach 2 ft. tall. Spread by rhizomes. Can grow in container 6 in. deep.	Use purchased transplants; does not seed well. Or, take root divisions in spring from estab-lished plants. Needs fertile, well-drained soil; keep moist with mulch. Cut back in early spring to encourage new growth.	Will do well in containers.
THYME ☐ ☾ or ☼	Leaves are tiny oval, dark green and depending on type may be rimmed with silver or gold. Generally low-growing and shrubby, reaching 8-12 in. tall. Trailing type also avail-able. Will grow in container at least 6 in. deep.	Start from purchased trans-plants or take root divisions from established plants in early spring. Provide well-drained, sandy, light soil; keep soil on the dry side.	Upright type forms attractive border. Trailing types grown in ground form dense mats; they're also good in hanging baskets or pots.

Culinary Use	Harvest and Preservation	Companion Planting	Varieties to Try
Use leaves sparingly in soups, sauces, salads; use with fish, poultry, veal, other vegetables.	Best used fresh. Cut to ground two or three times during season to encourage new leaf growth. Remove central stringy rib from each leaf before using.	. . . .	. . . .
Use fresh or dried with poultry, fish, vegetables, eggs, cheese. Use in white sauces and to flavor vinegar. Use sparingly or flavor will overpower other flavors.	To harvest, cut 2 in. of stem as needed. To preserve, strip leaves from stem and place in airy dry, warm spot not above 90°F or leaves will turn brown. Store in airtight container.	. . . .	Note that Russian tarragon is not as pleasing in flavor and aroma.
Use fresh or dried with red meat or fish. Use in chowders, soups, stuffings, jellies. Flavor is not overwhelming, so can be used liberally. Important ingredient in bouquet garni.	Harvest as needed for fresh use by clipping sprigs from base of plant before flowering. For preserving, cut from only upper third of plant. Dry stems on screen in warm, shady spot. When dry, rub leaves off stems and discard stems. Store in airtight container.	Plant near cole crops; said to deter cabbage worm. If allowed to flower, will attract pollinating bees.	Both upright and trailing types avilable. Silver Thyme: leaves edged with silver. Lemon Thyme: leaves taste and smell lemony. Gold Thyme: leaves edged with gold.

CHAPTER 7

Getting Ready for Gardening

There are a few more things you should consider before you rush out to plant the first lettuce or radishes. At first glance the topics that follow may seem like strange companions. But each one is important in its own right and together they will prepare you comfortably for the fun ahead and introduce you to the techniques to be discussed in the rest of the book. Here are some suggestions, then, on choosing garden tools, choosing proper clothing for the job, and preparing yourself with exercise as carefully as you prepare the soil to receive the seeds. These are followed by a brief overview of the gardening principles and practices that you will learn how to put to good use in Chapters 8 through 13.

There's No Tool Like an Old Tool

There are garden tools which become personal favorites, simply because of three things:

they are well made

they do the job that they were designed to do efficiently

they feel comfortable in your hand

When shopping for garden tools it is wise, then, to judge the tool by those standards. Make sure when buying tools that you take into consideration your own strength, stature and work habits. Then buy only the best. A top quality tool, properly maintained, will last for many years and always be a joy to use.

There are literally hundreds of different gardening tools, aids, and gadgets. The new gardener, when confronted with such a vast array, can be totally bewildered. You are faced with having to make a choice between many versions of the same tool, each designed in a slightly different shape, but made to perform exactly the same function. Fortunately, small space home gardening does not require a large investment in heavy machinery, as farming does. The beginning gardener can get away with buying only a few basic tools.

In the garden you will need to dig, rake, weed and cultivate. Therefore, to start with, you'll need four long-handled tools that do these jobs: a spade, a fork, a rake and a hoe. In addition to these four basic long-handled tools, a trowel for transplanting and a hand cultivator and hoe for chopping weeds and loosening soil for planting will be a nice addition and all you'll need to get you started for up-close work.

Some gardeners prefer a kneeling position for better control or when gardening in containers. It gives them a special feeling of closeness with the earth. For these gardeners, smaller hand tools are easier to use than long-handled ones.

Properly cared for, garden tools will have a long and useful life. To keep your tools in good condition after each use clean them by wiping with an oily cloth. Be sure to store them in a weather-protected place. Some gardeners keep on hand a pail of sand mixed with oil, and they dig their tools into it a few times before wiping them off with a clean rag.

In winter, you can give your tools a good going over. Remove any rust with an emery cloth or rust remover. Oil all moving parts and put a light coating of oil over all metal parts and working edges. Keep the cutting edges of any shears and clippers you have well sharpened. I have my tools sharpened at a knife and scissors sharpening shop halfway through the season and again before I put them away for the winter. The best way to store your tools is to hang them on cup or pegboard hooks, taking special care to secure the sharp tools and placing them in a place where they will not be dangerous. Tools have a way of disappearing when you put them down in tall grass or on the ground, but putting a strip of red or yellow fluorescent tape on the handle will help you spot where you put them last. While working in the garden, another good safety habit to get into is to keep sharp pointed edges toward the ground at all times.

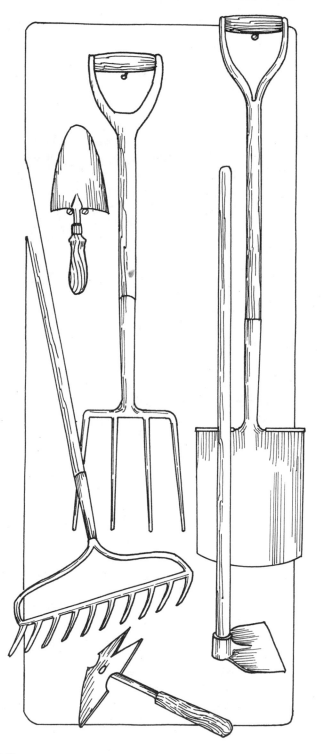

The only garden tools you really need are (clockwise from bottom) a hand cultivator for small beds and containers, a rake, a sturdy trowel, a fork, a spade and a long-handled hoe.

Salvaged Tools for the Garden

The hoe is over 4,000 years old and has amply proven its worth as a garden tool. Gardeners still rely on the hoe as a basic implement, but you don't have to stick to only such time-honored tools for gardening. There are plenty of implements you can devise yourself and put to work in the garden. When raided with a bit of imagination, most households yield up a gold mine of cost-free utensils that have outlived their original purpose and can be used as garden tools. Here is an inspirational sampling of household objects that creative gardeners can adapt for their use:

Spoons, forks and knives can dig up small weeds and seedlings, as well as being used to cultivate plants. They are especially helpful in container gardens where plants are close together.

Pencils make holes for seeds at planting time.

Wooden ice cream sticks and ice cream spoons make great plant identification markers. Use a waterproof felt-tip marker to write on them.

Large turkey basters, the kind with the rubber bulb on one end, can be used to give supplemental feedings of fish emulsion or manure "tea" to individual plants.

Coffee, tuna and beer cans can be used in a hundred ways. With tops and bottoms removed, they can become cutworm collars for newly planted seedlings. Tuna cans buried to their rims and filled with stale beer or sourdough starter can be used to trap slugs. Be sure to wash and rinse the cans thoroughly before you use them!

Plastic water or bleach jugs with the bottoms cut off make wonderful hot caps to protect seedlings from the cold.

A screwdriver can be used to pry up stubborn weeds like dandelions that have long taproots.

Use tweezers to remove bugs from individual plants.

Cheesecloth draped over fruit trees or berry bushes keeps birds from stealing the fruit and still allows sunlight, rain and air to reach the plants.

A magnifying glass is indispensable for identifying bugs.

Old nylon pantyhose have a multitude of uses. They can tie up trailing plants or attach climbers to a trellis. You can fill them with animal repellent, like hair cuttings to keep deer away, or stuff them with straw and make a scarecrow.

Wire clothes hangers offer myriad uses in construction (see Chapter 11).

Plastic containers, egg cartons, cottage cheese and butter tubs, disposable but usable aluminum foil trays are all handy containers to use for starting seeds and growing seedlings.

Most of all, remember that gardening doesn't have to cost a lot of money, for when it comes down to it, the best-designed tools of all are your own bare hands.

Manure Couture: What to Wear in the Garden

A nongardening friend of mine once remarked that the best way to enjoy gardening was to put a wide-brimmed straw hat on your head, wear unstarched, lightweight, loose-fitting clothing, hold a trowel in one hand and a cool drink in the other—and tell someone else where to dig. When you are not

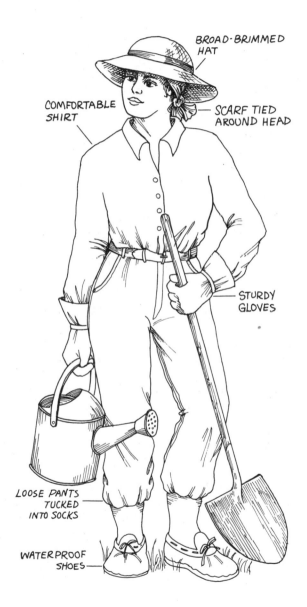

BROAD-BRIMMED HAT

SCARF TIED AROUND HEAD

COMFORTABLE SHIRT

STURDY GLOVES

LOOSE PANTS TUCKED INTO SOCKS

WATERPROOF SHOES

Manure couture—what to wear for comfortable gardening.

dressed appropriately and protectively, no doubt you would agree with my friend. Gardening is a sneaky and pleasant way to exercise in the fresh air and sunshine, but unlike jogging or golf or tennis, there are no shops that sell special clothing to outfit the gardener from head to toe. On the contrary, we gardeners have a special corner way in the back of our closets where we save comfortable and out-of-style clothing. These old clothes may not make us look like fashion plates, but they are broken-in, comfortable to wear, and have our personal body imprint. They let us bend and move easily and without constriction.

Gardening is not recognized as an athletic sport (even though to my mind it is). But gardeners walk, bend, stretch, lift, twist and pull—and that's what I call outdoor exercise. However, as anyone who has spent any time gardening outdoors knows, the bloom is soon off the rose when your arms and legs are covered with maddeningly itchy stings and bites, when the sun's ultraviolet rays burn you to a crisp, and when you are sweating and dehydrated. The good news is that all of these discomforts can be avoided or lessened to a great degree simply by wearing the right kind of clothing. Here are some specific suggestions for your comfort and well-being while working in the garden:

Avoid bright, colorful clothing (especially yellow) which will attract bugs.

Don't wear perfume or cologne while gardening. Sweet scents also attract bugs.

If mosquitoes plague you, a good insect repellent (such as Cutter's or Deep Woods OFF) sprayed on clothing is helpful. Or rub pennyroyal leaves or oil of eucalyptus on your skin to keep bugs away. A beekeeper's hat and netting can protect your face and neck from insects.

Gauntlet-style soft leather gloves protect wrists and hands from scratchy brambles and poison ivy.

If you forget to wear gloves and get dirty fingernails, twist the tips of your fingers in half of a lemon, or clean them with baking soda.

Do not wear sandals in the garden; stubbed toes and broken toenails will result.

Backless slippers, kept at the door, remind you to remove dirty shoes outside (in case the phone rings).

Do some limbering-up exercises in the spring before tackling the season's gardening chores. If you have had a sedentary winter, a sudden spurt of exertion will leave you sore and stiff. (Some exercises are described in the next section of this chapter.)

Don't put excess stress on your back. Learn to lift heavy loads with bent knees, and use a wheelbarrow or other sort of wheeled conveyor whenever possible to haul things.

When you're working in the hot sun, drink lots of water and wear a hat, plus loose clothing that covers you, to avoid heat exhaustion.

For especially hot weather, put a damp washcloth in a plastic bag in the refrigerator or freezer for about 15 minutes before going outdoors and then wear it under your hat to keep you cool.

Apply a total sun-block type of sunscreen lotion to your face, ears, and neck (the only parts of you not covered by clothing).

Cover two large sponges with terrycloth and sew velcro tape on each. Attach two pieces of velcro to the knees of your work pants. Attach the sponges when you kneel down to work. They are lots cheaper than buying knee pads, and are easy to remove when you don't need them.

No Strain, No Pain
Exercises for the Gardener

Gardening is a subtle, marvelous exercise. It is a totally absorbing activity without a moment of boredom. That's one of its problems: you have such a good time doing it that you forget that like any other physical activity it requires warmups. Any heavy work is tiring if you're out of condition, and gardening without pain requires preparation through exercise. With a rush of sudden vigorous activity, like the usual weekend gardening binge, will come those seasonal aches and pains that make you feel as if a herd of elephants have tap danced over your body.

The most important piece of machinery that every gardener needs and uses constantly is his or her own body. Like any other tool, it can't be allowed to get rusty or it will not carry out its function properly. Routine garden chores—raking, hoeing, digging, planting seeds, pulling weeds, clipping shrubs—require as much energy as any other athletic activity. Getting yourself into shape for gardening with the following exercises will help to prevent back strain or injury, or exhaustion after a sedentary winter. Start at least a month before it's warm enough to work in the garden and build up your sessions slowly from 10 minutes to a half hour a day. By the time spring arrives, you will be able to enjoy it enthusiastically. These exercises were designed by exercise specialist and author Lilian Rowan*. They are coordinated with muscle groups which are engaged during special gardening activities. They will stretch your muscles, improve flexibility and strengthen your body before you take hoe in hand.

*If you're interested in getting more involved in exercising, I recommend you read Lilian's books, *Working Woman's Body Book*, Lilian Rowan and Barbara Winkler (Rowson Wade, 1978), or *Speedwalking*, Lilian Rowan and D. S. Laiken (G. P. Putnam Sons, 1980).

First movement in walk and lift exercise

Second movement in walk and lift

For Bending and Crouching

All gardening chores require these positions; therefore, you should feel comfortable while in them. This exercise is designed to strengthen your thighs and give you better control and increased ability to raise and lower your body weight easily from a standing to a kneeling or crouching position.

Walk and Lift: Squat down with your right foot flat on the floor in front of your other foot, and your left knee on the floor. While you scoop up an imaginary object from the floor with your left hand, straighten up and take a step forward with your left foot. Squat down again so your right knee touches the floor and scoop with your right hand. Start with 10 steps and work up to 30 steps.

For Pulling and Tugging

This is the motion you use to pull a rake across the ground and to tug at weeds. The exercise, a type of push-up for beginners, is designed to strengthen your upper arms, upper back and shoulders.

The Push-up: Lie on your stomach, with hands near shoulders and elbows bent. Push body slowly off the floor until you are on your hands and knees. Keep your back straight as you push—don't arch it. Slowly lower your body to starting position. Start with three push-ups and work up to ten.

The pushup

For Lifting and Carrying

There is *always* something to lift and carry in the garden—soil, tools, compost. Here are two exercises to help you get in shape. The first will help strengthen back and stomach muscles, and the second will strengthen your thigh muscles and teach you the correct position for lifting heavy objects.

Bent-Knee Sit-up: First there is a sit-up with bent knees. Anchor your feet under a heavy object (or have someone hold them down). From this starting position, slowly roll your body into an upright sitting position. Then just as slowly roll yourself back down to the starting position. Begin with five sit-ups and work up to twenty.

The Lift: Second, try the lift. In a standing position, place your feet shoulder width apart. Keeping your back straight, lower your buttocks below knee level, and then return to knee level. In this position, bounce up and down four times. Then come up to a standing, straight-knee position. Repeat the entire exercise ten times. Shake out your legs to relax them.

For Digging and Shoveling

Shoveling requires that you lunge, lift a weight, and then swing or twist your torso. If

Bent knee sit-up

you're not careful you can easily injure your back. This exercise is designed to improve flexibility and strengthen the back.

Lunge and Twist: Take a big step with your right leg while bringing your right arm forward. Bend your right knee deeply while keeping your left leg outstretched behind you. Most of your weight will now be on your right leg. Slowly twist from the waist toward the left, attempting to reach your left leg which is outstretched behind you. Hold this position for a few seconds, and return to starting position. Repeat with the other leg. Alternate legs; start with three repetitions on each side and work up to five.

First movement in lunge and twist exercise

Second movement, lunge and twist

For Pushing

You may need to push a lawn mower or rotary tiller if you have a large garden or lawn. This exercise will help strengthen your back, legs and shoulders, as well as tighten your stomach muscles.

Bicycle Sit-up: Lie on your back, hands at your sides, and bend your knees in toward your chest. Move your legs as if you were pedaling a bicycle. Keeping your chin tucked in to your chest to avoid straining your lower back, try to sit up and then lie down with a rounded back and without interrupting the pedaling motion. Start with three up and down movements, working up to five. Only pedal as long in each position as is comfortable for you.

For Clipping and Pruning

When you prune trees and tall bushes your arms are raised and stretched above your head. Clipping involves the pectoral muscles of the chest as well as the upper arms.

Bicycle sit-up

Overhead press

Forearm press

The following two exercises are designed to strengthen arms, shoulders and chest.

Overhead Press: First, to strengthen your arms and shoulders for pruning, press upward. Raise your arms above your head, bending your elbows so your hands are next to your ears. Stretch your arms and bend your elbows quickly up and down. Start with 20 repetitions and work up to 40. To increase muscle strength, do this exercise holding a 1 pound can of food in each hand, but don't exceed 20 repetitions with the added weight.

Forearm Press: Second, try this chest strengthener to get ready for clipping chores. Grasp your forearms with your hands and squeeze hard while simultaneously pushing skin toward elbows. Release and repeat, starting with 10 repetitions and increasing to 30.

With your muscles strengthened and your body now supple, with your new tools sharp and clean as a whistle, newly outfitted from head to toe, you are now probably champing at the bit and raring to go out into the fresh spring air to start your garden. Go right on outdoors, but take this book with you and take a few moments more to read over the next section on some good-sense gardening techniques that will serve you well.

The Organic Way:
Good Sense Gardening

Just as the old song says, the best things in life are free. The sun, the air, water and the earth are all basic elements which support plant life. And all are found in nature, free for the taking. In the past, it seems that we took them too much for granted, until we finally realized that the supply of these elements is not infinite, as we used to think. What is removed, we learned, must be conserved and replenished or the earth will one day become barren and die.

Organic gardening beliefs are based on cycles found in nature where organisms (vegetable and animal) are born, live and die, then decompose and return to the earth where they once more enrich the soil for the fresh growth of a host of new organisms. There is, in fact, an innate logic in *all* the gentle principles of organic gardening, since they mimic nature and try to duplicate these cycles. Organic gardening just makes plain good sense. By respecting the natural cycles present in the land, the organic gardener returns what he has taken away from the soil and tries not to upset this delicate balance. By composting lawn clippings, food wastes and other things that are normally thrown away, organic gardeners have found a way to mimic nature's own recycling process, constantly improving and replenishing the soil structure and fertility. Thus, an interconnection of all parts of the garden working together in harmony is established. This kind of "holistic horticulture" provides a desirable environment for the proper bacteria, earthworms, and beneficial insects that inhabit the soil naturally.

No synthetic fertilizers or chemical insecticides or weed killers are ever used in an organic garden. The birds eat the weed seeds, and the gardener pulls the rest of the weeds or smothers them with organic mulches, which in turn break down in time and add to the structure and fertility of the soil.

Birds, when supplied with places to nest and berries and seeds to eat, will take up residence around the garden to do their job of devouring many unwanted insects. They should by all means be enticed to remain in the neighborhood, but they can stay only if we refuse to use poisons which will harm them.

Besides the birds, there are other "good guys" that can help you make chemicals unnecessary in the garden. Bees spread pollen and fertilize flowering fruits and vegetables. Earthworms aerate and help fertilize the soil with their castings. Beneficial insects like the praying mantis and the ladybug, nature's vacuum cleaners, love to eat destructive insects. (for more information, see the chart on The Good Guys in Chapter 12). In addition, there are numerous plants and flowers that when included in your garden will help repel harmful insects from your crops.

The interactions of the community of creatures and plants that make up the ecosystem of your yard and garden generally coexist in a natural system of checks and balances. Organic gardeners seek to preserve that balance. Our position on the use of pesticides is a valid one, I believe, because it calls attention to the dangers of destroying these normal checks and controls in the garden environment. We are guided by the realization that we cannot fight the unchangeable laws of nature. And, as the saying goes, when you can't fight it, you join it.

There is much that is not only sound but is also very important about gardening organically, and it is the small scale home gardener who is perhaps in the best position to make a personal contribution to the earth on which we live. We may not be able to convert the whole world to organic methods, but we can certainly use them in our own gardens. Best of all, we will begin to see some definite results within a year, at least in our own little plot of ground, and we can also act as role models for others.

Until our collective environmental consciousness was raised in the last fifteen years or so, many gardeners went along with the use of synthetic chemical fertilizers and pesticides. Yes, chemically based fertilizers are a quick fix, but they supply no organic matter and do nothing to improve the structure of the soil. Relying on them to nourish your garden allows the organic matter content and overall quality of your soil to gradually decline over the years until it reaches a point where it can no longer support the many varied populations of earthworms and bacteria that are essential to a healthy ecosystem. By contrast, organic fertilizers add organic matter to the soil, and release their nutrients to plants through the soil slowly, over a longer period of time. Over a number of years, organic fertilizers will improve the overall quality of your soil.

Home gardeners are in the vanguard of the organic front. Although more and more commercial farmers are returning to organic methods, the progress is gradual. Organic wastes from farms and feedlots are still not being recycled to the extent that they once were, and that they should be. But nonetheless, the movement is spreading. Have you ever heard the old story that if one person lights a candle in Madison Square Garden it is still dark, but when a capacity audience of 24,000 people each light a candle you can indeed see everything more brightly and clearly? So it is with organic gardeners who are spreading the word and fighting for the changes that will not damage our environment. We are no longer one candle in the dark.

Easier Does It

Good organic gardeners have found that some specific planting techniques are effective in keeping small spaces in constant production throughout the growing season. Most of these methods have been practiced instinctively by knowledgeable gardeners for many years. Other techniques, such as the intensive method of growing vegetables, are newer in approach and save time and labor as well as space. These methods break the rules of traditional linear row gardens, for crops are planted very close together in raised beds of rich soil. The techniques outlined here will all be discussed at greater length in the next several chapters. When you plan your garden space, keep them in mind for maximum yields in small spaces:

Interplanting involves simultaneously planting fast-maturing vegetables between slower-maturing, more widely spaced varieties.

Companion planting is planting next to one another pairs of plants which have a symbiotic relationship in which they help each other to grow better or repel insects.

Succession planting means sowing a new crop as soon as the preceding one is harvested to keep up constant production.

Catch cropping is a way to take maximum advantage of the growing season by planting fast-maturing vegetables where you have just harvested slower-maturing varieties.

Crop rotation insures protection of the soil. Vegetables which make specific demands for basic soil nutrients (such as celery and cabbage, which are heavy feeders) are grown together and put in a different part of the garden each year. Crops such as legumes, which enrich the soil, are planted where the heavy feeders were the year before. Rotating your crops keeps your soil from becoming depleted.

Extending the growing season, planting vegetables in containers and using space-saving vertical methods are all ways to get more food out of small spaces. You can use these limited areas themselves or as adjuncts to larger spaces.

Some Sources of Tools and Equipment

This list tells you where to find some specialized dealers that supply both common and uncommon tools for gardeners. This isn't by any means a comprehensive list, but it does contain my favorite sources.

Gardener's Eden
P.O. Box 7307
San Francisco, CA 94120

Every refinement you would like to own, plus many adaptable ideas to try if you are handy, are beautifully pictured in the pages of this full color catalog.

A. M. Leonard, Inc.
6665 Spiker Rd.
Pique, OH 45356

The most complete selection of horticulture supplies, tools, gadgets and machinery for both the farmer and home gardener. Includes hard-to-find, heavy-duty, smaller-sized gardening gloves for women, plus special small-sized hand tools designed for close work in crowded borders and beds. Catalog free.

Mellinger's
2310 West South Range
North Lima, OH 44452

Vegetable seeds, fruit trees, vines, flowers, organic insect controls and fertilizers, plus every conceivable tool and garden accessory that seems to be on the market. An excellent source for rare and imported seeds, too. Catalog free.

Walter Nicke
Box 667 G
Hudson, NY 12534

Gadgets galore, many from England where they are selected by the London Design Council. Includes the hard-to-find Rumsey clip, which neatly holds two panes of glass together to form a collapsible A-frame cloche. Also a source for practical, large-size plastic plant markers with enough space to write all pertinent information. Catalog 50¢.

Smith and Hawken Tool Co.
68 Homer
Palo Alto, CA 94301

Large selection of finest quality hand tools and supplies available. Manufactured in England where they must pass the test of an advisory board for performance and durability. A "Rolls-Royce" selection of garden tools for those who wish to invest in quality. Catalog free.

One additional source of information I'd like to point out is a book, *How to Select, Use and Maintain Garden Equipment* (Ortho Books, 1982). I have found this an extremely helpful aid to choosing tools, using them correctly, and caring for them properly. It may save you money and confusion as you choose from the vast numbers and styles of hand tools available.

Home Gardeners' Handy Helpers

Here's a list of some gadgets and containers I've found immensely helpful but hard to find. Sources are listed, too.

Firm Grip Weed Puller, the Cut and Hold Flower Gatherer

Both tools have 2½-foot-long extensions. A perfect no-stoop solution for gardeners who get tired of bending or who have back problems or are confined to a wheelchair. The original functions of these tools were to reach, hold, cut or weed flowers in inaccessible places, but other uses, such as trimming hanging plants, make both tools especially worthwhile.

Available from Walter Nicke, Box 667, Hudson, NY 12534.

Headlamp

For people who garden at night after work or who want to gather nightcrawlers and slugs from the garden. Portable and battery operated, this lamp frees your hands. The beam adjusts from a spot to a broad beam and lights wherever you look. Can also be used by cyclists, campers and spelunkers.

Available from Brookstone Co., 127 Vose Farm Rd., Peterborough, NH 03458. Catalog free.

Folding Magnifying Glass

Worn on a neck string by nearsighted bug seekers.

Available from the New York Botanical Garden Shop, Bronx, NY 10458.

All-Metal Permanent Rustproof Identification Labels

In ten different shapes and sizes, one of which is 21 inches tall so it can't get lost among the greenery. Use waterproof crayon for writing on these zinc nameplates.

Available from Paw Paw Everlast Label Co., Box 93 HQ, Paw Paw, MI 49079.

5-Way Hose Connector

With flow control valves that deliver the same amount of water to each hose. Lets you water five different areas at once, so you can water five times as fast.

Available from Gurney Seed & Nursery Co., Yankton, SD 57079. Catalog free.

Solid Oak, Country Wine Half-Barrels

These attractive, large, long-lasting con-tainers are perfect for tub-farming, dwarf trees and berry bushes. They are 17 inches high and 24 inches in diameter. Some garden centers carry them, but they are getting increasingly difficult to find as local cooperages are becoming scarce.

Available from J. E. Miller Nurseries, Inc., Canandaigua, NY 14424. Catalog free.

Low-Cost Biodegradable Molded Fiber Pots

Lightweight, durable and available in 30 sizes and shapes. Large tubs and matching saucers are the perfect answer for balcony, patio and rooftop vegetable gardens.

Manufactured by Western Nursery Pots. Look for these versatile containers at garden stores and nurseries in your area.

Bushel and Half-Bushel Baskets

These large baskets are hard to find and perfect for growing vegetables when lined with a large plastic bag. An inexpensive way to have an instant food garden if you rent your living quarters and don't want to invest in more costly containers. Can also be used to mix and store potting soil.

Available from the Garden Way Country Kitchen Catalog, Charlotte, VT 05445.

CHAPTER 8

The Secrets of the Soil

When we consider that we see only the top half of our vegetables as they grow and that the bottom half, the root system, is a buried, hidden mystery, we begin to wonder what's really going on under the surface. So let's start "talking dirty," and find out what the optimum soil conditions are, how to test and correct soil that is less than ideal (as most of it is) and how to maintain soil once you get it in good condition. Since we have to put our gardens on whatever land is available to us, we are usually stuck with less than ideal soil. But soil can be conditioned in both spring and fall, and you will find that what goes into it will determine the quality of the vegetables, herbs and fruit that come out of it.

Ideal Soil

Directions for planting seeds usually include the words " . . . and place seeds (or seedlings) into rich, fertile, well-drained loam." That description pretty well sums up the characteristics of the ideal garden soil, which should have all the following properties:

Open, crumbly texture

Porous structure that retains moisture while allowing air and water to drain through

Rich supply of composted organic matter (humus)

Balanced levels of nutrients which are constantly replenished for growing plants

Correct acid-alkaline (pH) balance

But let's face it, this kind of soil is rare. Most gardens don't start out with it. It should be a goal we strive for—a standard of optimum quality. What most of us *do* have is "dirt," untreated soil which falls into one or a combination of the following three basic types of soil.

Basic Soil Types

Loam is closest to ideal soil. It's a mixture of sand, clay and silt particles, plus humus. Loamy soil holds water and nutrients but still drains well.

Sand is made up of very large particles with lots of space between them. Water drains through this type of soil very quickly, and nutrients are easily leached out of the root zone of plants.

Clay soil consists of many tiny, flat particles which pack together tightly. The dense structure of clay prevents air, water and nutrients from penetrating. Clay soil is often soggy and poorly drained.

Pure clay or sand soils are extreme examples of structureless soil; most soils are really variations of these three types.

Testing for pH and Other Factors

After soil texture and density or weight are established, it's a good idea to test your soil for proper acid-alkaline (pH) balance, particularly if you are selecting a new site for a garden. Actually, pH (the letters stand for percentage of hydrogen) measures the concentration of hydrogen in the soil; the more hydrogen that is present, the more acid is the soil. The degree of acidity or alkalinity has a direct influence on the quality and quantity of the harvest. A pH level that is too high or too low for plants will restrict their growth and reduce the availability of nutrients to them.

The pH scale devised by scientists to measure the level of acidity can be visualized as something resembling a fever thermometer. A value of 7.0 is considered neutral; higher readings indicate alkalinity and lower readings indicate acidity. A pH of 6.2 to 6.8 is considered best for most vegetables. The scale is based on a logarithmic system, and each number indicates a tenfold increase or decrease in acidity. A soil with a pH of 5.0 is *ten times*

Other Services from the County Extension

Many other USDA services are available to gardeners through county extension agents. Your agent can give you information about your growing season and particular vegetable and fruit varieties that do well in your area. You can also get advice on identifying and controlling pest infestations and disease outbreaks among your plants. Following are descriptions of some of the services available to you.

Growing Season Information

You can request information on the average garden environment in your zone, including the average dates of last spring frost and first fall frost for your own county. You can also ask for suggested vegetable varieties which will grow best in your climate and within your growing season. You may want special information on container vegetable gardening as well.

Identifying Insects and Plant Diseases

For local infestations and controls, again, mention your organic preference, so harmful petro-chemical insecticides will not be suggested as a remedy. You cannot send live insects in the mail, and if you kill one by smashing it, it obviously cannot be readily identified. So, capture the insect on a leaf by slipping a plastic bag over your hand while holding the stem of the leaf, and then inverting the bag by pulling over your hand. Pour a bit of rubbing alcohol into the plastic bag to kill the insect painlessly. Remove it with tweezers, and dry on paper towels.

Pack the bug carefully in a cotton-lined box so the insect will not be crushed in transit. Include a note giving a description of the plant on which the insect was found. It is also a good idea to include a stamped self-addressed envelope with your inquiry.

This service is usually free.

To Diagnose a Sick Plant

Cut off a leaf and keep it refrigerated in a plastic bag to retain moisture until ready to mail. Mail as soon as possible, keeping the leaf in its plastic bag. If you live near an extension office, you can drop it off yourself during business hours.

Educational Programs

The Cooperative Extension Service also sponsors various educational programs. These can be enormously helpful to gardeners, so by all means look into them.

Master gardener series: Lectures on various topics by people in the field of horticulture from the state university.

Free fact sheets, booklets and newsletters: With information on all kinds of gardening activities in the local community.

more acid than a soil with a pH of 6.0. Since soil is a living community that changes constantly, it is important to test your pH periodically.

A do-it-yourself home test kit or meter, available from most seed companies, is quite adequate for a simple pH test, and a handy thing to have around. Although a simple pH test will not tell you anything about the organic content, structure, or type of soil, it will tell you whether your soil is acid or alkaline.

Soil Tests from the USDA

In addition to soil pH, you may also want to know about the availability of nutrients in your soil—whether there is too much nitrogen present, or perhaps too little phosphorus, for example. If so, a more precise laboratory soil test can give you that complete information. A number of soil tests are available through your Cooperative Extension agent of the USDA.

Having your soil analyzed by experts is as inexpensive (about $3.50) and as easy as sending a soil sample to your local Cooperative Extension office, usually branch of your local state agricultural college. When the USDA began making soil tests and other information available years ago, their orientation was primarily toward farmers. But in the last fifteen years or so, extension offices have been swamped with requests from backyard gardeners for specific local information. As a result, the extension office services now cover almost every phase of home gardening, in addition to offering help to farmers.

The information provided is extremely localized, by county, in every state. Unfortunately, there is no uniform way to locate the "county agent" in your telephone directory. You may be obliged to look under several different listings for county government offices, and the name you may find it under could be Cooperative Extension Service, or Agricultural Extension Service. If you have difficulty with the telephone directory, you can write to the nearest state college of agriculture and request a list of county extension offices.

Here's how to get a pH Test and a Soil Nutrition Test from your county extension office.

pH Factor Test: A simple, acid-alkaline pH soil test is available free of charge, and is conducted in the county agent's office. To obtain this test, follow the procedure described here:

Take 1 tablespoon of soil from the top 4 inches of your garden space, from five different locations.

Mix the samples together and dry the soil on paper towels.

When dry, put the soil into a sealed plastic bag, and send it off in a small box with your return address. Include a note to explain your request.

Soil Nutrient Test: For a more complete soil analysis there is a nominal fee that varies regionally. Find out what the fee is in your county, and mail a check to your county extension office along with a note explaining what you want. Do this *before* collecting your sample. In return, you will receive a questionnaire, instructions and a little box in which to return your soil sample by mail. This more elaborate test is actually five different tests which are conducted in the horticulture laboratory at the state university. Your soil will be analyzed for pH, nitrates, phosphorus, potassium, and soluble salts (street salt residue). Therefore, a larger quantity of soil is needed. Here are some tips on obtaining this more detailed soil test:

Collect at least 1 cup of soil in the same manner as detailed for the pH factor test.

When calling or writing your extension agent, mention what you intend to grow (trees, fruit, vegetables, etc.).

Tell the agent where your garden will be located: a city lot, a suburban backyard, or

Your Best Friend Could Be a Worm

These humble creatures can be a gardener's best friend. Sandy soils and heavy clay soils do not invite them. But when the organic content of such soils increase, their population explodes dramatically—sometimes by as much as 3 million worms per acre!

Earthworms act somewhat like food processors by mixing organic surface residues with the underlying soil. Their tunneling through the ground helps to increase the vital flow of air and water into and through the soil. No wonder they are so desirable to have around. Their presence signals that soil conditions in your garden are favorable enough for them to flourish. Earthworms increase the soil's fertility as well as improve its structure. When feeding, earthworms ingest soil and organic waste material, which pass through their bodies and are expelled in the form of "castings," a kind of worm manure, that is richer in nutrients than the original soil.

The earthworm's most intense activity usually occurs in the top 6 inches of the soil. However, they are susceptible to extreme conditions and will burrow deeper during hot, dry or cold weather. Their microscopic egg clusters are present and will increase in soils that have been cultivated and enriched with plenty of organic matter, so it's not necessary to buy them.

Years ago, with minimal knowledge about the habits of the earthworm, I saw a sign on a country road offering them for sale. Vaguely remembering that they would be of great help to the soil, I thought they would find a happy home in the large barrels which support my city rooftop garden. I stopped the car to buy 1,000 of them to take back to the city with me. It was an extremely hot summer's day and I was faced with a nine-hour drive before reaching home. I began to fear for their well-being after an hour in a hot car. Concerned with their welfare, I bought a Styrofoam cooler and some ice cubes from a roadside machine and continued driving.

When I reached my destination, it was late at night. I quickly distributed the worms on top of the soil and noted that they were still wriggling happily after their cooling voyage. The next day, about 11 A.M., having overslept, I decided to see how they had spent their first night in an urban environment. I expected they would have channeled their way deep into the soil, and I visioned that they had already set up housekeeping. To my chagrin, what greeted me that morning on that sultry rooftop was the sight of 1,000 worms, not alive and happy in the soil, but fried to a crisp on the hot tile floor! Obviously the soil was dry and compacted, and the worms crept out of their containers. As the heat of the sun was absorbed by the quarry tile floor (and since they are not noted to be among nature's speediest creatures) the poor worms were cooked in their tracks. I confess that my conscience has been burdened lo these many years with their terrible fate. Now that I know more after years of gardening, I try to be more considerate of the worm population and provide these friends of the garden with a more hospitable home.

---

other site, and describe your growing conditions as best as you can.

Mention that you are an organic gardener, so that any amendments suggested to improve your soil will not be chemical ones.

It is also a good idea to do this test in the fall, since Cooperative Extension offices are usually swamped in the spring. A fall test will also enable you to collect the necessary soil amendments and apply them to the garden in autumn, so they will break down and be ready by spring planting time.

Adjusting the Soil's Acid-Alkaline Balance

Once you have obtained the results of your soil test, you can then make the neces-

Lime Guidelines

Given here are approximate amounts of liming agents per 100 square feet required to raise soil pH 1 unit in soils of different texture.

	Calcic (Agricultural) Lime	Dolomitic Limestone	Wood Ash (Quantity varies depending upon hard or soft wood)
Light, sandy soils	2½ to 5 pounds	2 to 3 pounds	3 to 6 pounds
Heavy, clay soils	6 to 8 pounds	5½ to 7 pounds	7 to 10 pounds

Note: To lower soil pH 1 unit add at least ⅓ the amount specified for lime of sawdust, acid, peat moss or ground bark.

Also, urban gardeners should be aware that rooftop container soil is very acid (pH about 5.5) due to carbons and hydrogen in the air, and acid rains (in the eastern U.S.).

sary adjustments. Lime is usually added to the soil to neutralize its acidity, since most soils tend to become acid. Lime also helps fertilizers to work more efficiently by unlocking nutrients and making them available to plants. If the soil pH is out of balance, plant foods are wasted and nutrients don't do their job efficiently. Lowering the pH to make the soil more acid is rarely necessary, except in very arid parts of the country (like Arizona). Acid soils are more common. But if your soil does test out alkaline, adding acidic organic materials such as peat moss, cottonseed meal, pine needles or composted oak leaves should help lower the pH.

Adjusting the soil pH is an easy thing to do, although at times a bit confusing. Many garden books tell you to "add lime to correct soil acidity" and let it go at that. But there are other considerations. How much lime to use and when to use it differs depending on whether the soil is sandy or clay. Sandy soils, for example, may lose lime faster than clay, since nutrients are leached out more quickly. If your soil is sandy, small but frequent applications of lime may be necessary. On the other hand, clay soils and soils high in organic matter require larger amounts of lime than sandy ones. In general, areas with light rainfall, such as our southwestern deserts, tend to have more alkaline soils; in areas where rainfall is heavy, soil tends to be more acid.

Materials to Use for Adjusting pH

Choosing a liming material can be confusing, since there are several kinds and some are harmful. Lime and other pH-raising materials go by different names, have different time-release characteristics and vary in their neutralizing power. Here are the most commonly used materials:

Dolomitic limestone, sometimes called "magnesic" limestone, is half calcium carbonate and up to 50% magnesium. It is preferred for gardens where a soil test has indicated low magnesium levels because it supplies both elements (although it is not a very good source of calcium).

Calcic limestone is often referred to as "agricultural" lime since it is mostly calcium carbonate. Calcic lime is a good choice for soils where magnesium levels are adequate.

Quicklime (also called burned lime) and hydrated lime (or slaked lime) are two kinds of lime that are *not* recommended for home gardens. Both materials are caustic, and can burn plant roots and human skin. Stay away from them.

Bone meal, more often regarded as a fertilizer, can also be used as a liming agent; it is a good supplier of calcium and phosphate.

Marl is another liming material, usually available only in coastal areas. It is composed, in part, of ground clam or oyster shells and contains about 50% calcium carbonate.

Wood ashes from your fireplace or woodburning stove can also be used to raise pH. Burned hardwoods have about one-third more calcium than softwood ash. Wood ash also is used as a potash source, so you may want to retest your soil nutrients after applying it to be sure they are still in balance. Note that coal ashes have almost no liming value and in some cases contain toxic substances. Do not use them in the garden.

Different types of soil with the same pH do not necessarily have the same lime requirements. To determine the correct amount to apply, and also to prevent over-liming, it's best to be gentle. See the chart, Lime Guidelines, for some extra pointers.

When and How to Apply Lime

The best time to apply lime is in the fall after the last crops have been harvested or, in colder climates, before the ground freezes. It takes several months for lime to react and change the pH of the soil. Sprinkle lime on the soil surface so it looks like snow. An easy way to do this is to fill a coffee can and pierce the top with a nail to make half-inch holes and make a sort of lime shaker to distribute it evenly. Then work the lime evenly into the soil with a long-pronged garden fork. If you want to see how the lime has worked, retest your soil in the spring before adding any more organic matter (some of which may be strongly enough acid or alkaline to affect the soil pH). You may also want to test again at the end of the growing season to find out if your pH is still within a range that will trigger the availability of all the nutrients you have added during the past year. Once you get the hang of it, it's not complicated at all. Just remember that liming is not permanent and must be repeated whenever a soil test says it's necessary.

Modifying Your Soil

Soil that is not ideal or even close to being the "well-drained garden loam" that we all aspire to is hard to manage. It fights you and can be a great discouragement to gardeners. It is not difficult to improve your soil, so why suffer with a poor grade? In fact, improving soil can become a good gardening habit, almost second nature, like brushing your teeth twice a day. Organic matter is added, in some form, before planting and after harvesting crops to improve the structure and enhance the fertility of the soil. Because it's an ongoing practice, a good motto for getting your soil into the best possible shape might be "never leave soil bare."

Always protect your soil with some sort of organic covering, such as mulch, a live, growing crop or a "green manure." All of these coverings, as well as the remains of your harvested crops, are either dug into the soil to decompose or are decomposed in a compost pile and then added to the garden. It may seem strange, but both light, sandy soils and heavy, clay soils are improved in the same way—by adding large amounts of organic matter.

How Organic Matter Works

Organic matter is the waste remains of animals and plants—anything that was once alive (and usually something you would throw away). Organic matter in the soil improves the physical characteristics of soil as it decomposes into that dark brown, gorgeous earthy-smelling stuff: humus. It is humus that gives healthy soil its spongy texture and its ability to hold in moisture and nutrients while permitting aeration. Air or oxygen is necessary in the soil. Plant roots need it for respiration, and soil microorganisms need it to break down organic matter. The amount of air in soil depends on the soil's texture and structure, and the quantity of organic matter it contains. Poorly drained, compacted soils have very little pore space available for oxygen to occupy. Soils with poor aeration tend to have excessively high levels of moisture, which then competes with oxygen for what little pore space there is available. When there's not enough oxygen in the soil, plants have trouble absorbing water and nutrients, root and shoot growth is inhibited, and the activity of soil microbes is retarded. Organic matter lightens heavy soils and creates more pore space for air to occupy, and also improves water drainage. Even earthworms, which will become your hardworking friends, will delight in this oxygen-rich environment.

Organic Matter for Problem Soils

Although organic matter improves the structure of both kinds of problem soils, since their properties are different, their requirements will also be different. Here's a quick guide to building better soil structure with organic matter.

Clay Soils

Problem: Fine clay particles form a dense mass, do not absorb or hold moisture well. Water moves through soil too slowly, sometimes runs off surface.

Solution: Add builder's sand or wood products to help separate the density of the soil, allowing for better drainage. You can use sawdust, ground bark, wood shavings, or buckwheat, cocoa or rice hulls. Hulls can also be used in ground form, but be aware that rice hulls may contain water-repellent silicates. Note also that wood products draw upon the soil for nitrogen as they decompose. Therefore, a source of additional nitrogen should be added to soil at the same time.

Sandy Soils

Problem: Water and nutrients move through coarse-textured soils very quickly, and plant roots do not have time to absorb what they need.

Solution: Add spongy materials designed to absorb and hold water and nutrients: sphagnum peat moss, animal manures, or compost.

It is wise, then, to put soil conditioning at the head of your list of gardening activities. It should have top priority, for organic gardeners and all other gardeners! And never stop adding organic matter to your garden—even when you've gotten your soil in good condition. You may need to add less eventually, but since humus forms and breaks down over a period of time, if you stop adding organic matter to the soil you'll eventually be right back where you started. Remember, the better the soil the better your garden will grow. It's that simple. The "Good Humus Man" is not an ice cream vendor with tinkling bells on his cart; he's you!

Many kinds of organic matter are available and there are many places to find it, sometimes free of charge. Organic matter can take the form of animal manures, sawdust or other ground wood products such as bark, peat moss or compost. See the box titled Organic Matter for Problem Soils, for some guidelines on using it. About one-third of the soil should be composed of organic matter, since the quantity added must be large enough to change the structure of the soil to make a difference.

In addition to humus, good soil must also contain adequate amounts of the three major nutrients to support plant growth, nitrogen (N), phosphorus (P) and potassium (K) along with the secondary nutrients, manganese, sulfur and calcium, and a host of trace elements including iron, magnesium, zinc, copper, boron, chlorine and molybdenum. All thirteen of these elements work hand in hand and are found in varying proportions in compost. For the organic gardener, compost is the "Cinderella Factor" of gardening—a viable way of changing ugly waste into beautiful humus. The marvelous side benefit of using composted organic materials is that the primary three soil nutrients (NPK) plus the various trace elements are all added at the same time. Compost, then, serves many purposes: when worked into the soil, it fertilizes as it conditions; spread on top of the soil it makes an excellent mulch.

Accumulating organic materials for making compost, or to use individually as soil conditioners, organic fertilizers or mulches can be a bit tedious, though, unless you know where to look for them. To help you get started I've included here a Scavenger's Manual as inspiration for your treasure hunt. In the next chapter we'll discuss how to make compost.

Peat Moss— A Versatile Soil Conditioner

Peat moss is a useful soil conditioner that can help lighten heavy soil and can serve as a stopgap source of organic matter you can use while you collect material to make a batch of compost. Most gardeners know it by name, but novices may be perplexed when confronted by the many names on the peat moss labels at the garden supply store. There is peat, peat moss, Michigan peat, Jersey peat, sphagnum moss, sedge peat, peat humus, reed peat, moss peat, and there may be others. How to make sense of it all? For a start, the names peat and peat moss are used interchangeably.

Peat is decayed vegetable matter that is partially carbonized and decomposed. It is "harvested" from bogs or marshes and comprised of sedges, grasses, sphagnum and sometimes decayed tree trunks and woody branches. Depending upon the major base materials available, packaged peats are either domestic or imported. Peat moss is sterile, weed-free and 100% organic, but unlike compost, it has very little fertilizer value. It does, however, contain very small amounts of nitrogen. Peat is generally very acidic, ranging anywhere from 3.5 to 4.5 on the pH scale. When you add large quantities to your soil, you may need to add some lime, too, as a corrective measure.

Although peat is called by many names there are basically only two kinds—Michigan peat and sphagnum peat.

Michigan peat is a domestic, woody peat derived from decayed trees and other vegetable matter, and it retains a good part of the coarse materials that went into it. It is very dark in color—a rich brownish black—and it does not have the water-holding capacity of sphagnum peat, although it will hold three to six times its own weight in water.

Sphagnum peat is a fibrous peat derived from sphagnum moss, reeds and sedges. It is coarse in texture, light brown in color, soft to

A Scavenger's Manual of Organic Materials

This scavenger's manual is designed to clue you into places to look for all sorts of organic materials. The key will tell you what they can be primarily used for. Most materials have some fertilizing ability as well, even though not specified as such. All of these materials can either be worked into the soil in fall or spring, top-dressed around growing plants, used as a mulch, or added to the compost pile.

Key

SC – Soil conditioner
CM – Compost material
F – Fertilizer
M – Mulching material

Where you live has a great deal to do with the kind of organic material that is available. Organic waste products are usually peculiar to whatever is processed or grown in a particular region. Some, however, are shipped from other areas and sold locally on the gardener's own stamping grounds. For example, New England is the home of many silk and woolen mills where wastes are available. Georgia has tobacco farms and granite rock, cotton fields and mills. Maryland has commercial poultry farms, and oyster shells and sea products from its coastline. Rice hulls can be had from the Carolina rice growers. Minnesota has breweries. The Midwest is the corn, soybean and wheat belt. California is a veritable gold mine with its many wineries, cattle ranches and volcanic mineral mines.

A Word to the Wise

Since this seems to be the age of specialization in agriculture, it is best to seek out the source— particularly when looking for manures. A poultry farmer who raises hens for eggs, or raises beef cattle or dairy cows, rarely raises field crops which need to be fertilized. These farms would be the logical ones to tap for a source of manure. Some may even allow you to haul it away free of charge, so come prepared: take along sturdy shoes and gloves to change into. Bring a shovel and several bushel baskets or heavy boxes lined with plastic. (Lining boxes with plastic keeps the bottom from falling out when wet.) Borrow or rent a truck or station wagon and line it with plastic sheets for easy clean up.

It is easier and more expected for gardeners in the country or suburbs to gather organic materials. In urban areas, you may be considered slightly flaky. Do not be daunted. You will meet some interesting people and find yourself in some unusual places where you can learn a great deal. It's fun and it's educational, and it's usually free.

When making a deal with some of your local suppliers to collect wastes, leave a plastic pail. Once you explain what you want it for, and pick up the waste regularly (and perhaps bring a gift of a homegrown tomato or green pepper) you'll be in. Just remember, what appears to be waste to one man is often a gardener's bonanza. If you need to, locate some of your sources through the Yellow Pages.

Fish scraps and bones, crustacean shells—SC, F, CM: Local fishmonger, wholesale fish markets, fishermen, lobstermen, fishing boats, seafood restaurants.

Eggshells—CM, F: Homes, restaurants, commercial bakeries. Tip: Crush in a blender, freeze and store eggshells until enough are accumulated, then spread on cookie sheet and put in oven when you bake. They will disintegrate more easily in a compost pile.

Straw and hay—SC, CM, M: Farms (ask for spoiled hay farmer can't use as feed), feed stores.

Seaweed—SC, CM, M, F: Beaches, bays. After a storm is a particularly good time to go collecting seaweed (and expand your seashell or driftwood collection).

Vegetable and fruit wastes—CM: Breweries (spent hops), processing and canning plants, supermarkets, green markets (spoiled produce), restaurants, large institutions (hospitals, schools, prisons), bakeries, building superintendents, spent crop residues (your own and neighbors'), ice cream parlors (banana skins from banana splits).

Pine needles and other conifer needles—SC, M, C: Pick up fallen needles wherever the trees grow.

Paper—M, CM: Local newspapers and magazine

printers, neighbors, rubbish collectors, homes. Note: Do not use colored comic sections—the inks contain lead and are toxic.

Wood shavings, chips, bark and sawdust—SC, CM, M: Carpenters, furniture factories, sawmills, paper mills, road maintenance crews (for wood chips), lumberyards, tree surgeons, private landscaping contractors.

Manures—CM, F, SC, M: Zoos, farms, stables, racetracks, packing houses, poultry and egg farms, riding academies, dairies, stockyards, feedlots, duck farms, rabbit farms, pig farms, sheep farms, any operation where horses are used (police constabulary, logging operation, mounted park rangers). Note: Manures of animals kept in restricted quarters tend to have a high salt content, particularly in areas of little rainfall. Rainfall leaches out salts while manure ages, but can also leach out nitrogen. Therefore, it is best to use feedlot manure for soil conditioner rather than fertilizer.

Hair clippings—CM: Hairdressers, barbershops, dog grooming parlors.

Wood ashes—SC, CM, F: Fireplaces, wood burning stoves, incinerators. Make sure you use only wood ashes in the garden.

Leaves and leaf mold—SC, CM, F, M: Nearby forests, back country roads, neighbors' lawns (in fall), municipal street crews, or local parks department. Many cities make leaves collected during the fall available to gardeners free for the taking. It's worth a phone call to find out.

Animal by-products—F, CM, SC: Numerous rendered, dried and ground by-products of animals can be obtained from slaughterhouses, and meat-processing plants. Products include dried blood meal, fish scraps, hoof and horn meal and steamed bone meal.

Tea and coffee grounds—CM: Homes, restaurants, large institutions.

Feathers—SC, CM: Live poultry markets, commercial poultry operations, zoo aviaries.

Grass clippings and weeds—SC, CM, M: Homes, neighbors, golf courses, cemeteries, baseball fields.

the touch when squeezed, and can hold up to twenty times its weight in water. It is effective in aerating and lightening heavy clay soils and is also used as an amendment for retaining moisture in very sandy soils. It is usually imported and sold compressed or "baled" in a dry, powdery form. When used as is, sphagnum peat will absorb like a sponge whatever moisture there is in the soil. Sphagnum moss, a source material for sphagnum peat, is a grayish-colored bog moss which is available in two forms. The coarse, fibrous kind is used by nurseries to wrap bare-rooted shrubs for shipping, and is also used to line open wire hanging baskets. Finely milled sphagnum is used for starting seeds and rooting cuttings.

Here are some tips to keep in mind when working with peat moss:

It should never be added to the soil without wetting it first. Before using, cut the top of the bale or bag open on three sides, to make a flap like a book cover. Leave a hose to trickle into the bale for a few hours, and then let stand overnight. Make sure the moss is thoroughly damp before using. Keep the bale or bag outdoors, with the flap open, where it can always catch the rain and stay moist.

For general conditioning, work into the top 6 inches of soil two weeks before spring planting a 6-cubic-foot bale for every 100 square feet of garden area. Use half again as much if your soil is particularly sandy or heavy clay.

There is a drawback to peat moss when used as a surface mulch—it dries out quickly and has a tendency to cake. When the garden is watered, peat moss absorbs moisture for itself first before allowing it to seep further into the soil. Peat also tends to blow away in the wind when it becomes dry.

Note that both Michigan peat and sphagnum peat are excellent soil conditioners, but Michigan peat tends to rob nitrogen from the soil, so be sure to add a nitrogen fertilizer like manure to your soil whenever you add Michigan peat.

Starting from Scratch: What to Do If Your Soil Seems Hopeless

Improving your soil with organic matter is all well and good, but what do you do if you don't have any soil to speak of? Sometimes the *terra firma* is much too firm for good gardening. Sometimes the backyard in a city townhouse or suburban rancher may only consist of hard-packed dirt scattered with rubble and debris or a thin layer of topsoil over fill, with nary a blade of grass and totally deficient in the things that plants need to grow.

Although even the most difficult soil can usually be improved with patience, time and compost, there's no need to wait years in order to start a garden. There are several alternatives to choose from even in this desperate situation, from improving the soil bit by bit to trucking in a load of topsoil to create a permanent garden right away. For the most part, the methods I'm going to tell you about involve growing vegetables on top of fresh, new, custom-blended soil mixtures that are laid directly over the stuff that is too difficult to improve. In raised bottomless boxes and in containers, you can concentrate good soil that you have found in the country, bought, or built up with compost mixed with any existing dirt. You can then start gardening with the distinct advantage of having immediately the kind of soil that provides the maximum degree of plant growth.

Topsoil

If your soil is unsuitable for any kind of gardening, or if you wish to start a rooftop container project, a few loads of purchased topsoil may be the answer, if you can afford it. Here are some suggestions for finding and buying topsoil:

Look in the Yellow Pages under Topsoil for suppliers.

Remember that when you're talking about topsoil, the expression "dirt cheap" no longer exists.

Topsoil is sold by the cubic yard and is usually cheaper by the truckload. It can be purchased by the bushel and in 50 to 100-pound bags for smaller gardens or containers.

There are various grades of topsoil available at varying prices. Ask for *screened* topsoil, even though the prices may be higher than for unscreened loam. Screened topsoil contains no foreign matter, such as rocks or debris, and it's sometimes enriched with humus.

When ordering, tell your dealer the depth as well as the length and width (or the diameter, if the area is round) you plan to fill with topsoil. You'll then have a better idea of the correct amount to order.

Before buying a large amount, request that a soil test be made on the soil you're going to purchase, or ask the dealer for the results of the test if one has already been done. You should be able to find out both pH and nutrient levels.

Whether your needs dictate ordering a truckload or only a single 100-pound bag of topsoil, it's less costly to blend your own soil mixture. You need purchase only one-third of the total amount you need in the form of really good, screened topsoil. The topsoil can then be augmented with organic conditioners and fertilizers as a basic soil mixture for a raised bed or container. Here's a good, simple recipe for a basic, all-purpose soil mix:

$1/3$ good screened topsoil

$^1/_3$ coarse builder's sand (you can substitute vermiculite or perlite for lightweight container gardens)

$^1/_6$ well-rotted manure or dried manure

$^1/_6$ peat moss

To this basic mix you can add a dry, organic fertilizer mixture (see page 182) and then use supplemental feedings of liquid fertilizer during the growing season and you're all set.

Tricks for Mixing Soil

Blending any soil mixture is best done outdoors on a large drop cloth. If you have a large amount of soil, mix the ingredients in two separate piles for easier handling. Then use a shovel to combine the two piles, making sure the ingredients are well incorporated.

"But I live in an apartment," I hear you say, "so how and where can I mix up large amounts of soil without making a mess in these cramped quarters?" Here's how: To avoid tedious cleanup when you have no outdoor mixing space, lay a plastic drop cloth in the bathtub and work there. Divide the mixture into several smaller amounts and shovel it into heavyweight plastic trash bags for easier removal and handling.

Soil for Balcony and Rooftop Gardens

There are, of course, other soil problems for balcony and rooftop gardeners to overcome. If you rent and there is a change of tenants, there may be some old, tired soil from the previous occupant. Don't throw it away; it's a windfall. It's a bothersome chore to drag soil up to a high-rise apartment rooftop, so reclaim and revitalize what's already there. In fact, when your sky garden is established, you should renew the soil every year, replenishing nutrients and adding soil conditioners to keep it from resembling concrete.

The weight of soil mixtures is another problem to consider when large tubs or barrels are used on rooftops or patios. The idea here is portability, which can be defeated when large containers are backbreaking to move around. But there are several ways to lighten the load. Here are some tips for lightening up:

Use large containers made of compressed recycled paper pulp. When empty, a pulp pot that is 18 inches in diameter and 12 inches deep weighs only about 3 pounds. When filled with plants and soil it can weigh almost 50 pounds! Terra cotta or wooden containers weigh more but will last longer.

Reduce the weight load even more by putting a 2-inch layer of Styrofoam packaging chips on the bottom of the container, covered with a plastic sheet that is pierced in a few places. Fill the rest of the container with your soil mix. The plastic sheet will prevent the soil from washing into the chips, and will also help hold water around the roots while letting the excess drain off slowly. Perlite or vermiculite can be used instead of the foam chips on the bottom, and additional quantities can be mixed into the soil. This will both aerate the soil and lighten the weight load.

If you use wooden containers, which are heavier to move around, group them together and keep them small. The visual effect is the same as that of a larger tub, but mobility is easier.

Getting Soil Ready for Planting

You're one step ahead of the game if the soil you plan to use for vegetables is already cultivated. If it is not loose and friable to a depth of at least 10 to 12 inches, then it's time to get out your tools and dig. Here are some tips to help you get ready for planting:

Prepare soil in the fall, adding organic matter and slow-acting fertilizers in advance of spring plating. Dig them in and leave the soil surface rough over the winter to mellow.

It's digging time in the spring when the soil is reasonably dry and will crumble easily in your hand when you squeeze it. If the soil sticks together in a ball when squeezed, it's still too early to dig.

In spring, spread a layer of organic matter about 4 inches thick on the surface, and a 1-inch layer of dry fertilizer mix (see page 182).

Spade or till, breaking up all clods, because many vegetable seeds are fine and easily lost in lumpy soil. Use a rake to make the soil even finer just before you plant. This is called "single digging."

If you want to garden in a spot now covered with grass, a rented rotary tiller will help loosen the soil if the area is large.

It's hard work in the beginning, but once planted, 15 minutes a day should be enough time for you to maintain the soil in 100 square feet of garden. More time is needed, of course, if the garden is larger.

How to Take It Easy
When Digging a Brand-New Garden

Here is a step-by-step procedure for preparing soil for brand-new intensive beds. It's a modification of the procedure used by Ecology Action Studies, an intensive gardening program run by apprentices of the late Alan Chadwick in Palo Alto, California. Work for only an hour or two at a time with rest periods in between.

1. Mark off the space to be used. (If you are removing a part of your lawn, use pieces of sod turned upside down as a layer in the compost pile.) Take a soil test for pH level and note results.

2. If the soil is hard, or a dry clay type, soak area to be dug with an overhead sprinkler for two hours.

3. Allow soil to dry out for two days.

4. Using a spading fork, loosen soil to a depth of 1 foot, removing weeds and adding them to the compost pile.

5. Let soil—and you—rest for a day. (If soil is heavy clay, add a 1-inch layer of builder's sand at this point to improve texture. Mix into the top 12 inches.)

6. Add a 3-inch layer of aged manure or compost plus 1 inch of top soil, and work in with the spading fork.

7. Let soil rest for another day.

8. Do limbering up exercises to prepare you for some hard work. (See page 146.)

9. With your newly limbered up body double-dig the soil with a flat spade to loosen the soil to a depth of 2 feet. Using a spade, dig the first row of soil with added amendments and remove it to the opposite end of the patch. Loosen the soil to a depth of 12 more inches with a spading fork. Dig another trench next to the first one, using that soil to fill the first trench. Then loosen the soil at the bottom of that trench with a fork. Repeat the procedure row by row until the entire bed is dug. The soil from the first trench that was carried to the other end of the garden is used to fill the last trench.

10. Smooth the bed into an even shape with a rake, making the sides slope gently inward toward the top of the bed (if you're a purist).

11. Take a hot bath, and let you and the soil rest for another day.

12. Add a layer of organic fertilizers, 2 to 3 inches deep, sifting lightly with a fork.

Rake bed once again. Tamp bed down lightly with a board to remove excess air. Another pH test at this time may show that an adjustment is needed before planting.

13. Take out your garden plans and plant.

The good news is that this procedure only needs to be followed once, at the onset of establishing the intensive growing soil area.

The following season, soil preparation time should be cut in half since soil will then have a better texture and require only 1 inch of compost plus ½ inch of organic fertilizers to be dug into the looser, more friable soil. You may not be able to get down to the required 24 inches the first year if your soil is compacted. If 15 to 18 inches is all you can reach, don't fret—there's always next time, which will be easier.

The Gardener's Magic Wands

The mysteries of making compost never cease to amaze me, particularly when I observe what seems to be a kind of garden sorcery happening in the compost pile. It's as if I were privileged to witness the results of the work of a fairy godmother who had with the wave of a wand and a few incantations, converted worthless garbage into precious humus. Indeed, compost and organic fertilizers are the handmaidens that help the soil continue to provide what plants need to grow.

Compost:
The Cinderella Factor

We Americans are used to being part of a disposable society. So much of what we consume comes in beautifully designed packages and containers that we use once and throw away. In our yards we gather lawn clippings, fallen leaves, pruned branches and spent plants, and either burn them up or tie them up in plastic bags and have them hauled to a dump. We gather our table wastes and shove them into an electric disposal unit to be ground into mush and flushed down the drain to end up who knows where.

But there is no need for such rampant wastefulness when you have a garden, for almost all these throwaway materials are grist for the compost mill. In fact, the daily kitchen wastes of just two people, diligently composted, can yield up to several *hundred* dark, fragrant pounds of humus in one year. This "sorcery" is accomplished quite simply. In fact, nature does it all the time in the woods and forests as it slowly but continually converts dead vegetation into leaf mold and humus. Composting is really just a faster, more controlled way of imitating nature's own recycling process.

Adding compost to the soil is probably one of the best ways to replenish the supply of nutrients used by growing plants, and at the same time maintain good soil structure. Vegetables grow quickly and they constantly deplete the garden soil of nutrients. This rapid growth, coupled with additional nutrient loss caused by rainfall or watering, makes it essential for gardeners to replace what's been lost. When compost is applied continuously during the growing season, either dug into the soil directly in the same way that peat moss is used or spread on top as a mulch, only occasionally supplemental fertilizing (with organic materials, of course) will be necessary. Allowing organic matter to decay into compost before putting it on the garden is better than digging fresh garbage into the ground, because the fresh material will rob nitrogen from the soil as it decomposes underground.

Making Compost

If you are new to gardening, or to organic gardening, the information in this section on how to make good compost will get you started in the right direction. Remember, *properly made compost does not smell bad.* This section will explain how to make sure your compost pile works the way it should. Veteran compost-makers can skip this section and turn directly to the compost recipes on page 171.

Use the Scavenger's Manual in Chapter 8 to locate organic materials for compost. When you're ready to get started, just remember that building a compost pile is a lot like preparing lasagna—they're both made in layers. You may vary any of the methods outlined here according to the amount of time and space you have available and the materials you've gathered. Since no two methods of preparing lasagna or compost are exactly alike, as long as you achieve a good end product you don't need to feel intimidated by precise formulas. Not only can you make compost by several methods, you can also make it in large or small quantities, depending upon the size of your garden. Suburban gardeners with small backyards and city gardeners who have difficulty finding a steady source of animal manure or getting transportation to haul it home will find that composting kitchen wastes and other materials that are readily available is a convenient way to have that essential supply of nutrient-rich humus always on hand.

Organic material decays when bacteria and fungi consume it. Bacteria can attack more surface area faster if material added to

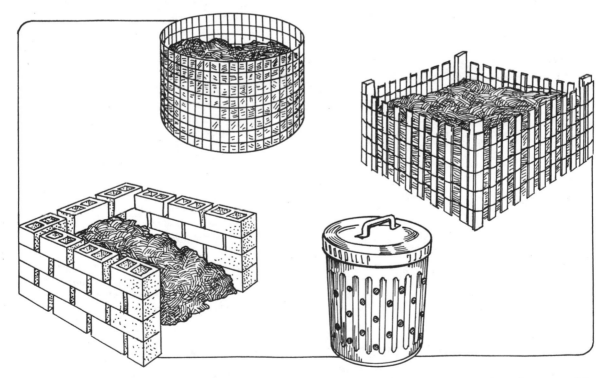

Four options for making compost are (clockwise from right) an enclosure made of easily removable snow fencing, a metal trash can with holes punched for aeration (used by Chris and Maria, interviewed on page 176), a cinderblock bin and a wire mesh pen.

Making The Good Earth Better

Sam Morrison lives down in Knoxville, Tennessee, where the growing season is long. Nice place to have a garden, I thought, but Sam explained that the location does give him gardening problems. "We're neither fish nor fowl," he says, "right between the number 6 and number 7 zones. So we can have frost in April or the thermometer can hit 90°F. The temperature range is very extreme." Sam, retired and now in his sixties, is philosophical about it all. "What we lose, we just replant!"

Sam has gardened for about 30 years, but very seriously only during the past 10. With the help of four part-time people, his raised-bed garden has become a testing ground for the All America Selections people, where he tests seeds and new varieties for them. He lives in a suburban house about a mile from the downtown shopping area, and people have commented that he has made a country place in the city. It is a comment of which he is justly proud.

When Sam wanted more garden space, he started to add boxes to the upper deck of his house. Now he has thirteen raised beds that range in size from 5 by 20 feet to 5 by 40 feet, plus a 14 by 16-foot greenhouse and a slightly larger solarium. Six boxes are located on a deck about 20 feet off the ground, right off the dining room. The beds are made of concrete blocks or redwood, and the sides that contain them are about 20 to 25 inches high. The boxes up on the deck are somewhat shallower because of the weight.

"I start all my own seeds," Sam says, "and I use the solarium for winter growing, hardening off the seedlings in the greenhouse. And, because of the long growing season, I plant outdoors as early as February and I harvest right through November." He also uses succession planting, getting up to three crops per bed (one succession he uses is peas, beans and then peas again). His vegetable crop includes just about everything; tomatoes, peppers, eggplant, zucchini, peas, beans, lettuce and beets all thrive in the beds. There's also lots of fruit from his trees—peaches, nectarines, apples, pears and cherries. Mrs. Morrison says, "He grows so much that anyone who comes here during the peak July-August season doesn't leave without at least 20 pounds of tomatoes!"

Sam's fertilizers include bone meal, alfalfa meal, cottonseed meal, wood ash and lime, and during the season he feeds with blood meal. In addition to that, he has nine compost bins, each of them 5 by 5 by 10 feet and made of chain link fencing. Since he can't get manure, every fall he has the city of Knoxville dump all the collected leaves in his bins and then he puts the leaves over all the beds, in a layer about 1 foot deep. He works the leaves into the soil in the spring. A tenth bin is located right off the top deck, and it's used for all the compostable table waste from the kitchen.

Sam's spirit is contagious—over the years he's encouraged most of his neighbors to become gardeners, including a gentleman across the street who just turned 85 and has started his first garden.

the compost pile is in small pieces. Cut up table scraps or garden waste before adding to the compost pile to insure faster decay. (If you are making lots of compost, a mechanical shredder will make this part of the job easier for you.)

Heaping or piling allows heat to be produced, and heat is needed for good bacterial action. The height of the pile influences the amount of heat that is generated. Too high a pile can become compressed, shutting off the air supply to bacteria. As bacterial activity slows, so does the decomposition process. If the pile isn't high enough, bacterial action is also slowed down and there will again be a loss of heat. For best results, a height of 4 to 6 feet is recommended. A compost pile must contain nitrogen in order for the bacteria to work quickly and produce the necessary heat. Otherwise the waste material will decompose more slowly and may not heat up as well. Fresh animal manure or another high-nitrogen organic fertilizer such as blood meal or cottonseed meal should be included in the pile.

Turning the pile with a pitchfork or shovel admits air and allows the raw material to decompose uniformly and quickly. Turn your pile by moving the material from the center to the outside of the pile and the material from the outside to the inside of the pile. If your pile is enclosed in a bottomless bin or pen, just lift it off the pile, place it alongside, and fork the ingredients into the new enclosure. Doing this once a month should provide good results. Moisture is also needed for decomposition to take place. When succulent materials such as fruit peels or vegetable wastes from the table are used, there is usually enough moisture. The pile should be damp but not wet. In dry climates an occasional light sprinkling of water with a hose may be needed if there is not adequate rainfall. If the pile is too wet, add shredded newspapers or straw to absorb the excess moisture.

The internal temperatures of any pile varies according to the regional climate, the time of the year, and the kind and the size of the particles of waste matter used. The average temperature of most compost piles is between 130°F and 160°F, and this is hot enough to kill weed seeds and insect larvae.

As the pile decomposes it is also reduced in volume. Most piles will shrink to about half of their original size. When "ripe" and ready to use, compost is crumbly, brown and earthy-smelling.

Some kind of bin or structure makes it easier and neater to stack compost to a proper height and still allow air to circulate freely (see illustration). If you're making a lot of compost, a three-bin system would be ideal. Use one bin to collect incoming material, one to hold compost in progress and the third to store finished compost until you're ready to use it. Three bins will give you a more continuous supply of compost to use throughout the gardening season.

Two types of bacteria can decompose organic matter into compost. One type, aerobic bacteria, operates when there is air, moisture and high temperatures, creating a fairly rapid breakdown with no odor. Anaerobic bacteria, on the other hand, thrive where there is no air and conditions are generally cooler; unless this compost is kept under wraps and tightly sealed until it's finished, you'll find that it does not smell quite like a rose before it is ready to use. Most likely, purists who attempt to duplicate nature's slower ways, and who carefully grind, turn, water and check internal temperatures with a thermometer will not approve of the anaerobic method. Nevertheless, here is some advice for making compost, from a gardener who is naturally lazy but no less successful.

A Recipe for Anaerobic Compost

If you have a very small garden on a rooftop or balcony, or if you live in a suburban or urban area, keeping your compost covered and out of sight is a sure way to avoid offending your neighbors' sensibilities. They won't even know your compost is there! This is the method I use for my own rooftop garden. Although my method is designed for impatient people, it works, and that's the most important thing. Here's how to do it:

Buy a 30-gallon garbage can with a cover, either heavy plastic or galvanized metal, and line it with a heavy-duty dark-colored plastic bag in a size to fit. Incidentally, if you don't want to use a garbage can, the plastic bag will do by itself, but the can gives extra protection in case the bag should tear.

In the bottom of the liner, place 2 to 3 inches of peat moss or soil.

Then start to add succulent kitchen and garden wastes. In my own kitchen I keep two covered plastic cans, one of which is used only for compost materials. On the lid, as a reminder, I have taped two lists. One list is headed "Yes" in big red letters; underneath is written what can go into this pail. Cut up vegetables and fruit peels, citrus rinds, coffee grounds, tea leaves, crushed egg shells, house plant trimmings, hair clippings (from combs and brushes and dog or cat hair) can all go into the compost can. The other list taped to the lid is headed "No" and includes noncompostable scraps—meat scraps, bones, and diseased plants.

Each day put your cut-up kitchen waste into the liner until the can is full. Then tie the bag tightly closed with a plastic wire twist, and cover the can to keep the air out. (If the mixture seems dry, add 2 cups of water.)

Place the can in the sun, and forget about it for a month until the heat of the sun cooks the contents into crumbly compost.

A Recipe for Aerobic Compost

This method allows for air penetration and is a more conventional way of making compost. This is the technique I use for my weekend seashore garden, since I find it easier to obtain grass clippings, spent garden plants and fallen leaves there. I can also accumulate these materials gradually and then add kitchen scraps on weekends, covering them with grass and leaves. You can build this kind of aerobic compost pile wherever there is sufficient space, on a large rooftop terrace or on the ground. Here's how to do it:

Begin by collecting materials in the fall, when summer crops are dying back and leaves are falling. This is the most joyous season for serious composters. Grass clippings, fallen leaves, kitchen wastes, fresh manure and topsoil are the major ingredients for compost.

Pick a corner with a northern exposure (The other exposures in your yard and garden are sunnier and make better places for growing crops, so don't waste the space.)

Enclose an area to contain the pile, or build it right on the ground without a bin. If you do decide to make an enclosure for your compost, try to make more than one, if you have the space. Extra bins make it easier to turn the compost. All you have to do is fork or shovel the pile from one bin to the other. As a guide for making a bin, 10 feet of wire fence will enclose a circular area roughly 3 feet in diameter.

If the compost pile will sit on a finished surface such as a concrete sidewalk, tiled rooftop or asphalt driveway, lay down several layers of heavy plastic to protect the surface. Then put down a loose 4-inch layer of thin vegetable stalks or twigs to provide some ventilation over the plastic (on bare earth, dig a shallow pit to the size of the pile and lay down the twigs).

Organic Materials as Nutrient Sources

Material and Characteristics	% of Nutrient
NITROGEN SOURCES (N)	
Animal tankage	8
Slaughterhouse by-products which are dried and ground or rendered.	
Bone meal	4-5
Used primarily for supplying phosphorus.	
Dried blood or blood meal	7-15
Can also be made into liquid supplement. (Use 1 tablespoon per gallon of water.) As dry fertilizer, mix with greensand and bone meal or rock phosphate.	
Hoof and horn meal	7-15
Activated sewage sludge	4-6
Processed by-product that has been heat-treated from purification of city sewage and is free of pathogenic organisms. Also used to improve soil. Sometimes marketed nationally as Agricultural Milorganite.	
Fish meal	8-10
Contains almost as much phosphorus as nitrogen. Can also be found in liquid form as fish emulsion.	
Cottonseed meal	6-9
An agricultural by-product, good for acid-loving plants.	
Animal manures	0.5-2.8
Highest in nitrogen and also used to improve soil structure. Best to use as a fertilizer when aged or decomposed.	
PHOSPHORUS SOURCES (P)	
Bone meal	22-35
Finely ground animal bones. Decomposes slowly. Available also as steamed bone meal, which is faster acting. Work well into soil.	
Rock phosphate	30
Finely ground rock powder. Also contains trace minerals. Very slow releasing.	
Fish meal	13
Contains almost equal amount of nitrogen plus 4% potassium.	
POTASSIUM SOURCES (K)	
Greensand	6-7
An iron-potassium-silicate material, derived from ocean deposits. Also contains trace elements and 2% phosphorus.	
Granite dust	7-8
Variable percentage depending on rock source. Also contains trace mineral nutrients.	
Wood ash	6-8
Makes soil more alkaline.	
Fish meal	4
Also contains 8-10% nitrogen, 13% phosphorus.	
Seaweed	5
Kelp meal	12
Long lasting, almost 1 year; high in trace minerals. Use sparingly.	

On top of the twigs add about 6 inches of soil, then 12 inches of plant remains from the kitchen and garden (leaves, grass, spent vegetable plants, weeds, etc.). Cover this with a 2-inch layer of fresh manure (if you don't have manure, substitute a smaller amount of blood meal or cottonseed meal). Over the manure spread a 2-inch layer of soil,

A Few Words About Grass Clippings and Dry Leaves

These are both popular compost ingredients because they're readily available. But they require a bit of special treatment before you add them to the compost pile. Therefore, it is best to collect them in separate piles. Fresh clippings tend to become soggy or slimy and then compacted. Keeping them in a separate pile for a week or two before adding to the compost heap will give the clippings a chance to "cure" and dry out. Or, if you wish, you can mix fresh grass with some soil before adding to the compost pile, or add the clippings only in very thin layers.

Dry leaves are self-composting and therefore also make good mulch. They decompose very slowly, though, and tend to blow away unless covered with a sprinkling of soil to weigh them down. Shredding dry leaves before adding them to the composting pile speeds up the decomposition. A sprinkling of nitrogen-rich fertilizer (cottonseed meal or blood meal) also helps. Leaf mold, the final product when leaves are allowed to decompose by themselves, is found in its natural state in the woods on the forest floor. It is a rich, black, earthy-smelling substance. Many suburban areas now have smoke control laws forbidding the burning of leaves, so they are easy to come by in large quantities in the fall. You can add them to your compost or make your own leaf mold separately. Leaf mold can sometimes be purchased regionally, but it is very costly.

followed by a sprinkling of bone meal or rock phosphate and wood ashes and some dolomitic limestone. In this pile, the manure supplies the necessary nitrogen, the bone meal, rock powder and ashes amplify the nutrient content of the finished product, and the limestone checks the acidity and helps to break down the organic matter.

If the plant materials used are very dry, it may be necessary to water them until they are moist like a wrung-out sponge. Repeat this layering procedure until the pile is 4 to 6 feet high. Then top off the pile with some soil and straw to retain the heat and make it look neat.

With a broom handle, poke several holes down through the pile to the bottom to allow air and rainwater to enter (or you can insert stakes when you build the pile and remove them when it's completed).

Turn the heap, from the inside out, in about a month (depending upon your climate) and turn it again two to three weeks later. By that time the pile should have collapsed to half its original size. If you started in fall, your compost will be ready to use for spring planting.

Before putting the compost on your garden, sift as much as you need through a piece of wide-mesh hardware cloth. If you come across any large pieces that are not fully decomposed, you can use them as I do to start another pile, or you can use them as a mulch for fruit trees and bushes.

Quick Food Processor Compost for Mini-Gardens

You can even make compost on a very small scale and use it in containers or window boxes. If your garden is tiny, try the following recipe. Use a 5-gallon plastic pail with a lid for your compost "bin." Pails that once contained wallboard compound or concrete patching material work well. Clean them thoroughly, of course. Have on hand a 25-pound bag of potting soil, a small bag of cottonseed meal or blood meal and some bone meal or rock phosphate.

Begin by placing a ½-inch layer of potting soil in the bottom of the pail.

Next cut up your day's accumulation of vegetable and fruit peels and rinds, coffee grounds and other items from the "Yes" list (see page 172). Put half of it in a food processor with some crushed egg shells, and make a wettish slurry. Leave the remainder of the food wastes roughly cut up to prevent your compost mixture from getting too wet.

Combine the slurry with the rest of the food wastes and put a 2-inch layer of this material on top of the layer of soil in the pail. Cover with another ½ inch of soil. Repeat the layers until the can is full, and be sure to end with a layer of soil.

The material must not become too wet or the correct bacterial action for decomposition will not take place. The contents of the pail should be only as wet as a squeezed-out sponge. If your layers are wetter, add some sawdust.

Stir the mixture often to keep it well aerated. If decomposition seems slow, sprinkle in some blood meal or cottonseed meal. Also add some bone meal or rock phosphate to boost nutrient value.

Keep the can in a warm room or outdoors if you have the space. The vegetable matter should be unrecognizable in about three to five days. When it is dark and crumbly your compost is ready to use.

Trench Compost

Some gardeners dig trenches or pits to bury their wastes, and just wait out the composting process. They claim that their compost is hidden and out of sight, and also

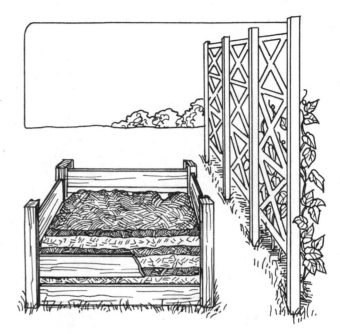

As shown in this cutaway view, good compost is made in alternating layers of organic waste matter and soil. The vine-covered trellis at right hides the compost bin from view of the house.

claim that small animals won't get into it. If the idea of keeping your compost truly out of sight appeals to you, give this method a try:

Dig several pits, deep holes, or trenches 2 feet deep by 18 to 24 inches wide by 3 feet long. Along the sides place retainer boards that rise about 6 inches above ground level. When the compost materials have been added you will need to cover this area with a wide board.

Another method is to sink a 30-gallon galvanized garbage pail with holes drilled all over it into a deep pit or hole. Cover with the top of the can, a board and some straw.

Place a layer of cut-up garbage on the bottom of the pit, trench or pail. Cover it with a layer of soil, grass clippings and weeds. Repeat layers until the trench or pit is full. Turn the contents several times to mix it all

Two Special Seaside Gardens

The two gardens that I'll describe here are both near the sea, located only a few miles from one another. And yet, the problems they posed to the gardeners were quite different, as were the solutions. One garden has blossomed from an original thick growth of brush and poison ivy, while the other one was lovingly nurtured in an arid, windswept patch of beach sand. Today, both are flourishing, remarkable gardens that provide a bounty of fresh vegetables and fruit throughout the season, a testament to the skill and devotion of the gardeners.

Maria Beqaj and Chris Jakimavicius

They are father and daughter, and they disagree on most of their garden philosophy, but the results are remarkable. Their gardens, just a few blocks from the sea, are exquisite oases that most strollers stop to admire. "Chris and I started our gardens about eight years ago," Maria says, "because I wanted my kids to learn and respect how food is grown. There was only sand, poison ivy and stubborn, deeply rooted fragmytes. Chris pulled them all up. And then came the chore of building the soil."

Not far from the village, the National Park Service rangers have a few horses quartered at the barracks, so Maria and Chris have all the free manure they can haul back on their little wagons. Chris believes in a proper compost, but Maria is afraid that it might attract rats, so they compromised. "I have my compost pile," Chris says proudly, "but I have it in a trash can buried in the sand up to the lid. Maria is more casual. She just marks off a garden area, buries the table wastes with some raw manure under the sand about 1 foot deep, and both of our methods work!"

Their methods certainly *do* work; their house is surrounded by bountiful gardens rich with a profusion of vegetables, fruit, herbs and flowers. An oblong fruit garden stretches off to one side of the large wooden deck that wraps around the house. Flourishing here are two apple trees, two pear trees, a plum tree and three peach trees that were grown from discarded peach pits. This part of the garden is edged with alpine strawberries. A grape arbor heavy with deep purple Concords graces a side deck, and some distance beyond it is the vegetable patch. The 28 by 60-foot vegetable garden is fenced on three sides to keep out rabbits and deer (the family dog helps, too). It holds tomatoes, cucumbers, zucchini, beets, collards and other favorite crops, and succession plantings are made throughout the season.

Between the deck and the vegetable garden are numerous planted "islands"—informally shaped beds that have been designed around existing mature holly trees, pitch pines, and highbush blueberries. These small island-shaped beds are framed with driftwood collected from the beach and chunks of concrete salvaged from a construction project in the nearby village. They charm the eye with a rich assortment of herbs and flowers. The islands are connected by a series of sandy pathways which are in turn surrounded by raspberry bushes, quince trees, strawberries, gooseberries, currants and nectarine trees.

Chris is a remarkable man, and Maria admits

that the gardens might not look the way they do except for his hard work. He is a true scavenger who believes, as I do, that everything can be used more than once. That's why the little island gardens are bordered by pieces of broken sidewalk, gathered a few at a time. Though they lovingly disagree about things like compost, both Maria and Chris are adamant about not using any kind of chemical sprays. They both feel that living on a fragile barrier island does not allow them to do any harm or change the environment's natural balance. They both love it too much. Maria laughs as she describes her gardens, "We do everything we're probably not supposed to do, but somehow it all works." And then she sums it up, "There's such a sense of privacy and quiet, interrupted only by the rhythmic sound of the ocean. Just to think you can have a garden so close to the sound of the sea is what amazes me most!"

Loretta Li

Chris and Maria's house was surrounded by the heavy underbrush that had to be torn out to make room for their gardens, but Loretta Li's house was surrounded by a large desert, buffeted by high winds and baked in the hot sun. There weren't even any trees, and yet Loretta's philosphy took hold and a garden now grows where sand once ruled. "I just think it's immoral to have space and not use it for growing food," she explains. "It's there and you've got to do it because it's part of living. Certainly it's a lot of work at first, but it gets easier as you learn more and more about it. Besides, I'm not in a hurry. Things that are enjoyable *should* take time!"

Loretta started her garden about ten years ago, with only lettuce and tomatoes. She experimented over the years, a little at a time, and now the garden boasts 60 different varieties of vegetables—seven or eight kinds of tomatoes alone—plus a hybrid melon imported from Israel because it was specifically developed for a hot, dry, sandy climate.

"It's possible to grow almost everything and I do try everything," she relates. "One year, I grew twelve Chinese vegetables. Sand can be a positive thing. You know exactly what you have, so you have complete control and you know what you have to put into

it to support your crops. On the other hand, it takes a long time to turn sand into soil."

Along the way, she asked the local market to save their old vegetables for composting. She gets manure from a friend who has a stable in another village, and in the beginning she bought peat moss and gathered the local seaweed. Loretta started with only one garden area. Now there are four, making it easier for her to rotate her crops. She also plants her crops very close to one another and uses no mulch, so that the plants create their own cool, shady environment. She waters daily because of the

summer heat, and unlike most other islanders she has no problem with slugs, because her property is so high and so dry. "We always plant more than we can use: some for us, some for the bugs, some for the birds, and some for the deer!"

The deer are protected on this island, and the herds have grown phenomenally since the first animals swam the bay about 300 years ago. "Last summer," Loretta says, "they ate our tulips. This summer they have been eating our peas. I have a low fence for rabbits and dogs, and I've created a large string 'cat's cradle' to tangle the deer when they try to come through. This year, I have a peach tree which is bearing fruit for the first time. The deer ate all but one. Every night, I tie it into a plastic bag and in the morning I remove the bag. I'm determined to see what *one* peach tastes like. Next year? More fencing, I guess!"

Dry Organic Fertilizers

Fertilizer	Amount per 100 Square Feet	When to Apply	Benefits
Compost	10-11 bushels	2-4 weeks before planting— and as a mulch and fertilizer side dressing	Excellent soil conditioner— provides major and minor nutrients
Animal Manures (cow, horse, pig, sheep, etc.)	10-15 pounds	Apply in fall, if not aged; 2-4 weeks before planting time if well aged	High in nitrogen, excellent soil conditioner
Dried Blood Meal	5 pounds	2 weeks before planting or as a side dressing	High in N (nitrogen)
Bone Meal	3-6 pounds	Apply 6 weeks before planting or in previous fall	High in P (phosphorus)
Fish Scrap (dried meal)	5 pounds	2 weeks before planting or as a side dressing	Good source for N; some P and trace minerals
Wood Ashes	5-10 pounds	Before planting time	High in K (potash)
Greensand	10-15 pounds	Apply in fall	High in K
Granite Dust	10-15 pounds	Apply in fall	High in K
Rock Phosphate	10-15 pounds	Apply in fall	High in P
Green Manure (vetch, winter rye, alfalfa, etc.)	2½ ounces of seed broadcast over raked soil	Plant in fall after harvest in North; very early spring, in Deep South	Protects topsoil from erosion; helps structure of soil and provides nutrients

Remarks
Screen to remove debris and any undecomposed material before using
Work thoroughly into top 6″ of soil; Can also be used in manure tea, as liquid supplemental fertilizer during growing season
Supposed to discourage rabbits from nibbling seedlings
Bone meal decomposes slowly
A similar liquid product, fish emulsion, is high in nitrogen; used a liquid supplemental fertilizer
Rain leaches out nutrients; raises soil pH; said to repel beetles, mites and aphids
Releases nutrients very slowly
Releases nutrients slowly
Releases nutrients very slowly
Allow to grow 4-6″ high then turn under into soil

together, cover with the board or lid, and let it mature for four to five months. (I've made compost this way from November to March.) You can start a second trench or pit while the first one is "in progress."

Learning the ABCs of NPK

An old adage states that the best fertilizer for any garden is the gardener's shadow. While it is true that tender loving care has always been the best nourishment for all growing things, we must remember another proverb that says (in part) "not by love alone." Plants need the same good nutrition that people do. Knowing what they require and learning to recognize early warning signals of malnutrition will let you keep both your soil and plants healthy. Diseases and insects are less likely to attack strong, healthy plants than weak, spindly ones.

Feeding Plants Organically

In contrast to chemical fertilizers, which provide a "quick fix" dose of nutrients to plants, organic fertilizers are by nature slower acting. They provide a more gradual but sustained nourishment to plants, releasing their nutrients slowly. They also improve soil texture and encourage the presence of earthworms and other helpful soil-dwelling creatures.

The chief concern of the organic gardener is simply to build better soil. Soil that is loose, friable and rich in organic matter usually contains the nutrients needed by plants. This kind of healthy soil requires little more in the form of fertilizer additions. All that's needed after your soil's in good shape is to replace the supply of nutrients used up by the crop after every harvest. Of course, there are many variables that can affect the nutrient content of even healthy soil. In an especially rainy year, for example, more nutrients may be leached out of the soil as the water drains away. And some crops take more from the soil as they grow than do others. These variables may affect the frequency of your soil-building activities, but the underlying principles remain unchanged.

Let's go on, now, to take a good look at some organic fertilizers that can give your soil an extra boost when it's needed. These fertilizers can be used in varying combinations depending on which nutrients you want to supply. They can also be incorporated into the compost pile to produce a richer compost.

Dry Organic Fertilizers

Compost and decomposed manures, although high in the nitrogen needed for healthy green leaves, will not supply large enough amounts of phosphorus and potassium, which are needed by flowering and root crops. During your annual spring soil preparation, the idea is to replace the nutrients removed by the vegetables that grew during the season before. However, the kind of soil you have to start with and types of vegetables you wish to plant will determine your nutrient replacement program.

Most organic fertilizers vary and they have very different properties from chemical fertilizers. Therefore, working by exact numbers is just not possible. The nature of the specific organic fertilizer itself, when and what you plan to plant and the type of soil and its pH level, all influence not only *when* you should apply fertilizers, but *what kind* to apply as well. The chart on Dry Organic Fertilizers, gives the approximate amounts of major nutrients in the various organic fertilizers. These materials also contain the minor nutrients and trace elements plants need. The most commonly available organic sources of phosphorus—bone meal and rock phosphate—require several months to become soluble and do not leach out of the soil quickly. Apply these fertilizers to the garden in fall if you want the phosphorus to be available for plants the following spring. These natural phosphorous materials require a soil pH of about 5.0 to break down efficiently, so it's often a good idea to add lime at the same time.

Natural mineral sources of potassium, such as greensand and granite dust, also take a long time to break down and become available to the plants. They should also be applied in the fall to benefit your spring crops (or, if you live where the growing season is very long, you can add them to the soil after each harvest for successive plantings). On the other hand seaweed and wood ashes, also sources for potassium, have a more rapid release rate of their nutrients. Wood ashes also contain lime and will raise the pH level of the soil. Apply wood ashes two to four weeks before spring planting and be sure they are well dispersed throughout the soil.

Animal Manures

Animal manures vary in nutrient content according to what kind of animal they come from and what the animal was fed. Even the age of the animal can be a factor of variance; older animals produce richer manure than younger animals that are using nutrients for their own growth and development. Some fresh animal manures, such as poultry manure, are very strong (that is, high in nitrogen) because they combine both manure and urine. Poultry manure must be composted before it goes into the garden or the abundant nitrogen could burn plants, and even then it should be used more sparingly than other manures (about 10 pounds per 100 square feet).

Other fresh manures, such as horse manure, are a bit lower in nitrogen and the microbes doing the decomposition take additional nitrogen from the soil to do their work. This, of course, diverts nitrogen from your plants. Also, chemicals are sometimes sprayed on horse manure to control flies in the stable. As a result, unless you know the source of your supply, it is better to compost the manure than use it fresh. And indeed, composting can make all the difference.

Composted horse manure is one of the best organic fertilizers there is.

Although well-rotted manure loses some of its nutritional value during decomposition, gardeners still prefer it to fresh for many reasons. Fresh manures contain a high percentage of water, and poultry manures usually contain some straw or sawdust from their stalls. Letting the manure compost lets the excess water evaporate and leaves you with a condensed manure that has more nourishment per pound. In addition, the nitrogen in well-rotted manure has gone through a bacterial process that leaves it in a form that is readily available to plants. Another plus is that rotted manure has no odor.

If you only have access to fresh horse or sheep manure, grab it anyhow. Pile it up on a plastic sheet to prevent leaching, and cover it with a layer of soil to eliminate any smell and to protect it from sun and rain. Then just let it sit and age for a few months, or add it to your compost pile. If you are an extremely impatient person who just can't wait, spread a layer of fresh manure on your garden in the fall and work it thoroughly into the top three or four inches of the soil, where it will decompose by spring.

As a last resort, most city and suburban gardeners must settle for packaged cow manure, which can be bought in bags, either composted or dehydrated. Dehydrated manure is dried in ovens and costs more to produce, and it is a bit higher in nitrogen content. Commercially composted manure is processed by spreading it on concrete slabs where it is turned and moistened regularly for five or six months until it is decomposed. This packaged manure has been sterilized, and sterilization has killed the bacteria that are one of its most valuable components as a starter in a compost pile. Therefore, it cannot be used like fresh (or partly rotted) manure for making compost. But if you are fortunate enough to have a source for animal manures, by all means take

advantage of this superb fertilizer.

One final word about manures: dog and cat droppings are *not* recommended for the garden. Cat droppings may contain certain microorganisms that are highly dangerous to humans, and droppings from an ill pet can also be injurious to your family. To be safe, it's best to avoid all pet manures completely.

Liquid Fertilizer Supplements

Plants absorb nutrients more quickly when they are in soluble form (dissolved in water) than when they're solid. Dry fertilizers begin to work only when sufficient soil moisture allows plants to use them. They are generally incorporated into the soil in early spring and once plants are up and growing, what is called a "side dressing" can be added either in dry form or as a liquid (soluble) fertilizer. Liquid organic fertilizers cannot harm plants by burning them, and they are convenient to use. They can either be applied at the base of the plant or sprayed onto the leaves (foliar feeding). Liquid fertilizers are an excellent crop booster when used every three to four weeks, especially for plants that are growing close together in a small, intensively planted garden. Two liquid fertilizers, manure "tea" and compost "tea," you make yourself and a third, fish emulsion, can be purchased at most garden centers.

Manure Tea

Although manure tea is *not* what you would brew and serve at a tea party, your vegetables will love it. To prepare it, first fill a large burlap bag or a large doubled piece of cheesecloth with 3 pounds of fresh horse or cow manure. If you don't have access to fresh manure, buy dried cow manure. Add a few tablespoons of bone meal and either greensand or wood ashes for a more complete supplement. Tie the bag tightly at the top with an extra long piece of rope.

Next, make a tripod from three 8-foot-long

Some Custom-Blended Fertilizers to Mix at Home

Here are some fertilizers you can blend at home. The approximate NPK analysis provided will guide you toward the proportions of each ingredient to use. In preparing your fertilizers, do not worry about exact numbers—they are not critical. Mix up a batch to have ready when you need it and store it in a plastic bag or pail.

There are also a few commercially available organic fertilizers listed in the back of the book; they can be ordered from seed catalogs. But like cooking from scratch, it's best to mix your own, so you know for sure what's in it.

All-Purpose Mix
for Root Crops and General Use

	N	P	K
1 part fish meal	10.5	6.0	0.0
1 part blood meal	12.5	1.3	0.7
2 parts bone meal	6.0	40.3	0.0
2 parts kelp meal	1.0	0.0	24.0
4 parts leaf mold	2.4	0.8	1.6
10 parts total	32.4	48.4	26.3
Analysis	3.2	4.8	2.6

High Nitrogen Mix for Leafy Plants

	N	P	K
2 parts blood meal	25.0	4.0	2.0
1 part fish meal	10.5	6.0	0.0
1 part hoof and horn meal	14.0	2.0	0.0
2 parts bone meal	6.0	40.0	0.0
4 parts wood ashes	0.0	6.0	28.0
10 parts total	55.5	58.0	30.0
Analysis	5.5	5.8	3.0

High Phosphorus Mix
for Flowering and Fruiting Plants

	N	P	K
1 part blood meal	12.5	2.0	1.0
2 parts fish meal	21.0	12.0	0.0
1 part bone meal	3.0	20.0	0.0
1 part rock phosphate	0.0	33.0	0.0
4 parts wood ashes	0.0	6.0	28.0
9 parts total	36.5	73.0	29.0
Analysis	4.0	8.1	3.22

pieces of 2 x 2 lumber or saplings. Tie the sticks together at the top and hang the rope of your manure "tea bag" from this frame. A wet bag of manure can be very heavy for a lightweight gardener—that's why you need all the rigamarole of tripod and rope suspension to help handle the weight load if you're a small or slender person.

Fill a 5-gallon bucket with water and put it beneath the tripod. Drop the suspended tea bag in it and leave it for about ten days. After the allotted time has passed, the water in the bucket should be the color of black coffee. This is a concentrated form of manure tea. Before you use the brew, dilute it to the color of weak tea.

Apply about a pint of diluted manure tea to the soil around the base of each plant, or use it as a foliar spray. Add the spent manure from the bag to the compost pile, or spade it directly into the soil.

Compost Tea

Another organic liquid fertilizer can be made with compost if you have some to spare. In a 5-gallon bucket, mix a large shovelful of compost with 2 gallons of water. Let stand for three to four days and then strain the liquid through a mesh screen. Use about 2 quarts of the strained liquid for each square foot of garden.

Fish Emulsion

This easily obtainable liquid concentrate is a mild fertilizer which makes an excellent supplement during the growing season. It usually contains about 5% nitrogen and 2% each of phosphorus and potassium. Dissolve a tablespoon of fish emulsion in a gallon of water and follow the instructions for use on the bottle.

Any of the liquid fertilizers can be made in larger amounts and kept ready for use during the growing season in a 60-gallon plastic garbage pail with a cover. Just tie a large soup ladle or dipper to the handle of the top of the can for easy removal of the liquid.

Supplemental Feeding

When you are growing a great many plants in a small space, it's a good idea to use supplemental feeding at critical times: when preparing the soil before planting, and during the growing season about once every three weeks. It's best not to overfeed; therefore, periodic applications of concentrated organic fertilizers are preferable to applying a lot of fertilizer all at one time. Unlike people, when plants are overfed they don't get fat, they *die*. So remember that twice as much is not twice as good, and go easy.

When plants begin to flower and fruit, apply either a liquid fertilizer or a side dressing of compost.

A Sample Fertilizer Schedule

There are so many options for fertilizing and feeding vegetables, that it's easy to become confused. If you're in doubt about when to apply organic fertilizers, here is a sample schedule that you can adjust to fit your own needs.

In the fall, add organic matter, animal manure, compost or a combination of all three to improve the soil structure and basic nutrient levels. To give your soil the balanced diet for your plants to thrive, the most important thing to do is add compost or other organic soil amendments.

When plants begin to flower or fruit, apply a liquid supplemental booster every three weeks, or use compost as a mulch or as a side dressing.

Always bear in mind that leafy crops need a higher nitrogen fertilizer, and fruit-bearing and root crops need a higher percentage of phosphorus and potassium.

CHAPTER 10

It Ain't Necessarily Sowed—
Seeds vs. Transplants

If you're a new gardener, you may not know beans about beans right now, but through exploring seed catalogs and studying the chart of vegetable varieties for small garden spaces in Chapter 6, you'll soon become familiar with beans and lots of other vegetables. You'll also learn to judge individual features of each one against your own needs. Most of all you'll become aware that the key to a nonstop garden is timing. And timing is the key to deciding whether to plant seeds directly in the garden outdoors or start them ahead of time indoors so you can put transplants out in the garden. The time it takes each vegetable to mature and the length of your frost-free growing season are the keys to figuring out a planting routine.

Maturity dates found both on seed packets and in catalogs clue you in to the approximate time it takes (give or take several days depending on yearly weather conditions and your location) for a vegetable to mature from the day the seed or transplant is put into the soil. This includes the amount of time required for different seeds to germinate (eggplant, for example, needs 14 days to germinate, while squash and tomatoes sprout in only 7). Times to maturity vary widely among different vegetables, and even among different varieties of the same vegetable. Most carrots, for example, take about 90 days to reach maturity, and celery takes 140 days. Radishes are usually ready to pop into your mouth in about 23 days, with germination taking place after only 2 or 3 days. So you can see that you have to plot your garden and and choose your crops carefully to make it right for your own growing season, particularly when you're working with a limited amount of space.

Some vegetables like it warm and others like it cool. Vegetables like peas and spinach thrive only during cooler weather and must be planted very early, but others such as eggplant and tomatoes demand warmer days and nights and will die in the first hard frost of fall. In climates or growing zones where there is a short season, if you want to have a continuous supply of vegetables you have to start seedlings indoors several weeks before it's time to plant them out in the garden. Or you can purchase transplants from a nursery in the spring when they are available, to set out into the garden at the proper time.

Using transplants shortens the time a vegetable spends in the garden and so does sowing seed at the right time. Whether you grow your own seedlings indoors or buy them is your own decision to make, but there are many advantages to growing your own from seed:

You have a much greater choice of varieties.

It is less costly to grow your own—it costs about 65¢ for 30 tomato seeds versus about $2.00 for four to six tomato transplants.

Staggering your seed sowing allows you to have an ever-ready supply of backup transplants to replace those that are harvested, or to use for intercropping with flowers or herbs in various sites around the garden.

Choosing your own starting dates also lets you lengthen the growing season by several months. In spring, you can get a head start and have early plants ready for the garden long before the nursery has transplants ready for sale. You will also have enough transplants to extend the season in the fall, when most nursery transplants are either picked over or sold out.

Some people consider the whole seedling scene to be too damp, messy and hard on the windowsills. They obviously do not possess enough of the nurturing instinct which is required. Also, some gardeners simply don't have the space or light needed to grow seedlings indoors. For them, the only acceptable way to have a garden may be to seed directly outdoors the early and fast-maturing vegetables, and replace them after harvest with warm-weather plants purchased at the nursery. On the other hand, there are those of us who wouldn't think of missing that first tentative emerging green, and who take the utmost pleasure in watching "our babies" grow and keeping them cozy, fed and watered for the several weeks they will probably need to be indoors.

If you're a novice gardener, you will never know which category you fit into until you attempt to start some of your own seeds indoors. It's not that difficult and if you have never done so, I urge you to try an experience not to be missed. Not only will you have an instant garden to set out when the time comes,

but I think you also will have found the most soul-satisfying way to do it: raising your own from seed to harvest.

To help you avoid some common errors and enjoy to the utmost the observation of this miracle of dried seed transformed into life-giving food, this chapter provides a step-by-step guide to get you off to a headstart on the season. Included are tips and advice and some do's and don'ts—many of them offered to me by some of my experienced gardening friends.

How Do You Decide *When* to Plant?

After you decide what to grow (see Chapter 6 for some helpful suggestions) you need to plan out when is the best time to plant each crop. Two key dates for all gardeners are the last frost in spring and the first frost in fall. Planting dates for spring crops are usually a certain number of weeks before or after the date of the last anticipated frost. Late crops are planted a given number of weeks before the date of the first expected fall frost. Your local county extension agent can provide you with information about frost dates in your zone. But remember, these dates vary from year to year, and local conditions can also have a marked effect on the actual dates. The dates your county agent gives you are only averages. The actual frost date in your garden may vary by a week or two, or even more.

When you have a fix on your frost dates, calculate the proper sowing date for each crop by a countdown. Count back from the actual outdoor planting date the number of days or weeks needed for seedlings to grow strong and big enough to be planted outdoors. This date is generally after the last frost, but several vegetables which are very hardy, such as broccoli, can be set out several weeks before the last frost, with some protection when nights are very cold. (See vegetable, fruit and herb charts in Chapter 6 for more specific information on hardiness.) Remember when doing your figuring to allow sufficient time for any special treatment your seeds may require for best germination (such as nicking the outer coat first or soaking the seed).

Instead of starting *all* your seeds at the same time, try to stagger your plantings so you will get a smaller and more continuous harvest. You can't eat more than one head of lettuce a day, and nothing is as depressing as a long row of bolted lettuce. A good motto to follow for starting vegetable seed is "a little, but often." Try to discipline the quantity of seed you plant for the amount of space you have, too. But do plant a few extras for succes-

sive plantings and for some of the mishaps which might occur. (Last year, half my hot pepper seedlings were gleefully gobbled up by a rambunctious puppy!)

How to Start Seeds Indoors

Gather together all the materials you will need: seeds (of course), a disease-free growing medium like the two described below, containers, some sort of tray for both bottom-watering and catching any drainage (to avoid water marks on furniture) and some water-soluble organic fertilizer such as fish emulsion.

The Growing Medium

First and foremost, the growing medium for starting seeds indoors must be pasteurized or sterilized; *don't* use soil directly from your garden. In addition to the fact that unless you live in a warm climate your garden soil is probably too frozen to dig up when it's time to start the first seeds in January, it can harbor bacteria that may kill tender seedlings. It may also contain weed seeds that will germinate along with the seeds you plant and then steal vital nourishment from your seedlings.

Soil must be loose and friable for seedlings to emerge easily. Use either a commercial premixed seed-starting medium (available under various trade names—check the label to make sure the one you choose contains no chemical fertilizers) or prepare your own medium from either of the recipes below. A 1-pound coffee can can be used as a handy quart measure.

Soilless Seed-Starting Mix
2 quarts fine sphagnum peat moss
2 quarts vermiculite
2 quarts perlite

Seed-Starting Mix Using Soil
2 quarts sterile potting soil
2 quarts fine sphagnum peat moss
2 quarts of builders' sand, perlite or
    vermiculite

How to Figure an Indoor Seed-Starting Date

Here's an example of how to calculate a seed sowing date. Let's assume you want to grow broccoli, and that your last frost date is around May 15. You find that the particular variety of broccoli you want to grow takes 112 days (sixteen weeks) to mature. Broccoli is a fairly hardy crop and plants can be set out four weeks before the last frost, on about April 23. Seeds usually take about a week to germinate indoors, and the plants should grow for about six weeks before you transplant them out. Counting back seven weeks from the planting-out date, you'll find that you should plant your seeds indoors on March 5. If all goes well, you can expect to start harvesting sixteen weeks later, about June 25.

This kind of calculation makes a good wintertime activity for new gardeners. As you gain experience, this will become second nature, and you will know when it's time to start seeds for your various vegetables without having to go through all this complicated figuring.

Measure all the ingredients into a large plastic bag (indoors, use the bathtub for easy cleanup), close the bag tightly and toss it around to mix the ingredients until all are well blended. Then open the bag and add 1 part water for each 4 parts of medium. Refasten the bag and let it sit for about 30 minutes until the moisture is evenly distributed. You can store the mix right in the plastic bag.

Containers for Starting Seeds

Almost anything from around the house that can hold the growing medium can be recycled into containers for seedlings. You can use Styrofoam drinking cups; margarine, cottage cheese, yogurt or butter tubs; milk cartons; plastic bleach or milk jugs—all sorts of containers can accommodate plants. Just make sure that you poke two or three holes in the bottom for drainage, and clean the containers thoroughly before you use them. Two commonly recommended seed-starting containers—egg cartons and eggshells—I don't recommend using because they hold very little soil and dry out quickly. Here are some tips to follow for seed-starting success:

Don't forget to label each container to indicate the variety and date planted.

After filling the planting containers with the moistened soil mix, tap the container smartly on a table top to settle the contents, and then level off the surface with the edge of a ruler. Tamp down lightly until the soil surface is about ½ inch below the container rim (don't tamp hard or you'll compact the soil).

Scatter seeds sparingly on the surface, then cover them with a layer of soil mix that is twice as deep as the diameter of the seeds (use an old salt shaker or restaurant-type sugar shaker to insure even coverage of soil if you're all thumbs). Note that seeds vary greatly in size—some are so tiny that a good healthy sneeze would blow them

Why Did Grandma Soak Her Seeds Before Planting?

Some seeds will awaken and germinate with the addition of only a few drops of water. In fact, viable seeds have been found in the ancient tombs of Egypt where they were kept cool and dry for centuries. When the seeds were taken into a laboratory and given moisture, they sprouted! However, some of the seeds you will plant in your garden will not germinate quite so easily. In the germination process, water is drawn from the soil to the seed surface and must first be absorbed before the outer seed coating splits open and unlocks the seed embryo. Since moisture is the key to germination, soaking seeds overnight in tepid water before planting them speeds germination and you end up with more plants that are off to a healthier start more quickly. Grandma did it, and I do it—and it works!

With larger vegetable seeds such as those of squash, pumpkins and cucumbers, I have had great success speeding germination when planting either indoors or outdoors by cutting off the end of each seed just enough to see the embryo within and then soaking them overnight. The seeds sprout in three days instead of the usual ten to fourteen.

away, while others are as big as a fingernail. Tiny seeds need only be pressed onto the soil surface and lightly covered with soil.

Press down lightly to put the seeds in full contact with the moist soil, then water the surface with a plant mister so the seeds are not dislodged by flooding. Keep misting the soil until it's moist all the way through. Do not water again until germination takes place. (And always water with tepid water, never cold water which lowers soil temperature.)

Cover the entire container, including the tray on which it sits, with a piece of glass or any kind of see-through plastic. This cover prevents moisture evaporation and helps to maintain the critical soil temperature, which should be about 70° to 80°F for most seeds you'd be likely to start indoors.

If you use a sheet of soft plastic as a cover, keep it from resting on the soil surface by propping it up with plant labels, sticks, or a wire coat hanger bent into an arch shape.

A nice, but certainly not essential, device to have is a covered propagating box with a heated cable or pad at the bottom. These units provide the uniform, gentle bottom heat that's ideal for germination.

If you don't have a propagation box, improvise. You can find free bottom heat for your seeds by setting the pots on top of a furnace, hot water heater, a TV set or even a radiator. To temper the heat, place seedlings on top of a few magazines or newspapers.

Make a daily check. As soon as the seedlings pop through the soil surface, remove the plastic covers and transfer the containers to the sunniest part of a room.

If you have sown your seeds too thickly, pull out some of the crowded plants with tweezers or snip them off at soil level with manicure scissors.

The Care and Feeding of Seedlings

Once your seeds have germinated you've got to keep the little plants alive and well until it's time to transplant them out to the garden. Here are some pointers:

Turn pots frequently so the seedlings don't bend and grow spindly reaching for sunlight

Don't kill them with kindness; water only when soil is dry just beneath the surface. Water from the bottom by pouring tepid water into the holding tray until the surface of the soil turns moist, usually indicated by a darker color.

If there is not too much direct light in your room, you can increase the amount of light your seedlings get by setting the pots on light-reflective white pebbles in the tray. Or make a tiny folding screen covered with silvery mylar to place behind the pots to reflect light from the windows. A mirror or sheet of white paper can be used the same way.

If you don't have any sunny windows at home, try your office. I have a dear friend who grows his seedlings in front of his office window where the light is better than in his apartment, and where he can keep a loving eye on them during the day.

If you have no sunny place or direct daylight at all, then you must resort to keeping your plants under fluorescent lights for 12 to 16 hours a day. In fact, when the days are short in January and February, you may need to supplement the natural light in this manner.

The first two leaves are the cotyledons, or seed leaves, and do not have the shape characteristic of the mature plant; they are somewhat like baby teeth in people, which are replaced by permanent ones. When the seedlings get to be about 2 inches tall and have formed their true leaves you must be cruel and ruthless and cut down the weakest plants with cuticle scissors, allowing only the strongest plants to survive. Although this may be a painful thing to do, it will give the survivors the space they need to grow healthy and strong. Besides, weak plants are more susceptible to pests and diseases out in the garden.

Then, transplant the remaining seedlings into their own 2-inch pots, or gently lift and replant them in a larger flat to give them more room to grow.

To transplant a seedling to a larger pot, use a pointed object such as a sharpened Popsicle stick to loosen the plant and pry it up and out of the pot. With your other hand, hold the plant gently by the leaves, not the stem. Set the plant in its new home, settle and gently firm the soil around the roots. Then, water with a ¼-strength dilution of fish emulsion or some weak manure tea, alternating weekly with plain water. Keep the transplants out of the sun for two days until they get acclimated, then put them

When seedlings are hardened off and ready to transplant, first remove them from the container. If using a plastic six-pack, push in on the bottom of the container while supporting the plant with your other hand.

Dig as many holes as you need at the correct spacing. Add water if the soil is dry.

Gently lower the plant into the hole and fill in soil around the roots.

If you're planting early in spring, cover the transplants with a glass or plastic cover for a few days until they become thoroughly acclimated to outdoor temperatures.

back in the full sun.

Going Out: The Garden Debut

Young plants, like people, can suffer from sunburn or windburn if they are exposed to the elements all at once. Their tenderness requires special consideration both before and after they are transplanted into the outdoor environment. The first thing you have to do to transplant seedlings starts a week or two *before* you actually want to do the transplanting. About ten to fourteen days before plants are to go into the garden, start to toughen them up by holding back on water and fertilizer, by gradually lowering the temperature around them, and by slowly increasing the light intensity. Set them outdoors in a partly shaded, sheltered spot for a few hours a day. Increase the amount of time the plants spend outdoors by an hour or two a day, to gradually introduce them to the sun and breeze. Once outside the plants may require more frequent watering because they are still in small pots and exposed to more air. After about a week, unless there is a danger of frost, keep the plants out all night.

After spending a few nights outdoors your seedlings will be ready to make their garden debut, provided weather conditions are O.K. Here are some tips for successful transplanting:

Transplant when outdoor conditions are gentlest—on a cloudy day, soon after a rain or in late afternoon when the sun's rays are weakest.

Determine how far apart to dig your planting holes.

About an hour before planting, dig holes in the garden that are slightly deeper than the root balls of the plants. Pour water into the holes.

Place one seedling into each hole and fill with soil. Press gently against soil to remove air pockets. Water, and when the water drains away, fill in with more soil. Leave a little depression around the base of the stem to hold water for the plant.

Tomatoes and vegetables in the cabbage family (broccoli, cauliflower, mustard greens) should be planted a bit deeper than most other vegetables. These plants should be buried to just below their bottom leaves. The buried stem on tomato plants will send out additional roots, and the cole crops need a strong root system to support their heavy top weight.

If you bought your transplants at a nursery, water them thoroughly and drain them before you take them out of their pots so that the soil sticks to their roots.

If your transplants are in plastic pots, flats or "six-packs," tap the bottom of the pot or press the soft bottom of a six-pack tray with your thumb to loosen the plant and release it into your other waiting hand. Never pull the plant out by its leaves.

Remember to set up vertical support for climbing plants or cutworm collars for plants which need them (such as tomatoes and cabbage).

If you are extending your growing season by planting early, your new transplants will need to be protected from the cold. In southern areas, or during spells of very warm weather the plants must be protected from the heat. Protective devices help plants become established in the outdoor environment with less stress.

The season-extending techniques discussed in Chapter 13 can be used for transplants, too.

Direct-Seeding Outdoors

When you're gardening in small areas the first thing you have to do is forget about the conventional spacing directions on the backs of seed packets. It's an unnecessary luxury to allow plants to be spaced 6 to 12 inches apart when they will grow just as well 4 inches apart—and they will, in the rich soil you have prepared for your intensive gardening beds. Soil quality is of prime importance when spacing is close.

When you space seed sparingly and carefully instead of scattering it thickly, you don't waste as many seeds and then end up having to thin them to the desired spacing. For a simplified way to plant seeds try this method, which saves both time and seeds:

After determining the distance needed for the mature plants (see vegetable chart in Chapter 6) use your finger to poke holes into the soil about 1 inch deep where you plan to put the seeds. Make all the holes before you plant any seeds.

Fill the holes halfway with vermiculite or any lightweight soil mix. If the seed is small, fill the hole three-quarters full; for really tiny seeds, fill the hole almost completely.

Drop one or two seeds into each hole. This sort of individual planting takes a little more time than dropping seeds into a furrow, but it will save you the work of thinning later on.

Cover the seeds with more vermiculite to fill the holes, and spray with a mister hose attachment to saturate the soil.

Soak a folded piece of newspaper and place it over the planted area, weighing it down with a few stones on the edges. This will keep the soil moist and warm for the seeds, and will also keep them from being dislodged by birds or heavy rains.

Check after a few days, and keep checking to see if the seeds have germinated. If they have, remove the newspaper. Leave covered any seeds that have not germinated. If one or two of the plants don't come up, just replant—you'll have lots of seed to spare.

What to Do About Leftover Seeds

Seed packets are stamped with dates to indicate freshness, just like milk cartons are. But unlike milk, you don't have to throw out seeds that don't get planted in time. If you have bought too much seed—and we all do—save the extra for a later planting or for next year. When properly stored in an airtight container in a cool, dry place, most seeds will stay viable for several years. You can even collect and save your own seed from plants you grow that are not hybrids (you can get this information from the seed packet or catalog).

When you want to use the leftover seed, if there is any doubt about its viability, test it for germination. Roll up about twenty seeds in dampened, doubled paper towels. Place the roll in a plastic bag and keep it damp and in a warm place for about ten days. Check the towel after five days and remoisten if it has dried out. If fifteen of your twenty seeds sprout there's no problem with the viability of the seed. If only ten seeds sprout, just plant twice as thickly as you would normally. If only a few seeds sprout, buy some new seed!

From year to year ardent gardeners are usually habitual savers of seed packets. But all those little envelopes have a way of getting scattered about in drawers or tool baskets. To store them in an orderly fashion, roll them up like cigars, and put them in jars in a cool, dry place. If you wish to combine both seed storage and record keeping, then empty the seeds into salvaged plastic pill vials or plastic containers from 35mm film, each marked with a number. Devise a simple indexing system whereby each numbered bottle has a corresponding page in a loose-leaf binder filled with transparent plastic folders that are divided into four 4 by 5-inch pockets—the kind usually used to store and display snapshots. Each sheet can hold four empty seed packets for at-a-glance information on both sides. Such a well-organized binder also becomes a working garden record when accompanied by an index card noting past performance of each variety. Over the years you will accumulate an invaluable reference guide that's geared to the conditions in your own garden.

You could also use index dividers to separate seeds according to their planting dates. Include a separate page for those you need to sow indoors at an earlier date. Another way to prevent that annual early spring rummaging for seed packets in the bottom drawer is to use a salvaged partitioned carton that formerly held soda or liquor bottles. Sort the seed by planting dates and label the partitions "Indoors" and "Outdoors." List all the planting dates to help you keep your plantings on schedule.

Nurturing Nature Along— Tips on Helping Growing Plants

The seeds are in the earth, and nature in its own remarkable way has pushed the first green leaves into the air. We gardeners, glowing proudly with the accomplishment of getting something to grow, now feel that we're more than repaid for our springtime toil by the sight of these brave, delicate seedlings. Certainly it is possible to sit back now and rock contentedly on the porch waiting for harvesttime. However, there are many things that can be done to help the crop along.

The magnetic pull of nurturing your "babies" into a thriving maturity will give you a hundred reasons to return to that prized garden of yours all through the growing season. Here are some excuses to sneak outdoors into the summer sunshine and see how you can help your plants along.

Playing a Supporting Role with the Spreaders and Sprawlers

People with small gardens are constantly searching for new ways to make their growing space more productive. They usually find it when they begin to think and look vertically instead of horizontally. Many favorite garden plants can be trained to climb trellises or strings and use up far less ground space. In fact, some of the most popular vegetables— tomatoes, pole beans, peas, cucumbers and squash—are those that take up the most room in the garden when allowed to sprawl. Luckily, they are also the best candidates for growing vertically. All of these vegetables grow on rambling stems or vines. Some will climb unassisted, by means of grasping tendrils, while others need to be attached to strings and still others need to be tied up to supports.

There is no need to sacrifice these vegetables when there is little space in your garden. Vertical gardening is the answer. The prime advantage is growing more vegetables in less space, but there are other less obvious benefits to vertical gardening.

Vertical crops can serve as a decorative screen, to divide one part of the garden from another or to hide a less-than-ideal view.

Plants that are off the ground are less vulnerable to ground rot, insect infestation and slugs, giving you greater yields and cleaner vegetables.

Climbing plants are handier to tend and pick. You don't need to bend over to get at them—a relief for aching backs.

The vegetables receive better air circulation and exposure to sunlight.

Eye-level bug control is another plus. You

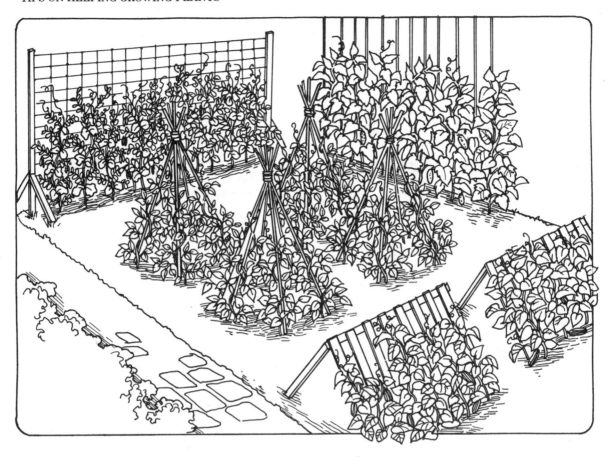

There are many ways to support climbing plants. Shown in this garden are (clockwise from front) wood A-frames for rambling zucchini, 6-foot teepees for pole beans, plastic netting attached to poles for tall-growing crops like sugar snap peas and heavy strings attached to a metal frame for fruiting crops like cucumbers and tomatoes.

can spot insects more easily and quickly, and get rid of them before they multiply into a hungry horde.

Vertical plants look attractive and neat.

There are two distinct types of vertical supports: cages and stakes for individual plants, or fences, frames and arbors of various design that support several plants. The latter can either stand next to a wall, such as a lattice-type trellis, or it can be free-standing like an A-frame trellis. Trellises, arbors, walls and fences are usually used to support berries, espaliered fruit trees and grape vines, but they might just as easily be used for long, vining vegetables such as cucumbers, pole beans, melons or sugar snap peas.

The range of materials that gardeners use to construct these vertical supports seems to be unlimited, and dictated by only one factor: the weight of the vegetable. From saplings and bamboo poles (used in the Far East), lumber of all kinds, steel water pipe, electrical conduit and plastic PVC (polyvinyl chloride) pipe, gardeners have designed structures of sizes and shapes that are determined only by the growth habits and strength of support required for a particular vegetable, and the builder's imagination.

These vertical aids are as personal as handwriting, fingerprints and hairstyles. Every gardener who is an innovative thinker seems to develop his or her own practical solutions to the gardening problems we all face. To say that any one structure or material is better than any other is unfair; what works for me may not work for you. Besides, I rather enjoy seeing the indomitable free spirit that is reflected in the limitless variety of materials, designs and construction techniques displayed in the many gardens I have seen all over the world. The fact is that gardeners everywhere must delight in this inventive bit of gardening creativity, for they have found all sorts of clever ways to get a maximum amount of food out of a small patch of earth.

Whether your supporting devices take the form of stakes, cages, fences, strings, towers, teepees, A-frames, poles, accordion or block trellises, ladders or arbors, they all serve the same purpose—to get plants up off the ground. Many of these supports play a dual role. They can be used as frames over which a sheet of plastic can be draped to protect plants in early spring (see Chapter 13), and some can be used to support plants growing in tubs and boxes. The possibilities are endless. And as the saying goes, "You just pays yer money and yer takes yer choice!" Study the illustrations on pages 194 and 196 for some ideas for useful plant supports.

To Weed or Not to Weed

When I weed my gardens, I have some frantic times when I am driven by a savage determination to clear away every bit of green weed that I feel is stealing nutrients away from my plants. But there are other times when the physical rhythm of weeding is more gentle, and my mind travels deeper into thought. A sort of hypnotic effect sometimes takes over while I work at tugging out an intruding plant or gently relocating a disturbed earthworm back into its home. It is at these times that the work-a-day circuits of my mind shut down, and I drift off into more serene realms of contemplation while my hands work mechanically.

Weeding can be a real chore, but its great virtue is that it gives you a reasonable excuse to be in the garden when you really ought to be doing something else. The ambivalent love-hate relationship that I have established with weeding over the years, is not as unique as I used to think it was, for many of the gardeners I've come to know admit to the same feelings.

Emerson wrote that a weed is a plant whose virtues have not been discovered. A British dictionary I once came across snobbishly defined a weed as "a plant hindering the growth of superior vegetation." I prefer to think of weeds in a more appreciative manner. Even as I bend over to pull and tug on them I am secretly grateful to them for allowing my thoughts to soar.

Of course this sort of philosophical daydreaming isn't for everyone. For some gardeners, pulling weeds is high on the list of wearisome tasks. Gardeners who don't enjoy pulling weeds can use a few tricks to keep them from growing in the first place, namely, they can cover their gardens with a layer of mulch.

Mulch Ado about Something

A mulch is nothing more than a protective blanket of inert material laid down on the surface of the ground around your growing plants. Mulching is also a lazy gardener's way of building better soil, for as the mulch ages, it slowly decomposes and adds to the organic storehouse of the soil below. There are many reasons to spread a layer of mulch on your garden:

Methods of supporting individual plants include holding a plant to a wood stake with two wire hoops made from bent coat hangers and taped to the stake; surrounding a multi-stemmed bush with stakes connected by string; tying a plant loosely to a wood stake with a cloth strip in a figure-8 pattern (to prevent stem damage), a simple trellis for a potted plant and a cylinder made of wire mesh.

Mulch reduces soil erosion caused by runoff rain water or irrigation.

The weight of heavy, pounding rains can create a hard, crusty soil surface. Mulch keeps this crust from forming and so increases the infiltration of water into the soil.

Also during heavy rains mulches keep vegetation clean by preventing soil splashback.

Mulch conserves soil moisture by reducing evaporation.

It acts as insulation, keeping the soil around plant roots cool and moist.

A thick layer of an organic mulch laid down in spring around fruit trees and berry bushes, along with some bone meal, lime and rotted manure, will not only keep roots cool in summer, but will make only a supplemental feeding necessary for the fruits.

Sprawling crops like watermelon love to rest on a cushion of mulch and will not mildew or rot as they do when they rest on the ground.

The most obvious reason for using mulches is that they suppress the growth of weeds which compete with your vegetables for water and nutrients.

Advantages of Winter Mulches

Mulches have special advantages in winter. Here are some:

Winter snow has been called the "poor man's mulch" because everyone can use it free of charge. Snow protects fruit trees and the roots of berry bushes and also serves as insulation for perennials and hardy vegetables. The melting snow will also water plant roots.

So called "trash mulches" of dead vegetable plants, flower stalks and vines can be chopped up and left on the ground as a protective winter covering. As this material decomposes, it offers a haven for earthworms that will carry organic matter and nutrients deep into the soil. Their tunneling allows for better water penetration, also. In fact, if you do not mulch in winter, earthworms may die or migrate to more protected areas.

A thick layer of a loose mulch, such as straw or hay, can be drawn around the base of frost-hardy vegetables to keep the roots from freezing and thus help to extend the harvest. Mulches are particularly useful for vegetables that taste better after a cold snap: kale, Brussels sprouts, parsnips and rutabagas, for example.

Remember to remove winter mulches (such as straw) or dig them (compost or grass clippings) in early spring to allow the soil to thaw and warm up.

What to Use for Mulch

When applied to the proper depth, a layer of almost any biodegradable material from newspapers to peanut hulls can be used as mulch. Some mulches, such as agricultural by-products, are usually available locally. Others are sold commercially, and still others are available free with a little ingenuity. See the chart on Organic Mulches for some suggestions on what to use and some tips on those materials that have quirky characteristics.

Plastic mulches, to my mind, score zero on the desirability scale, even though they are sold specifically to be used as mulch. The plastics will indeed retain moisture and reduce weeds, but just as important is the fact that they do not improve the soil quality by adding organic matter, as organic mulches do. Several synthetic mulches come in rolls, and these are designed to keep weeds down to prevent trailing fruits such as strawberries and melons from rotting as they touch the ground. Although the plastic mulches are convenient, I still prefer organic mulches for general use. But I do sometimes use synthetic mulches for the purposes outlined below:

Polyethylene films: Available 1½ mils thick and 3 to 6 feet wide. Clear plastic heats the soil about 10°F, so it can be used to promote early germination of cool season vegetables and to speed up production of warm season crops. Clear plastic, with its see-through quality, will not smother weeds as black plastic will.

Black plastic: Heats the soil 3° to 6°F and will accelerate growth of warmth-loving crops by absorbing the sun's heat and radiating it to the air above it, rather than transferring it to the soil. Therefore, it is good for extending the growing season into fall. Because it doesn't transmit light, black plastic is also useful on pathways, when laid as an undercover to smother weeds.

Light blue plastic: Has the same uses as the clear, but is supposed to have some insect-repellent properties.

Aluminum foil: Also sold as a mulch, foil is better used in shady parts of the garden to increase reflected light. When laid on the ground, it lowers soil temperature about 10°F. It may also help control aphids, we are told, by confusing them with the reflected light.

Biodegradable plastic: A fairly new product which comes in rolls and can be worked into the soil at the end of the season. This product is not yet universally available, so check garden catalogs to find out who may have it in your area.

Organic Mulches

Some mulches can be purchased throughout the country. Others are only available locally as by-products of agriculture or industry. Their properties differ and there are some quirks in their use.

Mulch	Availability	Comments
Aged animal manures	Locally available from farms.	Use 2 to 3 inches deep. Use only aged manures; fresh manures will burn plants.
Apple and grape pomace, spent hops	Growers and producers of wine, beer and cider.	Use 4 inches deep; turn under at season's end to condition soil.
Compost	Do-it-yourself mulch (see Chapter 9).	Sift compost and use only coarse remains as mulch. Use 4 inches deep.
Dried leaves	Not sold commercially, but a fresh supply falls annually.	Best to shred and add to compost pile. Blows very easily when dry and gets slimy and compacted when wet. Use 6 inches deep with 2 inches of soil on top to prevent blowing.
Grass clippings	Plentiful. See Scavenger's Manual in Chapter 8 for sources; cannot be bought.	Use 2 inches deep. Preferable to spread out loosely in thin layer to dry first. Avoid grass where weedkillers have been used.* Sprinkle cottonseed meal or blood meal to allow for additional nitrogen if fresh clippings are used.
Ground corn-cobs, bagasse (sugar cane wastes), tobacco stems	Farms and processors.	Must be shredded or ground. Use 3 to 4 inches deep. Add nitrogen fertilizer.
Hay and straw; cured grasses	Farms and garden suppliers, feed stores.	Good protection, but catches fire if smokers are careless. Use 6 to 8-inch depth. Good winter protection for containers.

*Cornell University suggests that a lawn treated with herbicides be mowed at least 3 times before collecting any grass clippings to use as mulch.

Mulch	Availability	Comments
Hulls: buckwheat, rice, peanut, cottonseed, cocoa bean	Look in phone directory Yellow Pages under processing; can be purchased locally.	Buckwheat and cottonseed may blow around; peanut hulls are attractive; rice repels water. Use a 4-inch layer of hulls covered with 2 inches of soil to keep mulch in place.
Mushroom compost	Can be bought where mushrooms are commercially grown.	Use 4 inches deep, turn under into soil at season's end to condition soil.
Newspaper	Available everywhere.	Use 4 to 8 sheets thick and cover with thin layer of soil. Do not use colored newspaper; inks are toxic.
Nut shells: almond, pecan, walnut	Purchase locally where they are grown or processed.	Long lasting; use about 4 to 6 inches deep. Mold sometimes forms on shells, just rake top layer under.
Peat moss	Expensive for large areas, but easily available.	Blows away easily when dry; once dry difficult to wet again; forms crusty surface, floats. It must be kept wet or it absorbs rather than keeps moisture in soil. Better used as a soil amendment.
Pine needles	Save discarded Christmas trees. Shake dry needles into plastic bag or use branches as winter mulch in rooftop gardens.	Use 6 inches deep. Good for alkaline soil or acid-loving plants like blueberries.
Sawdust, wood shavings, wood chips, shredded bark	Mills, carpenters, furniture factories, lumber companies, tree removal services. Chips and bark can be purchased from nursery suppliers, and chips are available in several sizes.	Apply wood chips and shavings 3 to 5 inches deep; sawdust, 2 inches deep. Add additional nitrogen to soil, since these mulches will draw upon the soil for nitrogen needed to break down. Use 4 to 6 inches of bark; if coarse, it can harbor ants.
Washed seaweed	Free for the gathering near beaches and bays.	Breaks down slowly, very attractive dark color. Wash well before using. Use 4 to 6 inches deep.

When and How to Apply Mulch

Mulching is the solution to many garden problems, but as with most gardening rules (which we have already determined to be practically nonexistent), the rules for how and when to apply mulches differ from one gardener to another. Here are a few general tips to help you get started with your own mulching program:

In early spring, wait until the ground is warm, seeds have sprouted and seedlings have been thinned before applying mulch.

Your seedlings are hard to spot with a 4 to 6-inch layer of mulch, so it's best to mulch all pathways and bare spots first, and then wait until your plants are at least 4 inches high before pulling a heavy mulch up to them.

As a rule of thumb, the finer the mulch, the thinner the layers need to be. For example, 2 to 3 inches of finely ground corncobs is usually thick enough; but straw, which is coarser, needs to be at least 6 inches thick to do any good.

If plant leaves nearest the ground begin to turn yellow, it's usually a sign that the mulch, as it breaks down, is drawing nitrogen from the soil below it. A liquid fertilizer high in nitrogen, such as fish emulsion, will correct this condition.

As the mulch condenses, add new material. Mulches should be maintained at their original depth.

Watering: Too Much Too Soon or Too Little Too Late

For some gardeners a kind of magic transpires when, with hose in hand, they go out to the garden to water their plants. Perhaps for these gardeners, watering satisfies an inborn nurturing instinct, like feeding a baby or watching a puppy clean its plate. For other gardeners, watering is an annoying, time-

Plastic sheeting is used in combination to protect these young transplants. A black plastic mulch around the plants keeps down weeds and helps warm chilly spring soil, and a cover of clear plastic makes the most of the sunlight. Clothespins attach the plastic cover to wires run around the top of the stakes.

consuming chore that should be gotten over with as quickly as possible. There is no denying that water is a vital element for growing plants, and love it or hate it, when the weather is dry, the gardener has to supply it to the garden. In recent years, below-normal amounts of rainfall and drought conditions in various parts of the country have made us realize that we cannot disregard water conservation any longer. We see now how precious a commodity fresh, pure water is. So, efficient techniques for watering are something all gardeners need to know.

To help you make the best use of available water, here are some water-saving suggestions for you to consider:

Add organic matter to the soil to improve water retaining capacity. Because of its spongelike texture, organic matter increases the ability of all types of soil to hold water, and it also promotes drainage and aeration.

Mulch everything in sight. Mulches not only stifle water-stealing weeds, but help to keep soil cool and slow the evaporation of soil moisture.

Water at ground level rather than from overhead to cut down on evaporation.

Apply water only as rapidly as the soil can absorb it; avoid overwatering that causes wasteful runoff.

Water in the early morning (the best time of day) or evening. Any water given during the heat of the day will evaporate much more quickly.

Where possible, redirect rain gutter downspouts into large drums to collect rainwater for garden and container crops.

When using unglazed clay containers, which are porous and dry out quickly, half-submerge bricks in a tub of water and set each clay pot on one of them. The bricks, which are also porous, absorb and transmit through the pot enough water to keep plants moist for several days.

On hot windy rooftops or balconies, group plants close together to create some shade and keep the humidity higher around the foliage, both of which help to slow moisture loss.

Perforated coffee cans or plastic milk jugs or other containers, when sunk into the ground next to plants and filled with water, are especially good for hillside planting to prevent surface water runoff and allow water to reach the roots, where it is needed most. Or, position them right next to melon and cucumber plants, which need large amounts of water.

Using water for growing food without wasting it is the responsibility of all good gardeners. Yet some of the most common misunderstandings among gardeners involve the amount of water plants need, how frequently they need it and how it can best be supplied.

How Much Water?

It is generally accepted by vegetable growing authorities that 1 inch of water per week is the minimum amount required for proper growth and development of most garden plants. The water content of vegetables ranges from 80 to 94%, with most of them in the 90% bracket. It's easy to understand, then, why the absence of water for even a short period changes their character and can cause injury from which they never fully recover.

The plants must be watered deeply, to the roots, in order to receive maximum benefits from the water. A good basic rule to follow is "more water, less often." If you sprinkle your garden for a brief period each day only the top few inches of the soil will be wet. Plant roots will grow closer to the soil surface in search of water, and a sudden hot spell could damage these shallow roots. Deep watering, on the other hand, sends roots downward to the cooler subsoil. When there is water stress, caused by insufficient water, flowers and immature fruits drop off the plants, and low yields of small, misshapen, poor quality vegetables or fruits will result.

When to Water?

Although plants need moisture throughout their growth, there are certain critical periods in their growth cycles when water stress is most detrimental. For most vegetables the critical times are during seed germination, when seedlings first emerge from the soil, and when young transplants are set out in the garden. Newly planted fruit trees and bushes also need plenty of moisture. A steady supply of water is essential during these critical times. These plant youngsters have not yet

Some methods of conserving water during summer dry spells include (clockwise from right) plastic milk jugs with holes in bottom, filled with water and set next to individual plants; a drip irrigation system that supplies water right where it's needed; a rain barrel connected to rain gutters and downspout; and grouping container plants together to conserve humidity right around the plants.

put down deep roots, the surface soil can dry out quickly, and *poof*! the plants are gone. Therefore, particularly when you are replanting during the hot summer months, make sure the plants or seeds are well watered.

Other critical times when vegetables may need to be watered are when they are flowering and setting their fruit. But for some vegetables the period of fruit development is one of the most critical times for watering. Broccoli, cabbage, cauliflower and lettuce need water when the heads are developing. Carrots, radishes and turnips need plenty of moisture when their roots are getting fat and round. Beans and peas need water when the pods are growing, and corn needs it when the ears

are developing.

Water is lost not only by transpiration through the leaves of the plant, but also by evaporation from the surface of the soil. These two processes will dictate the amount and frequency of water your garden needs, and only you, through trial and error and observation, will be able to discover the most efficient watering program for your plants.

Confusion often sets in because the "1-inch-weekly" rule cannot be applied to *all* gardens everywhere since watering requirements change and are influenced by the type of soil, the temperature and length of day, the regional cloud covering, the wind, relative humidity, the type and size of vegetables growing, the density or number of plants growing in a given space, whether or not mulches are used, and the amount of rainfall in a given season. So you can see that just turning on the hose won't do. Understanding your own garden's needs for water and then choosing a method or combination of methods, will help to conserve water without denying your plants this most vital source.

To test how long it takes you to give your garden 1 inch of water, set out a number of empty cans, pressing them into the garden soil to steady them. Turn on the hose or sprinkler as you normally would and see how long it takes for one inch of water to accumulate in the cans. One inch of water usually penetrates about 6 inches deep into the ground, although soils vary and no one rule can really be made. The following guidelines for seasonal watering may be helpful to you in gauging your watering during these critical times.

Early Spring: Many gardens experience rain, melting snow, and spring thaws at this time of year. The only watering that is usually necessary is the initial watering you do when sowing seeds or transplanting seedlings for early crops. However, if the soil surface looks dry where seeds are planted, water lightly with a mister attachment or lightweight watering wand, or a hose extender with a breaker nozzle wand so seeds will not be dislodged.

Late Spring and Early Summer: These are the months when tender crop transplants are set out (tomatoes, cucumbers, peppers, and eggplant). Use your judgment—it is best to soak the planting area before planting and again after transplants are set into the ground.

Full Summer: This is the time when most water is needed, since the summer heat dries out soil very quickly. Plants are larger and therefore thirstier. It's a critical time to make daily visits to the garden to see if water is needed. You will probably be going to the garden anyway, since this is when you'll be harvesting early crops and replanting succession crops to replace those that have been picked.

How to Water?

There are two basic ways to water your garden: from overhead and at ground level. Some gardeners insist that watering from above more closely approximates rain and is therefore a more natural way to water plants. Others believe just as ardently that the best way is to water directly onto the ground. There are advantages and disadvantages to both methods, plus gadgets galore to satisfy both schools of thought. There are times when you may want to switch methods, and when only one way of watering will be more practical for your needs.

Since a substantial amount of water is lost through evaporation, overhead sprinklers used on windy days or in windy climates are wasteful. It is better under these conditions to use a ground soaker or some type of drip irrigation. If you insist on overhead watering, do it in the morning or evening when there is less wind and the rate of evaporation is lower. Watering in the morning allows plants to dry off a bit during the day. In foggy or very humid areas, overhead watering, especially in the evening, may also encourage mildew.

Overhead watering is easier and usually less costly than ground level methods since the watering devices themselves are cheaper to buy and are available in many forms to suit the needs of many kinds of gardens. Nonmovable overhead sprinklers have holes that sprinkle water in square, rectangular or circular patterns up to 100 square feet in area. This limited range is perfect for small gardens. There are other oscillating, rotating or pulsing devices that attach to a hose. There are also wands and fine-spray hose attachments that deliver a light, gentle spray of water to seeds and seedlings or to wash soot off leaves in a rooftop garden. Indeed, there is something

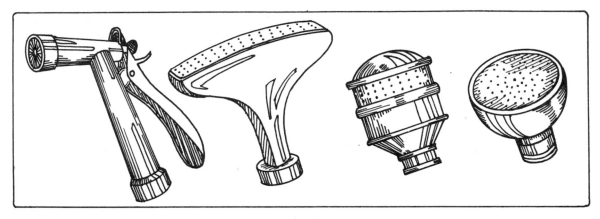

Hose attachments to provide different water flows include (left to right) a pistol nozzle for a narrow stream, a fan, a bubbler and a circular sprayer.

for everyone, and garden catalogs and nurseries detail some of these attachments (see illustration above).

Proponents of ground watering say that about 50% of the water applied by an overhead sprinkling system can be saved by using their preferred method. Ground watering devices also abound: a soaker hose with lengths of porous tubing, a drip-emitter of some sort or even a plain old ditch to catch water, or a hose with a hose and bubbler attachment can do the trick for you. One point to remember is that it will take longer to deliver a given amount of water to the root zone when using a ground watering system, but the extra time may be worthwhile because evaporation loss is greatly lessened.

No matter how you water your garden, the diameter of the hose affects the delivery time. For example, a ¾-inch-diameter hose delivers over 3⅓ gallons in ten seconds, while a ½-inch hose delivers only 1⅓ gallons in the same amount of time. Choose your tools accordingly.

Special Watering Needs

If you are the kind of gardener who considers standing in the garden at the end of the day with hose in hand sprinkling everything in sight to be one of life's special joys and thought-provoking activities, you will be glad to know that you should not deny yourself this pleasure, for it will not harm your plants. Not watering at all is more harmful than occasionally overwatering. But if you are a busy or impatient person who doesn't like to stand around hosing down the "south forty," a drip irrigation system with a timer has its merits. Rooftop water pressure is notoriously low most of the time and hours can go by while water trickles slowly into each container. It is difficult to find a neighbor willing to take over your tedious hose-watering chores if you are away. This was a problem with my own rooftop barrel garden. Although initially more costly and time-consuming to install, a drip emitter system with the timer set to deliver the required amount of water has saved me 4 hours of daily watering. Now I set the timer before going to bed and in the morning I awaken to find birds bathing in some of the puddles left in the depressions in the terrace floor—an added and unexpected delight. (One manufacturer of drip systems is Chapin Watermatics, 368 N. Colorado Ave., Watertown, NY 13601.)

Plants growing in city rooftop gardens also must have soot cleaned off their foliage with a fine spray of water that gets rid of any pollution accumulation. In really hot weather, a light sprinkling with a hose keeps vegetables in containers from "fainting" in the heat. The hose sprinkling is used as a supplement to the regular watering program. If you cannot get a friend to water your balcony or rooftop garden while you are away, water it yourself in the early morning or late evening and then enclose the container (not the plant) in plastic sheeting, or cover the soil with a plastic bag to retain moisture.

Container plants are exposed to drying air on all sides. The smaller the container, the more susceptible it is to drying, so check the soil daily by sticking your finger into the soil an inch deep. If it's dry, then water thoroughly with a watering can or bubbler hose. Large hardware stores carry adapters for bathroom or kitchen sinks that will enable you to hook up a hose that can be run out to the plants if there is no outside supply of water. A source of water can always be found. If there isn't a spigot on your roof a plumber can put one in, or you can use the adapter method.

Watering your vegetables gives you a chance to really see what's happening to them. You come to develop an intimacy with your garden that you may not have any other way. You putter around, pulling a weed or two, picking off a dead leaf or an insect; it is a time for caring. Somehow we creatures of the earth are always drawn to water. The evolutionary theories that we may have emerged from the sea could account in part for our love of water. Or perhaps it is a primal memory of our comfortable, floating watery prenatal bed which makes us once again drift into a dreamy state whenever we hear the trickle of a hose, the rush of a stream or the crash of the sea.

The tilling, the planting and preparation of the earth have been replaced during the growing season by something we might well call "puttering." But this puttering is the best antidote I know for a tension-filled day at work. In the garden, you can empty your head of everyday worries and fill your mind with the anticipation of the harvest that will soon come . . . if all goes well.

CHAPTER 12

The Good Guys and the Bad Guys

Beginning gardeners live in a simple and innocent world of absolutes: there are good guys and bad guys. The good guys are all the vegetables, fruit, herbs and flowers, the birds (although they can sometimes be seductive invaders), the predatory insects and toads. The bad guys are the weeds, the four-legged furry nuisances, everything slimy that creeps on the ground, and the diseases and destructive bugs. Since life outdoors doesn't come prepackaged for comfort, it requires a certain amount of tailoring.

The novice gardener may not be aware that many insects do not harm plants and a great number, in fact, perform positively useful roles as pollinators and predators. To many new gardeners, all bugs are nasty things that chew, chomp, suck and burrow their way into the garden. They are an enemy that has arrived uninvited and is determined to stay, so they must be fought by fair means or foul, by hand-to-hand combat or chemical warfare. What compounds the problem for these gardeners is that so many creatures are invisible enemies. At least they *seem* to be invisible, and there is something disturbing and disquieting about an enemy that lurks in daytime hiding places and sneaks into the garden at night, an enemy that hides among leaves and flowers, taking on their shapes and colors.

The enraged novice gardener often feels like challenging these hidden nocturnal creatures and in frustration may dust, spray and fumigate them all to an untimely demise. The bugs, good and bad alike, are stopped dead in their tracks by an arsenal of expensive and environmentally damaging chemical pesticides. Victorious at last, the gardener watches his enemies drop to the ground. That's one way to get rid of your bug problems. But enlightened gardeners know that there are better ways of sharing the earth with nature's creatures, and although at times we may feel like crying out "Help, everyone's eating my garden but me!" we take the time to learn not to harm the environment with chemicals. Releasing a few thousand natural predators, inviting bug-eating birds to the garden, and practicing a compromise called I.P.M. (Integrated Pest Management) are all techniques which are slower and quieter. But they work even though you usually cannot see or hear them at work. The organic defense, then, is as hidden as the enemy, but it is considerate of the environment and a fairer exchange with nature. You can be a discriminating executioner and target only the harmful bugs in a "search-and-destroy" mission, sparing the good bugs to do their jobs.

Some Guidelines for Insect and Disease Control

Since the organic gardener is his own best defense against pest problems, the first step in any insect and disease control program is always prevention. In addition to preventive measures involving good garden management, the use of natural methods and agents as alternatives to the use of chemical pesticides should be your goal. Here are some measures to take:

Build up your soil until it is balanced in nutrients and full of organic matter. Rich, well-drained soil normally promotes and sustains vigorous, healthy plants and when plants are healthy they are more resistant to harmful insects and diseases.

Practice good garden hygiene. Be neat. Don't leave piles of wood, stones, or plant debris around the garden for wintering pests to find shelter in. Rid the garden of infested plant material promptly, to reduce the possibility of spreading infection to others. Do not compost diseased plant material for the same reason.

Elevate growing areas by means of raised beds, hanging pots and containers to keep some insects from crawling into the garden.

Make sure your garden gets plenty of light and that air circulates freely, to help fight fungus, mildew and other diseases.

Select vegetable varieties that are known to be resistant to specific pests and diseases that tend to be problems in your neighborhood.

Deceive and counterattack with timing. The time of planting some vegetables can be an important aid in controlling pests. Sometimes planting earlier or later in the season is helpful, or staggering the same crops, or using early or late varieties. These techniques allow vegetables to escape periods

Other Garden Friends

Besides the good guys (insects) and birds, there are some other creatures that eat pests in your garden. These other garden friends should be welcome in your garden, although their identities may come as a surprise to you.

Toads: Snare an estimated 10,000 insect pests per summer with their swift sticky tongues. They live about ten years and have a strong homing instinct; they will come and stay in your garden as long as the living is easy. To persuade them to remain in the garden to eat a variety of pests, provide them with a few "toad houses." Each house is simply a clay pot turned upside down, with a "door" chipped out of the side. Put the pots in a shady spot and include a shallow pan of water nearby. If you capture the toads and bring them to your garden, keep them penned up for a few days before releasing them, so they become acquainted with their new environment. They will soon settle in and set up housekeeping.

Lizards: May be purchased in some pet shops. These fast-running reptiles want nothing more than to be free and go about hunting their dinner. They lay eggs twice each summer and their young, when they reach 1″ long, move on to new territory. I once found a lizard living in my seventeenth-floor New York City roof garden. I identified it through a book on reptiles as a "five-lined skink." He became an oddity visited by our friends because of his seemingly unnatural choice of life-style. Louis Lizard, as he came to be known, kept us from putting on our window screens for the entire summer. In one of our barrels there is a sign to commemorate his existence and his demise. It reads, Here lies Louis Lizard: R.I.P.?

Box turtles: Slow, but steady. These exquisitely patterned creatures require no provisions except water. They will eat grubs, worms, slugs and bugs, and any fruit or vegetables that drop to the ground. Just leave a few rinds or vegetables on top of the compost heap for the turtle's diet supplement. When cold weather comes, they will dig down into the ground for extra warmth and hibernate for the winter.

Some Common Bad Guys

Insect	Description	Vegetables Affected	Feeding Habits and Plant Symptoms
Sucking Insects			
Aphids	Green, pink, black or yellow; tiny, sometimes winged soft-bodied insects.	Most vegetables.	Lives and feeds in colonies, sucks leaves and stems. Foliage curls, puckers and yellows. Plants become weak and stunted. Buds and flowers deformed. Spreads viral diseases.
Leafhoppers	Small wedge-shaped, green or brownish color. Moves quickly and sideways, holds wings in tentlike position above body.	Eggplant, beets, corn, celery, potatoes, grapes, tomatoes and others.	Nymphs and adults suck leaf juices and transmit various diseases. Leaves yellow and stipple, then curl and brown at tips and margins.
Mites	Oval shape, yellow, green or red; only $\frac{1}{50}''$ long.	Beans, peas, tomatoes, celery, fruits.	Sucks plant juices. Most prolific in dry weather. Fine silvery webbing under and over foliage. Mottled, speckled, curled and wilting foliage.
Whiteflies	White, powder-covered bodies, resemble small moths. When disturbed fly up erratically like a cloud of snow.	Peppers, tomatoes, most other vegetables.	Hides under leaves, sucking plant juices from leaves, stems and flower buds. Yellowish nymphs attach and feed on leaf undersides; plants stunted and weak, fruit yields reduced.
Bugs	Wings overlap. Form transparent tips shield shape. Triangle on backs.		
	Harlequin Bug: red & black shiny pattern, ¼″ long.	Cabbage, cauliflower, radishes, turnips, Brussels sprouts, kohlrabi.	Sucks leaves, causes white blotches; leaves wilt and die.
	Squash Bug: ½″ long, brownish black, light grey nymphs.	Cucumbers, squash, pumpkins.	Damages vines, sucks leaves, causing plant to wilt and die.

Some Natural Controls

Home remedies: Spray with mild soapy water solution, then clear rinse. Aluminum foil reflectors as a mulch. Natural predators, e.g. ladybugs and aphid lions.
Commercially available controls: Safer's soap spray, rotenone, pyrethrum.

Home remedies: Cover small plants with fine netting in early summer.
Commercially available controls: diatomaceous earth (Permaguard), Safer's soap spray, pyrethrum, rotenone.

Home remedies: Destroy garden debris so mites don't overwinter. Natural predators, ladybugs.
Commercially available controls: use dormant oil spray in early spring for fruits.

Home remedies: Paint boards yellow, coat with sticky substance, and hang over affected plants. Mulch with light-reflective aluminum foil to disorient insect. Soapy water. Ladybugs, natural predator.
Commercially available controls: Safer's soap spray.

Home remedies: Handpick;
plant decoy crop of turnips near maincrop. Plant resistant varieties, practice crop rotation; get rid of garden debris.
Commercially available controls: Safer's soap spray, rotenone, pyrethrum.

when pests lay their eggs or are especially abundant.

Learn to recognize pests on sight, and also be aware of the less obvious clues that they leave behind. Study and observe their lifestyles: when they appear, what their diet preferences are; and study their lifecycles.

Become familiar with the control options for pests you see frequently (see the chart Some Common Bad Guys).

Once the insect is identified as harmful, if it is large enough to see and remove, the next step is what I call "the hand-pick and foot-stomp method." If not gotten rid of quickly, insects seem to invite their friends and relatives for three meals a day. So before invasion by the many, try the next three suggestions for the few.

Inspect daily. If you are fastidious, squeamish or nearsighted there's no excuse. The squeamish can wear garden gloves and use tweezers for easy removal. The nearsighted can use an inexpensive hand-held magnifying glass to see and identify the minute eggs and offspring of some of the tiny common garden pests. Dispose of them in a coffee can with an inch of alcohol or kerosene in the bottom.

Practice crop rotation. Even with a small garden or containers it is feasible to move each group of plants into another area of the garden every year. Crop rotation foils insects by depriving them of their preferred host plants.

Utilize companion planting. Although not altogether scientifically proven, companion planting has been used by gardeners to control insects since ancient times. Make the insect-repellent plants do double duty in small gardens and plant edible companion crops such as kitchen herbs and members of the onion family (chives, garlic,

Insect	Description	Vegetables Affected	Feeding Habits and Plant Symptoms
	Tarnished Plant Bug: brownish yellow, ¼″ long.	Most vegetables.	Sucks tips of stem, fruit and buds. Causes black spots.
	Green Stink Bug: ¼″ long, light green color.	Legume crops, peas and beans.	Sucks leaf and stem juices. Distorted growth, brown blotches.
Leaf Chewers Beetles	Large diverse group different sizes and patterns; all have hard, opaque wing covers divided in the center. Group includes Mexican bean beetle. Colorado potato beetle, cucumber, blister, asparagus and flea beetles.	Almost all vegetables.	Some chew leaves leaving holes, others stems. Transmit viral and bacterial diseases. Grubs (larvae) live beneath soil—chew roots.
	Colorado potato beetle: yellow with black stripes on wing covers, dark dots behind head; $1/3″$ long.	Eggplant, peppers, potatoes, tomatoes.	Adults and grubs chew leaves.
	Flea beetle: shiny black, hops away when disturbed; tiny—$1/10″$ long.	Various species attack most vegetables.	Adults and larvae chew tiny holes in leaves.
	Striped blister beetle: yellow with black stripes, elongated shape, ½″ long.	Beans, beets, melons, peas, potatoes, tomatoes, and other vegetables.	Feeds on leaves and fruit.
Slugs, snails	Soft fat tan bodies, some with spots. Can measure up to 3″ when adults. Snails have hard shells.	All vegetables and fruit.	Active during wet, or cloudy days—active during early morning, evenings. Hides during day under boards, mulches. Leaves silvery trail of slime. Can eat entire plant. Makes holes in leaves.

Some Natural Controls

Home remedies: Handpick; destroy garden debris so they will not overwinter. Garlic, hot pepper spray. Natural predator, praying mantis. Commercially available controls: rotenone, pyrethrum.

Predator—ground beetle.

Diatomaceous earth, rotenone.

Handpick but wear gloves; bugs secrete skin irritant.

Home remedies: Handpick with tweezers. Sprinkle with salt. Leave saucers of stale beer on ground. Sprinkle ground surface with coarse sand, wood ashes. Keep garden clean of hiding places.

onions) as borders. Or intercrop companions with vegetables, or plant an entire herb garden near your vegetable garden to offer a collection of many different kinds of edible, insect-repelling companions.

Some Good Guys to Know

Insect pollinators and predators, along with larger creatures like birds, lizards and toads, consume mountains of harmful insects daily. They are the good guys in the garden and wise gardeners value them. But the indiscriminate use of insecticides can backfire and destroy these beneficial, indispensable and often beautiful creatures. Just imagine a summer day without the fluttering patterns of butterfly wings, or a morning without birdsong. How sad it would be. It's important to learn which are the helpful insects and creatures, for when you can identify them you will be able to welcome and protect these sentries (see the chart on The Good Guys).

In general, most of the garden "spoilers" are vegetarians, whose diets consist mostly of leaves, stems, roots and fruit. Ironically, the good guys are not only carnivorous and eat other insects, but some are cannibals as well, and they'll eat one another. The helpful insects fall into two categories, predators and parasites. The predators are considered by entomologists to be much more effective biological control agents than the parasites, since they destroy a large number of insects during their life cycle. Parasites, on the other hand, usually kill only a single victim. No matter. They are still the allies of the gardener and a good line of defense against the spoilers (even though it may be difficult to love and to accept cannibals).

Inviting Helpful Birds and Discouraging the Pigeons

For advanced garden sluggards, relying on birds is a sly but effective way to cut down on the harmful insect population without

Insect	Description	Vegetables Affected	Feeding Habits and Plant Symptoms
Caterpillars and worms	Larval stage of moths and butterflies. Diverse group, some smooth some hairy.		
	Cabbage looper: Bright green with stripes, hunches back into loop as it walks; 1½" long.	Cabbage, cauliflower, kale, parsley, celery, lettuce, broccoli, beans, peas, tomatoes, potatoes.	Chews leaves, prefers cabbage or cole family—holes and ragged edges plus black droppings indicate their presence.
	Imported cabbage worm: bright green with one yellow stripe. Larvae of white moth, 1½" long.	All members of cole family.	Chews holes in leaves. Leaves soft green droppings.
	Corn earworm: larvae stage of brown moth. Greenish color worm, 1½" long.	Prefers corn; when not available will eat tomatoes, okra and pea pods.	Moth lays eggs on corn silks, larvae chew way into kernels. Chew other vegetable stems, buds. Stunt plants, destroy crop.
	Tomato hornworm: Green with spike or horn at end of tail; 8 diagonal stripes on sides; 3-4" long.	Tomatoes, peppers, eggplant.	Chews leaves and fruit.
Burrowing Insects Borers	Diverse group includes peach borer.		
	European corn borer: grayish pink caterpillar with dark head and spots on top of each segment; 1" long. Adult moth is yellowish brown in color.	Prefers corn, but will also eat stems and leaves of other plants such as beans or peppers.	Burrows into stalks and corn ears after moth lays egg mass on leaves.
	Squash vine borer: larvae of moth with double set of wings— front opaque, rear wings transparent.	Squash and pumpkins, cucumbers, melons.	Eggs hatch and borers enter stem at ground level. Feed on stem tissue leaving small piles of yellow frass. Vines wilt and die very quickly.

Some Natural Controls

Home remedies: Handpick, or sprinkle worms with flour or salt.
Commercially available controls: *Bacillus thuringiensis* (BT), a bacterial disease affecting caterpillars only. Use for heavy infestation of all listed caterpillars.

Home remedies: Handpick; use garlic, hot pepper spray.

Home remedies: As soon as cornsilks appear, trickle mineral oil onto silks with an eye dropper.

Home remedies: Handpick wearing gloves or use tweezers.

Home remedies: Handpick; use resistant seed varieties, plant in relays; slit stalk and remove borer, destroy stalks after harvest.
Commercially available controls: rotenone.

Home remedies: Plant several relay plantings. Slit vine at soil level. Remove and kill borer with knife point. Bind slit stem with twist 'em. Heap soil over wound to encourage rerooting. Clean up and destroy diseased plants.

lifting a finger. Birds add color and song to the landscape and will come to your garden if they are welcome there. Attracting local and migratory birds with well-placed feeding and watering stations will result not only in a sharp increase in the local bird population but also a drop in insect damage. And you get the added bonus of more hours to spend in restful observation and fewer hours to spend fighting bugs.

To attract birds that eat insects, especially in the North, gardeners must also provide for them during the winter. After autumn, their food supply dwindles and although birds develop extra fat to carry them through the cold, they must eat three times their weight each day to maintain warmth. If you take care of the birds in the winter, they will help you and your garden during the rest of the year. Besides, it's fun to watch these "flowers of winter" and feeding them is a rewarding, soul-satisfying project. Here is some advice on feeding birds during the winter:

Find or build an appropriate bird feeder. (A good mail-order source of feeders and practically everything else you'd need to attract and feed birds is Duncraft—For the Birds, Penacook, NH 03303.)

Place the feeder in a sunny, wind-free spot where the birds will be close to trees or shrubs and can flee if they feel threatened. They will not be lured to a feeder in an open area.

The commercial bird feed mix sold in supermarkets is likely to go uneaten. Local birds often reject this mixture of wheat, milo and millet, and prefer fine cracked corn, peanut hearts, sunflower seed and black thistle. Always read labels before buying bird food.

Provide some suet or beef fat for extra warmth and energy when it's very cold.

Feed from first frost (around the end of

Insect	Description	Vegetables Affected	Feeding Habits and Plant Symptoms
	Has bright red abdomen. Larva is fat, white, 1″ long, with brown head.		
Underground Pests			
Wireworms	Larvae yellowish brown, 1½″ long. Adult black beetle lays eggs in soil.	Carrots, radishes, beets, potatoes, onions and others.	Feeds underground on seeds and seedlings—bores holes into root crops, tubers.
Cutworms	Hairless caterpillars, many different kinds: brown, black, spotted, or striped. Curl up when disturbed. Brownish moth lays eggs in soil.	All garden vegetables, particularly seedlings.	Hides in soil during day, feeds at night. Cuts off seedlings at ground level, destroying plant.
Grubs	Larvae, plump greyish white with brown head. Black or brown beetle lays eggs in soil.	Strawberries, potatoes.	Lives in soil, chews roots of crops.

October in my area) until spring, gradually weaning the birds from the feed and encouraging them to eat from the wild around your garden area. Make sure there are enough trees or bushes with berries nearby, such as mulberry, firethorn and inkberry. Most libraries are good sources of books with suggestions on what local birds will eat in your area.

Particularly in urban areas where there are no ponds or puddles, provide some water in a shallow bowl. Change the water occasionally, and check regularly to see that it's not frozen over.

In the spring, nesting birds are on the lookout for building material. Fill a mesh bag with string, pieces of yarn, or small strips of cloth and a feather or two and hang it on a tree or fence, then sit back and watch the birds' industrious activity.

One bird that town and city dwellers abhor is the pigeon. While most rooftop and balcony gardeners may respect the pigeons' survival instincts and clever adaptability to an urban environment, they spend a good deal of time trying to outwit them. Pigeons come as uninvited dinner guests and push the smaller insect-eating birds aside. They

Some Natural Controls

Commercially available controls: early dusting of rotenone at base of vine before moths emerge.

Home remedies: Regular use of compost and wood ashes—rotate crops, cultivate soil.
Trap: Cut potato, run stick through middle, bury 1″ deep for 2-3 days, then dig up and remove wireworms.

Home remedies: Place collars made of paper or aluminum foil around base of plant when seedlings are set out.
Commercially available controls: Diatomaceous earth, sprinkle *Bacillus thuringiensis* around plants.

Home remedies: Birds are natural predators.
Commercially available controls: Milky spore disease (*Bacillus popilliae*; sold as Doom).

that requires birds to perch on a dowel to get at the food. They must stand flat footed while they eat.

A feeder placed where any seed that spills can fall onto a heavily planted area is helpful—bigger birds can't get in to pick up the seed.

A deep, rough mulch such as bark chips underneath the feeder also helps to foil the pigeons. They don't look very hard for their food, and don't see the seeds between the chips.

When you feed the birds, you won't be

pull up new seedlings and leave their messy droppings over everything. They build nests in unexpected places—like air conditioners, for example—and worst of all, they *never* eat insects. It's easy to see what a problem these big bullies cause for the urban gardener who tries to supplement with bird seed the meager natural wintertime food supply for the little birds. To help you avoid the presence of pigeons while caring for the insect eating birds, there are a few pointers I can pass on to you, based on things I have observed in my own city rooftop garden:

Pigeons will not dine at the type of feeder

How to feed helpful birds without encouraging pigeons: try this kind of bird feeder, which has a dowel across the front. Pigeons can't grasp the dowel with their feet, so they'll have to find other sources of food outside your garden.

Some Garden Good Guys

Good Guy	Description	Benefit
Ground beetles and tiger beetles	Most are shiny black or brown, although they come in different colors as well as sizes. They have long oval bodies, narrow heads. Their grubs are slender with two projections at the tail end.	Although these beetles hide during the day, and scurry away when disturbed, leave them be—particularly their grubs which eat more than the parents do. Very fond of caterpillar family.
Praying mantis	Light green, 2½-4″ long with papery wings. Wedge-shaped heads can swivel from side to side, creating an eerie feeling of being watched by them as you move. Folded forelegs are adapted for grasping, giving them a praying appearance.	The young feed on aphids. Adults feed on many kinds of larger insects such as beetles, flies, aphids, leafhoppers, bugs, moths, caterpillars, mosquitoes. They are cannibals and may eat each other.

Parasites

Good Guy	Description	Benefit
Tachinid fly	Bristly, gray or brown in color, about ½″ long. Look like common houseflies.	Lay eggs on victim or foliage that victim eats. Larva eats by feeding within the body and killing the host insect, which can be European corn borers, bean beetles, gypsy moths, caterpillars.
Braconid wasp	Adult wasp is about ¼″ long, dark bodied, with transparent wings.	If you see a moribund caterpillar (the tomato hornworm in particular) with tiny, white, ricelike pouches attached to it, don't destroy it. The braconid adult has stung and paralyzed the host and inserted its eggs on to its back. The larvae then proceed to chew up and demolish the host insect. Another helpful wasp, the *Tiphia* wasp, is a parasite of the Japanese beetle, the *Ichneumon* wasp is a borer killer.
Trichogramma wasp	Minute, yellowish body with brownish abdomen.	Parasitizes over 200 species of insects by laying up to 25 eggs in 1 host egg. Host eggs then turn black.

Good Guy	Description	Benefit
Pollinators		
Honey Bees	Familiar sight in most gardens. Brownish yellow, striped, with darker thorax. Smaller and more slender than bumblebees (which are less efficient pollinators).	Probably the best-known pollinator of garden flowers, including those of vegetables, herbs and fruits.
Syrphid fly (Hover fly)	Four winged fly—adults have abdomens banded with black and yellow stripes.	Although most flies suffer from a bad reputation, the syrphid fly does not. It looks and behaves more like a bee and "hovers" (hence its nickname) among flowers, acting as a pollinator like the honey bee, while sipping nectar and gathering pollen. The white egg larvae of this fly feed on scale insects or aphids, sucking out their bodily contents.
Carnivores		
Ladybug (Ladybird beetle)	Adult ladybug is a fat oval ¼″ long; most common ones are shiny tan or orange red with black spots, although there are about 350 species of these beetles found throughout the world.	Famous for their role in pest control as predatory beetles; can eat 40 aphids an hour.
Larvae	Their larvae are elongated, tapered with somewhat warty surface. They are wingless creatures that do not resemble their parents at all. They are about $1/_{16}$″ in size, have six legs and are different colors; grayish, orange or blue.	The ladybug larvae have insatiable appetites; they are like little vacuum cleaners.
Lacewing (adult)	Fragile gauzy wings and golden eyes. Yellow green color. Fragile, hairlike antennae; long, narrow, slender tapering body. Sickle-shaped jaws. ⅜″ long, hair, grayish brown larvae.	Useful as an indicator that their larvae are probably present.
Larvae (Doodle-bug, Aphid-Lion, Ant-Lion)		Lacewing larvae are adept predators that feed on aphids, mealybugs, scales, thrips, mites

Good Guy	Description	Benefit
		and other insects. They have earned the title of "aphid-lion" for their ability to consume up to 100 aphids per day. Larvae of other lacewing species build conical shaped pits, usually in dry sandy places, and wait in the bottom for insects to tumble in and be consumed.
Assassin bugs	Dark-hued, some spotted or banded with red. Oblong in shape (½″ long) with narrow heads and long legs like spiders, for which they are sometimes mistaken. Count their legs; bugs have six—spiders have eight.	Earned their name from the way in which they attack and stab their victims, inject them with liquids that dissolve their insides and then proceed to suck them dry. Their prey varies; wasps, caterpillars, grasshoppers—even some other good guys, e.g., bees, praying mantises—anything. Don't handle them—they may also inflict a painful bite if humans provoke them.

alone; nature centers, feed and grain outlets, hardware stores, supermarkets and mail-order suppliers, in a combined estimate compiled by the Stanford Seed Company, figured that 17 million pounds of seed were sold in 1982 alone.

The Four-Footed Connoisseurs

As much as you may love animals, it's sometimes important to get the message across to those four-legged gate crashers that they are not always welcome in the garden. Keeping your garden off limits to the free-loading *al fresco* diners can be a year-round frustration for friends of animals who wish them no harm, but simply prefer that they would stick to eating wild food.

Wildlife habitats are regularly destroyed as building and land development projects expand in ever-widening circles from metropolitan regions. As we invade their territory, suddenly the animals appear closer to where *we* live. To some extent, we can coexist in densely populated areas that were once their private wild domain. But there are greater pressures for their survival under these conditions and they must move closer to man in order to survive.

When winters are hard, natural food supplies dwindle rapidly, and wild animals may either die of starvation or browse and forage nearer to home gardens, or they may do both. In some years, losses of plant life, particularly in fruit orchards, are staggering. After a couple of years of seeing the fruit trees gnawed and the garden invaded, the gardener may start to feel that the deer, rabbits, raccoons, squirrels and mice are always lurking someplace unseen, watching for their chance to nibble at everything in sight.

Although no measure is completely foolproof, there are several ways to outwit these nightly raiders and send the wildlife elsewhere for their dinners. Knowing who or what is likely to stop by for a garden raid, and what its dining preferences are, is the first step in pest-proofing. Although we never object to sharing a bit of our garden with hungry animals, we do balk at the idea of their getting it all. So when it becomes clear that everything is eating your garden but you, it is time to experiment with some strategies to outwit this inventive lot. None of the remedies suggested here for waging this "cold war" involve chemicals or killing—it just is not our way. The repellents described here are actually more in the nature barriers, which are either physical, visual, olfactory or auditory. All of them are also easy to prepare or buy, and have been used by fellow gardeners over the years. Here is our list.

Sound, Visual and Physical Barriers

A good fence, partially buried underground, is the best device for keeping out all furry animals (see below for more information). Some gardeners, however, hate the look of a fence and consider it a prison or a barrier between them and nature. For them, there are other remedies.

Thorny branches placed in front of mole tunnels may force the moles to abandon their homes. Moles don't like getting cuts and bruises since they bleed heavily. One gardening friend suggested inducing diarrhea by dropping laxative pills down into their burrows, forcing them to scurry away elsewhere!

Raid the local toy store for plastic pinwheels and stick them into the ground. It may or may not work for you (reports are mixed), but it will certainly give the garden a festive atmosphere. In fact, some gardeners favor stringing up anything that dangles and moves in the wind, or that shines and catches reflective light.

Bury three long-necked empty bottles of different sizes in a row between or surrounding your vegetables, leaving two inches at the top exposed. Wind blowing over the openings creates weird underground sounds that are said to frighten moles and rabbits. Ring the bottle tops with reflective paint or tape so two-legged creatures don't stumble over them.

Build a scarecrow. They don't always frighten anything or anyone but they are another "oldtime remedy" that gardeners still love to use.

Toy rubber snakes or several old pieces of garden hose placed among the plants to look like snakes have been known to scare animals away.

A family cat or dog sometimes works, depending upon the character of the animal. If your dog will sleep through anything and doesn't like to hunt, don't count on it to keep the critters out of your garden.

A transistor radio in a plastic bag (in case of rain) tuned in to a talkative all night disc jockey (low volume preferred at night) will either scare the animals away, or at least give them music to dance to.

Fences

The most commonly used and most effective method of keeping all animal pests out of your garden is to put up a fence. Although initially expensive, a good fence seems to be the most acceptable solution for most gardens in the long run. Your choice of fencing materials will depend upon your personal needs: the type of animals you want to keep out, the size of the plot to be enclosed and, of course, your budget.

Low-Voltage Electric Fences: An electric fence will keep out all of the nimble nuisance animals. If they are a major problem in your area, a low-voltage electric fence will control them most effectively, although it is also the most expensive kind of fence to buy and set up. The fence is hooked up to a controller that is either connected to house current or powered by a battery. The animal receives a small shock on contact that makes it wary about returning. But the low voltage is not enough to harm the animal. To be effective, the wires should be placed at intervals 3 inches, 8 inches and 30 inches from the ground, and wound around ceramic insulators mounted on metal or fiberglass fence posts. Note: This type of fence is not recommended for anyone wearing a pacemaker or where there are small children.

Nylon Mesh and Plastic Pipe Fence: Using 1-inch plastic pipe, it is easy to build a framework around any size raised bed. Tie fishing weights to anchor a length of nylon mesh and drape it over the beds. Adjust the height of the pipe structure depending upon how tall the vegetables are that are growing. This simple fence is effective against birds, deer and rabbits.

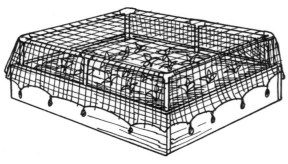

To cover a single bed, attach a framework of plastic pipe to the wood frame enclosing the bed and cover the pipe with a piece of netting. Use fishing weights to hold down the edges of the netting and keep it in place.

Screenhouse Structure: A totally enclosed screenhouse with an entry door is another structure that can be built. Use posts 8½ feet high and make the framework of pine 2 by 4s in whatever length you need to enclose the entire garden, including the top. A discarded screen door with a hook and eye fastener makes the entry way. Screening or chicken wire or nylon mesh or netting can be attached

If your garden is small and your animal problems are severe, you can enclose the whole garden in a screenhouse.

to the framework to enclose the garden.

Bent Wire Half Hoops and Petticoat Fabric: Bend pieces of stiff wire to make a support to cover small vegetable patches, pockets, or container plants. Cover the wire hoops with stiff nylon petticoat fabric, which can be purchased by the yard in shops selling sewing supplies and yard goods. Secure the fabric to the ground with large-size hair pins to hold it in place.

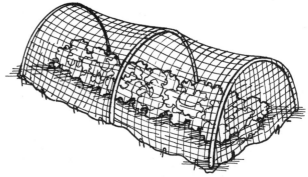

To cover a row or just a few plants, stretch a length of netting over hoops formed from pieces of heavy wire (coat hangers work fine).

Two Special Fences: Raccoons—those masked marauders—require a specially structured barrier in order to be kept out of the garden, and you can build one easily. Insert 2½-foot-long posts into the ground around the garden, 1 foot deep and bent outward at about a 30 degree angle. Fasten some chicken wire around the bottom of the posts, leaving the top half of the chicken wire unfastened. As the raccoon climbs the chicken wire covering, its body weight will pull the unfastened part of the fence over on top of it, causing the animal to drop to the ground.

For woodchucks you will need a 2-foot-high wire mesh fence that goes 1 foot underground and then curves out away from the fence for another foot. It is the most difficult kind of fence to build, but an ordinary fence will not keep out woodchucks.

Scent and Taste Repellents

It was the late entertainer Jimmy Durante who always said, "Nobody knows, but the nose knows." He could have said the same thing of animals. Most are extremely sensitive to scents and tastes, particularly unpleasant ones. The following are all stop-gap repellent measures that you can try:

Deer have been repelled by a whole range of tactics including hanging nylon mesh bags full of dirty human hair, dried blood, mothballs, or rotten eggs. The bags are hung from fruit trees, or left on the ground outside the garden patch.

One gardener suggests lion dung (the big cats are the natural predators of the deer family, and our wild deer supposedly retain a vestigial instinct that warns them away from the scent). So make friends with a circus trainer or zookeeper if you want to try this exotic approach.

The Weyerhaeuser Company Research Department has developed a deer repellent derived from rotten eggs; it is now available at some nurseries to use on fruit trees and bushes and may be worth investigating. The product is sold as MCK Big Game Repellent (can be ordered from Shemin Nurseries, 1081 King St., Greenwich, CT 06830) or as Deer-Away (available from Deer-Away, 712 Fifteenth Ave., Minneapolis, MN 55413). More information about this deer repellent can be found in *Control of Wildlife Damage in Homes and Gardens* by James W. Caslick and Daniel Decker. (Available for $2.50 from Distribution Center, 7 Research Park, Cornell University, Ithaca, NY 14850. It's bulletin #176.)

Dried blood meal sprinkled around plants is supposed to keep away rabbits and deer. It must be reapplied after rain. It is also a high-nitrogen fertilizer, so use it only around leafy greens.

For rabbits, plant a "trap-crop" border of soybeans around the perimeter of the garden. The idea is to give the rabbits plenty of soybeans to eat (it seems to be a favorite food) so they won't venture further into the garden.

Interplant with marigolds, onions or dusty miller. Bunnies hate the smell and taste of these plants.

Soak a thick rope, pieces of absorbent felt or rags in creosote, and hang them around the outside of the garden to repel deer.

Mothballs scattered around are also used to repel rabbits, but I have seen some young rabbits develop a taste for them and nibble them with obvious relish.

There are numerous sprays you can concoct at home to keep deer, rabbits and raccoons out of ripening corn and squirrels out of city gardens. These sprays should help discourage everything from aphids to rabbits.

Home-Brewed Garlic Hot Pepper Stay Away Spray: In an electric blender put a whole head of garlic (peel off outermost skin, but it is not necessary to peel individual cloves). Quarter an unpeeled onion and add it. Then add 2 tablespoons of cayenne pepper and 2 to 3 cups of water. Puree together and mix with 1 gallon of water in a pail and let stand overnight. Strain the mixture through a strainer lined with dampened cheesecloth or an old nylon stocking, to remove any debris that would clog a sprayer. Then add 1 tablespoon of a mild soap powder, like Ivory Snow, to give the mixture sticking power. Use with a portable hand-sprayer and renew after each rain. Do not use this spray on vegetables you cook without peeling (such as beans) since there may be a taste residue. Vegetables should all be washed off thoroughly before using.

Liver Spray Rabbit Repellent: Steep ¼ pound of fresh beef liver cut into chunks in 1 gallon of hot water for 1 hour. Strain the liquid and spray with a hand sprayer. The North American Fruit Explorers recommend spraying this concoction on fruit trees and brambles to repel rabbits. You can also just rub a piece of liver on the tree trunks.

Slug Nutty

At the top of my list of most-hated garden pests, perhaps because of their visibility, the obvious damage they cause and their obnoxious demeanor, are slugs. No matter how benevolent I may feel toward the creatures of the earth, I find it hard to love these hermaphroditic gastropods, these slimy, shell-less mollusks. I have waged a personal war against slugs that may rival the Hundred Years' War in Europe. Slugs thrive in moisture, and hide in dank, dark places during the day. You can find them under rocks and boards, under thick vegetation, clustered under bricks and paving stones. In the evening or on dark days they sneak out, sliding about 8 inches a minute on a flat, muscular organ called a foot, aided by a trail of mucusy slime that they secrete. When you see this trail during the day when it is dry and it becomes shiny white,

beware. It means that slugs are lurking in the garden, voraciously consuming 30 to 40 times their own weight daily of the herbs, flowers and vegetables you have so lovingly planted.

Over the years I have tried lots of different methods of slug destruction. The ones listed below have all worked for me. I have to admit, with only the smallest twinge of guilt, that slugs are one of the few creatures (along with my other pet peeves, squash vine borers and mosquitoes) whose immediate demise gives me great pleasure.

At dusk, set out shallow cans (from tuna or cat food) sunk into the ground up their rims, and fill the cans with either stale beer or sourdough bread starter. (To make sourdough starter, mix ½ cup of flour with 1 teaspoon yeast and 4 cups of warm water. Let stand for several days in a warm place before filling cans to the brim.) Slugs are attracted to the fermentation, fall into the can and drown in the brew.

The direct salt-shaker attack is another method. Slugs shrivel when you sprinkle salt on them, and can be picked up with tweezers and dropped into a jar of water with kerosene floated on top.

Slices of fresh cucumber, cabbage or lettuce leaves, or citrus skins left on top of the soil make good hiding places for slugs during the day. At dusk lift up the vegetables and shake off the slugs into a can of coarse Kosher-style salt.

If you just want to keep slugs away and not necessarily kill them, design your garden with a 2-foot path around the outside, made of rough-surfaced materials such as cinders or crushed seashells or rocks. Snails do not like to cross rough textures. Crushed eggshells help, too, in smaller gardens.

I have also tried sprinkling sawdust, wood ashes, hydrated lime, tobacco dust and coarse sand around my plants. Sometimes everything works, sometimes it's only me who works.

Some Special Tips on Fighting Squash-Vine Borers

An exasperated young school teacher I knew long ago, who taught in an ethnically mixed grade school, once exclaimed at the end of a trying day that she was really very democratic; she hated *all* her pupils equally. I feel similarly democratic about squash-vine borers and slugs—I hate them *both* equally. Perhaps since the first specialty cookbook I wrote dealt with the many ways of cooking squash, borers are a personal nemesis of mine.

Borers also seem to be very democratic—they eat all kinds of squash, cucumbers, melons and pumpkins. The borers are the larvae of a small, clear-winged moth that has a bright red underbelly. The moth lays eggs on the host plant and they hatch into larvae. The larvae bore into the vine stems near ground level where they feed on the succulent inner tissues, causing the plant above to wilt almost overnight, and leaving greenish masses of frass around the stem holes. The borers themselves look like inch-long wrinkled white caterpillars with brown heads.

There are two methods you can successfully use to save your vine crops (especially if you are a weekend gardener who is not always around to notice the first signs of damage). One is to bypass the borer problem by planting two crops, one in spring just after the last frost and the other later in midsummer. One crop may be sacrificed to the borers, but the next one should produce well. The other method is to get rid of borers once you have them; use a razor blade to slit the stems they're hiding in just below the soil line and remove the white borer with tweezers. Heap the earth back in a mound around the stem to cover it.

A Sampling of Organic-Base Pesticides

When all else fails, there are tougher organic solutions. Several insecticides are avail-

A simple hand-held sprayer like this one is easy to operate and can be used for homemade organic sprays.

able that are not considered hazardous to wildlife, birds, kids or dogs, and that don't cause a residual buildup in the environment. Some of these pesticides are derived from plants. Among those most widely available from garden supply shops and seed catalogs are:

Pyrethrum. Derived from the dried white flower heads of a member of the chrysanthemum family, pyrethrum controls dozens of fruit and vegetable pests including aphids, spider mites, leaf mines, mealybugs and thrips. It is nontoxic to mammals, bees and ladybugs.

Rotenone. An extract from tropical leguminous plants, this is a broad-spectrum organic insect killer with low toxicity to warm-blooded animals. However, it is harmful to fish and will also kill some of the garden allies, including bees. Use it selectively and carefully against cabbage worms, bean beetles, leaf miners, aphids and mealybugs, and don't allow the wind to carry it toward any body of water where fish live.

Bacillus thuringiensis. This powder can be used against any worm or leaf-chewing

Several Ugly Plant Diseases

Pathogen	Vegetables Usually Affected	Identifying Symptoms
Bacteria		
Bacterial Wilt	Cucumbers, melons, squash.	Usually spread by cucumber beetles. Wilting and drying of leaves, vine, runners, or the entire plant.
Bacterial Blight	Peas, beans.	During wet weather, water spots develop and enlarge on pods, leaves and stems. Spots dry up in dry weather.
Bacterial Soft Rot	Primarily lettuce, cabbage, onions; also other fruits and vegetables.	Rapid change within 3-5 days after small rot spots appear. Spots enlarge and become soft and watery.
Scab	Beets, potatoes.	Raised or pitted corky rough spots on roots or tubers which enlarge as disease spreads.
Fungi		
Anthracnose	Lima beans, peas, snap beans.	Sunken, dark brown lesions develop on pods. May also affect underside of leaves and stems and exude a pinkish liquid.
Black Rot	Sweet potatoes, winter squash, pumpkins, cabbage.	Starts as a pale-colored, irregular-shaped spot which turns black. The flesh under the rind of the fruit also rots.
Club Root	Cabbage, cauliflower and most other crops of the brassica family.	Parts above ground wilt, particularly during hot days. Leaves are pale, growth stunted. Roots enlarge and form galls or clubs. Spores are persistent and may remain dormant in soil for many years.
Downy Mildew	Grapes, cucumbers, lettuce, onions, melons.	Especially in wet humid weather, upper surface yellows and undersurface has a white furry growth. Leaves often turn brown.
Powdery Mildew	Squash, cucumbers, many melons, beans.	Thrives in wet conditions. Powdery white patches on leaves and stems.
Early Blight	Tomatoes, potatoes.	Brown spots first appear and form concentric rings on leaf like a target. Infected spots spread and merge and at times entire plant is defoliated.
Late Blight	Potatoes, tomatoes.	Spreads in cool damp weather. Dark irregular spots on leaves; light mold on leaf undersurface.
Fusarium and Verticillium Wilt	Tomatoes, peppers, vine crops, potatoes, eggplants.	During heat of day, leaves curl up and wilt—although they recover at night. Later, plant wilts and dies. Brown discoloration.

Preventive Measures

The bacterium overwinters in cucumber beetles, which enter the plant. Control early in the season with rotenone.

Rotate crops; avoid working amid wet foliage, which can cause disease to spread; do not use homegrown seed, which can harbor the bacteria. Destroy crop residues—do not compost.

Well-drained soil and proper air circulation between plants. Destroy infected plants and remove crop debris.

More of a problem in sandy alkaline soils. Do not add lime, wood ash or manures where potatoes will grow. Dig up and destroy tubers.

Rotate crops; destroy diseased plants. Plant disease-resistant varieties.

Rotate crops; destroy diseased plants.

Lime the soil to achieve more alkaline (over 7.2 pH) balance where brassicas grow. Practice long-term rotation.

Plant disease-resistant varieties, rotate crops, destroy diseased plants.

Plant disease-resistant varieties, try not to water overhead, destroy diseased plants.

Since seedlings are usually affected, plant only healthy varieties. Rotate crops, destroy diseased plants.

Same as above.

Plant only varieties having the initials "VF" after their names—these varieties are resistant to both diseases. Destroy infected plants at end of season.

caterpillar or other insect that passes through a chrysalis stage (from caterpillar to moth). This bacterial killer works by paralyzing the digestive systems of worms. It is sold commercially as Dipel or Thuricide.

Quassia. A product derived from the wood chips of a South American tree, quassia can be made into a harmless spray. The base of the spray, quassia chips, is available at pharmacies (One source is Kiehl's Pharmacy, 109 Third Ave., New York, NY 10003; cost is $4.50 per quarter pound.) To prepare, use 1 gallon of water and 2 ounces of quassia. Boil for 2 hours and strain through a nylon stocking. Add 1 tablespoon of mild liquid dishwashing soap and dilute with 5 parts of water before using. Wash vegetables thoroughly before eating if you use this spray. Although it won't kill friendly ladybugs or harm warm-blooded beings, it makes the vegetables taste bitter.

Safer Agro-Chem's Insecticidal Soap. A fairly new product that is harmless to people and pets, this soap spray effectively controls whiteflies, mealybugs, aphids and many other pests. It has been cleared by the Environmental Protection Agency for use on edible crops and has no residual effect. However, frequent applications, at weekly intervals, are necessary to keep down populations of rapidly reproductive insects such as those listed above.

Oil sprays. Dormant oil sprays have long been used on fruit trees to control a host of chewing and sucking insects. Dormant oil must be sprayed on trees before the buds open, and should contain 97% petroleum oil and no toxic chemicals such as arsenate of lead. Newer oil sprays developed especially for horticultural use are also available, and are reported to work better than dormant oil sprays. The newer sprays are less viscous and will not clog leaf pores, and can be used when trees are in full leaf.

Pathogen	Vegetables Usually Affected	Identifying Symptoms
Smut	Corn, onions.	Small, white and green galls form on ears, stalks, leaves, and tassels, then break open to release more fungus spores. Stunted and withered plants a problem in dry warm areas.
Viruses		
Mosaic disease	Peppers, cucumbers, corn; most plants.	Yellow and green mottled leaf pattern. Plants are stunted with light splotches and a bumpy surface.
Yellows (mycoplasmas)	Beets, cabbage, carrots, lettuce, spinach.	Yellowing of new leaves, curling; stunted growth; lettuce heads prematurely; carrots become hairy.

Horticultural oil sprays are available at most garden centers under various names. Read the labels to make sure the one you choose contains no toxic insecticides or fungicides.

I would be remiss not to mention a few tips for using these sprays correctly and carefully:

Read the instructions and follow them carefully.

Water the garden well before you spray.

Spray on a calm day, not when it's windy, to avoid drifting.

It's best to spray in the evening when most insects are at home and munching on your plants (except for our friend the bee, who is most active in the morning and by evening has safely returned to the hive).

For small balcony or terrace gardens, a quart-size, hand-held, trigger-topped plastic sprayer is sufficient.

For larger backyards, or rooftops, a hand-held metal slide type sprayer is more efficient (see illustration on page 223).

Thoroughly clean spray equipment and yourself after spraying.

Store insecticides, even organic ones, on a high shelf or in a securely locked cabinet, away from children and pets.

Remember, more than 95% of our insect pests are controlled by natural means such as the weather, companion plants and beneficial insects, predators, or mechanical controls such as lures or traps. Sometimes nature is slower than we would like it to be and there are some insect problems that may get out of hand. Only after exhausting all the methods of insect management outlined on page 207 should you resort to even the most harmless of organic sprays. They should be your last line of defense.

About Diseases and Disorders

No matter how long you may garden, you will probably never see all the vegetable pests, diseases and disorders that exist. My intention in this chapter has certainly not been to discourage your gardening efforts. On the contrary, my purpose is to take the worry out of problems that you notice but can't identify, and to provide you with the ability

Preventive Measures

Use resistant hybrids. Cut and destroy infected plants before galls burst open. Rotate crops.

Use disease-resistant varieties, control aphids which spread the disease.

Transmitted by insects, usually aphids or leaf hoppers. Keep area weed-free so it will not harbor insect carriers; rotate crops; do not plant susceptible crops near each other; use resistant varieties (of cabbage); destroy infected plants.

to deal with and correct pest and disease problems when they do arise.

Ugly to look at, plant diseases have ugly names to match: rot, scab, smut, wilt, spot, blotch. Plant pathogens are similar to the fungi, viruses and bacteria which affect man. They are divided into three main groups. Bacteria are microscopic organisms which enter a plant through injured tissues or other openings. Diseases caused by bacteria include bacterial wilts and blights, soft rot and scab. Fungi are the largest cause of plant disease. Fungi reproduce by spores, and they cause mildews, wilts, rusts, cankers and leaf spots. Viruses, the third major cause of disease, multiply by entering the plant or being injected by insects, rather than through direct penetration. Common virus diseases include mosaic disease, ring spot and "the yellows." No control agents known at the present time will cure viruses in a diseased plant. The only real defense is to take preventive measures.

In fact, the best way for organic gardeners to cope with all sorts of disease problems can be summed up in a single word: prevention. The nice thing is that the odds are in your favor when you practice "preventive medicine"

in your garden. Plant disease can strike whenever three key elements are present:

The disease-causing agent (bacteria, mold spores, etc.) must be harbored in the soil, waiting for a suitable host crop.

A host crop that is susceptible to the disease must be growing in the garden.

The right combination of weather conditions must exist for the disease to assert itself. High humidity, very high or low temperature and lack of air circulation can often favor the development of plant disease.

Plant disorders are very similar problems that you may also have to deal with. Unlike plant diseases, which are caused by living organisms that are transmitted from one plant to another, a plant disorder is usually caused by unfavorable growing conditions and environmental influences. Disorders may look like diseases if similar symptoms are present, but most disorders can usually be corrected by a proper balance of nutrients and adjustment of the soil for better drainage, or by providing more sun, wind or frost protection in the growing environment (the microclimate).

A preventive program of good gardening practices will help to keep both diseases and disorders out of your garden, so follow these few golden rules to stay out of trouble:

Prepare the soil properly. Provide enough compost or other organic matter to encourage healthy, vigorous growth and good nutrient balance. Remember, the nutrient potassium helps to make plants resistant to disease by conditioning the whole plant. Good drainage is also essential for healthy plants.

Plant disease-resistant varieties of seeds and transplants. Choose carefully from the seed catalogs.

Plant only healthy seedlings. Spindly, weak transplants are more vulnerable to disease than are sturdy, stocky young plants.

Water correctly. Many diseases enter plants when the foliage is wet, and they need wet conditions to spread. Watering early in the day is best, no matter if you're watering from overhead or at ground level, because it allows plants to dry off before nightfall.

Don't work in the garden when it's wet. You could easily spread a developing disease as you move from plant to plant. Beans and vine crops in particular should never be handled when wet.

Practice good garden hygiene. Overall cleanliness, destroying diseased plants promptly and cleaning up garden debris regularly gets rid of the hiding places where insects and disease pathogens can overwinter.

Keep tools clean. Sterilize garden tools with fire to disinfect them if you suspect that they were used on diseased plants.

Rotate your crops. Soil troubles and nutrient deficiencies build up if you grow the same crop year after year in the same area. Rotation prevents disease from gaining a foothold. Slight damage one year may be devastating the following year if the same host plant is there. Disease agents die off when they are deprived of their hosts.

Finally, you should make it a point to learn as much as you can about plant diseases. Learn how to identify them and become familiar with the ailments that are common in your area. The chart Several Ugly Plant Diseases is a beginner's guide to identifying some common garden maladies. Above all, when you do notice signs of disease in any of your plants, take action quickly, before the problem has a chance to spread.

Making the Season Last Longer

The sun is still one of the best things in life that remains free, and sun power can be harnessed to stretch the growing season at both ends—weeks before the first frost in fall and weeks after the last one in spring. There are several simple, practical and effective ways to extend the growing season: mulches, cloches and other protective devices, cold frames and, of course, greenhouses. Essentially, they are all used to provide plants with a warm, protected environment that lets in the sun's light and warmth but keeps out cold winds. Since all these season-extending methods achieve their aims in slightly different ways, I'll give you a rundown of their possibilities to make it easier for you to choose what's best for your garden. The subject of greenhouses is complicated and beyond the scope of this book, so our discussion here will be limited to mulches, cloches and covers, and cold frames.

Mulches As Season-Stretchers

Although mulches are used primarily during the growing season to keep weeds down and to help the soil stay cool and moist, some mulches offer multiple blessings. There are mulches that absorb heat and transmit it to the soil underneath, and other mulches that collect heat and radiate it to plants growing nearby. These are the sorts of mulches that you can use to get an earlier start in your spring garden and to prolong the life of your fall garden.

Dark-hued, flat-surfaced stones are perhaps the most primitive and least costly sun collectors you can use as a mulch. They are laid faceup, usually on a bed of hay or seaweed, around and between plants and rows where they will absorb heat from the sun during the day and radiate it back at night to the plants around them. A couple of drawbacks to this kind of mulch are that stones are heavy and are not always available, depending on your local terrain.

Inventive gardeners have employed a principle used in greenhouses for heat collectors— that of storing heat in black containers full of water. These devices also release heat slowly at night, and some gardeners lay these collectors all over their gardens to take the place of stone mulch. All sorts of things have been used—garbage cans painted black and filled with water, plastic water jugs or milk jugs filled with water tinted black with India ink, old black automobile and truck tires filled with water (tires can also be used as plant containers when you need additional soil heat). A garden full of jugs or tires may *look* a little strange, but if it lets you have a few extra weeks to enjoy your fresh garden produce, the aesthetic sacrifice is worth it, since it's only a temporary measure.

Black plastic is another popular mulch which absorbs the sun's heat and transmits the heat to surrounding vegetables. It has the added advantage of smothering weeds, too. Black plastic is a favorite mulch with many New England gardeners who find that it extends their short growing season and increases their yields of warm-season vegetables such as tomatoes, eggplant and peppers. Sheets of plastic should be laid between rows and around plants at the end of the growing season when nights are cool and frost begins to threaten. Black plastic does heat the soil and accelerate plant growth at the end of a season, but it is not advisable for use in warm weather, because it could heat the soil *too* much and harm plant roots.

Clear plastic is a good mulch to use in early spring, to get your soil warmed up for early crops. Clear plastic lets sunlight penetrate to the ground below, and provides two to three times more heat to the soil than does black plastic. It can be used before any crops are planted, to destroy pathogens that may have wintered over in the soil, and the warmth it provides will give seedlings that needed headstart, too. Of course, it also gives a headstart to the weeds. Although clear plastic can be used as a mulch and soil warmer, it is more often used by gardeners to improvise structures and protective devices that act in much the same way as the more elaborate and more costly greenhouse does.

Cloches, Covers and Other Plant Protectors

At its simplest level, extending the growing season and protecting plants from damage by the elements, birds or insects means merely placing some sort of protective cover over an individual plant, a row or block of plants, or even an entire garden bed. These devices to moderate the climate give you the advantage of allowing transplants or seeds to be set outdoors several weeks earlier than normal in spring (as much as four to six weeks before the last frost, when temperatures would not normally support growth) and lets your garden keep producing as much as eight weeks after the first fall frost.

In essence any plastic-covered structure, whether it takes the form of a hot cap, cloche, tunnel or cold frame can be considered a sort of minigreenhouse. All these devices trap warm air and hold it around plants when the outside air is cold.

The protectors range from the most inexpensive devices you construct yourself (from materials you have on hand or recreate out of recycled objects) to more costly and sophisticated types of cloches like those designed by Leandre Poisson, a noted solar engineer in New Hampshire. Poisson has designed season extenders made of semirigid, fiberglass-reinforced plastic that was developed for use in solar collectors.

The cheapest kind of protective devices you can buy ready-made are hot caps made of heavy waxed paper. But the most fun way to protect your garden—and the cheapest of all—is to adapt materials you find or have available into suitable protective devices.

The traditional cloches that originated in French market gardens and in England were glass bell jars that were and are still used to cover individual plants. Today the term "cloche" is often used to refer to any protective covering that is transparent. And in fact, plastic is most often used by gardeners today. Plastic cloches are easier to handle and store, they don't break, and they weigh less than glass.

A few words are in order here about the types of plastics available and how to use them as covers. There are two basic kinds of plastic available, rigid sheets such as Fiberglass or Plexiglas and flexible sheeting that

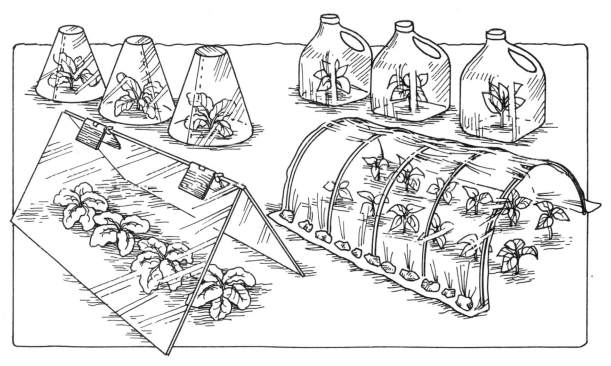

Some devices to protect late crops from cold fall weather include (clockwise from front) a tunnel of plastic stretched over wire hoops to cover a row (weigh down the edges of the plastic with stones), a cloche made of two pieces of glass or Plexiglas held together with hinged clips, translucent wax paper cones for individual plants and plastic milk jugs with the bottoms removed.

comes in rolls, such as polyethylene. My favorite is the fairly new wire-reinforced, ultraviolet-stabilized polyethylene which is 5 mils thick. The plastic is laminated to a wire grid for additional strength. This sturdy plastic can be cut with scissors and formed into any kind of shape. You can even use as a top for a cold frame. The material is called Key-Lite and can be ordered through Mellinger's catalog, or purchased at garden centers. (See the list of tool suppliers at the back of Chapter 7 for Mellinger's address.)

When you're shopping for plastic you'll choose, basically, between rigid and flexible materials. The rigid plastics are more expensive, but they are windproof and rainproof, and they last longer. On the other hand, polyethylene and other flexible soft plastic sheetings are less costly but can be wind damaged. They don't hold up as well, but they are easy to work with and can be stretched to fit any particular frame.

The plastic can be supported by wire mesh fencing, wood of all kinds, or wire coat hangers bent into various shapes. Some resourceful gardeners have even tried a combination of black plastic mulch, held down with wire mesh, and a clear plastic canopy in the hope of both collecting and storing heat. The clear plastic also protects plants from wind and birds. Your protective devices can be cones, jars or bottles, A-frames, or tunnels.

Some devices are used solely for sun and wind protection and these can be made of opaque material. There are even some models which can cover and enclose an entire raised bed. (See the illustration on the next page for some ideas.)

To use your cloches in spring, set them in place ten days before planting, to let the soil warm up. When the young plants are up, leave the cloches in place until the plant leaves touch the sides. It's important to provide ventilation, though, or remove the cloches during the warmest part of the day to prevent too much heat buildup. Even at this time of year, the sun is strong enough to "cook" tender seedlings in an unventilated plastic cover.

Cold Frames

The simplest cold frame is merely a bottomless box that rests on the earth and is provided with a removable transparent top. Experienced gardeners consider a cold frame an indispensable aid, for it is designed to capture the sun's warming rays and offer protection from unfavorable weather conditions. Cold frames work on the principle of storing heat and taking warmth from surrounding structures, thus creating a "greenhouse" effect. Sunlight streams through the transparent cover by day and its warmth is trapped or absorbed inside, making the interior of the cold frame significantly warmer than the air outside it. Since the cold frame gets all its heat from the sun, it has to be angled so its glass or plastic cover faces south, to get the maximum exposure to sunlight.

During a very sunny day, the lid must be propped open a few inches for ventilation, since the heat buildup within can be damaging to the tender plants. By late afternoon, you will have to close the top to trap the heat for nighttime warmth. In really cold weather, cover the cold frame at night with a blanket or rug for additional insulation. If you are not home during the day to open and close the cold frame whenever it is necessary, then it may pay you to invest in an automatic solar-powered vent controller, which raises or lowers the top for the cold frame as needed. The top of your cold frame must weigh under 30 pounds for the lifting force to operate properly. It adjusts to open the frame when the temperature reaches between 60° and 80°F. A vent controller called Solarvent is available through Mellinger's catalog, and Burpee sells a kit for building your own cold frame with automatic vent.

Like every gardening aid available, cold frames range from the costly solar pod, with an automatically controlled venting system—the Rolls Royce of cold frames—to the kind that you can improvise out of found objects and a bit of construction, even if you are a dropout from the "smashed-thumb" school of carpentry. Here are some suggestions on how to build a simple cold frame of your own.

Half-inch exterior plywood or scrap lumber can be used for the base, but first give the wood a coat of protective Cuprinol to keep it from rotting. If you have an old storm window that you no longer need, then your cold frame is half completed. Simply measure the window and build a wooden box to fit it. There are only a few general things to consider when planning a cold frame.

For the cover, you can use glass or rigid plastic sheeting. You can also use discarded old windows from salvage yards or house wrecking companies. Clear acrylic can also be used, and is usually sold in precut sheets, and fiberglass is available either flat or corrugated in 2, 4 and 6-foot widths. Flexible plastic film (6 mil) will probably have to be replaced annually, but it is the least expensive to use. If you do use plastic film, stretch one sheet over the frame for the cover and another sheet under the frame to create a 1-inch air space between the layers for better

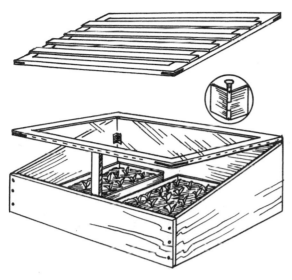

Make a simple collapsible cold frame or holding bed for late summer transplants from boards attached at the corners with pin hinges. Pins are removable. Interchangeable tops can be made from artist's canvas stretchers.

insulation. If you want to use your cold frame as a nursery during the summer when the weather is hot, replace the glass or plastic top with a cover made of window screening or small-gauge wire mesh, to let in plenty of air.

You can even make a top frame from the wooden canvas stretchers used by artists (if you hate carpentry as I do). These stretchers have notches and slots in the corners, and you put them together without nails or glue. Just buy some stretchers that are in proportion to the top of your cold frame (they come

in many sizes), and then stretch and staple cheesecloth or nylon mesh over the frame for summertime use, or nail some lath strips or shade cloth over it for sun protection, or staple plastic over it for cold-weather use. Having several interchangeable tops allows you to use your cold frame more frequently than only at the beginning and end of the season. The top can be quickly attached or replaced if you use hinges with a removable center pin. A cold frame can be used in the following ways at various times of the year:

To harden off young seedlings for outdoor transplants, and to protect them from wind and sudden frosts.

To start seeds in late summer for fall crop transplants.

To keep seedlings coming along during the growing season and to serve as a holding bed for a continuous supply of transplants for succession crops and for filling empty spots in the garden.

To grow some hardy winter salad greens and herbs and harvest them right from the cold frame, even in winter.

In urban areas, a cold frame can also offer protection from birds, and from cat and dog nuisances, too.

One last bit of advice for building your cold frame: a Rodale Press book, *Build It Better Yourself* has loads of ideas for building cold frames. There's even one made of cinder blocks for those who want to avoid carpentry completely. You might investigate this book at your local library.

Epilogue

"Although I am an old man, I am but a young gardener."
—Thomas Jefferson

No matter how detailed written instructions may be, no matter how vividly you may paint a descriptive picture, no matter how you demonstrate, a beginner cannot learn to swim on dry land. The real lessons begin only when that first plunge is taken into the water. Then, as a teacher, you can only walk along the side of the pool and gently call out a hint here and there—the actual swimming can only be done by the person in the water.

So it is, too, with even the most knowledgeable gardeners and the most informative gardening books. Just as Thomas Jefferson said, in spite of years of experience I, too, am still learning. I can only hope that with the gentle encouragement in this book, you will "take the plunge" and use some of the ideas and approaches offered here for your own garden. Like the swimming coach, I can only call out advice from the sidelines and hope that your gardening efforts will be newly inspired.

In the end it's all up to you. You have to feel the dark, warm, fragrant earth in your own two hands and under your own two feet. You have to experience the struggle of growing plants through all their stages, and you must do it by yourself. When you first take your tools in hand and you begin to give shape to your garden, only then will you become a member of a society that is ancient and far-reaching, stretching in an unbroken succession from the first garden—the one in Eden—to your own garden today that may be only as large as a few spadefuls of earth. A green thumb is a working thumb, and it can be yours just as certainly as it's mine.

So take heart. Neither the art nor the science of gardening is difficult. The art is a simple one, the science is elementary. The tools are light and you can work at your own pace. No one will pressure you to go on if you don't want to. You can stop whenever you feel the need to lean upon your spade or hoe just to contemplate the sky. You will find yourself during these moments in a quiet place where you can listen to the song of a bird or follow its flight toward the heavens. Unlike the farmer, who must till the soil in the hot sun for profit, you as a gardener have the privilege of working only for the pleasure of your senses and the enhancement of your table. Take time to enjoy it.

In contrast to the flower garden, the food garden is fundamentally utilitarian. But it can also permit you to become aware of the beauties of nature. You will find yourself moved if you let yourself be, by the sleek dark purple oval of an eggplant or the crisp green beauty of a lettuce bed.

Every garden, no matter where it is or how small it is, is a living testament to our ability to defeat seemingly impossible odds. Your own garden is a private victory over poor soil, insects and capricious weather. What is the reward for your work and your caring? The ultimate, final pleasure comes when your dinner menu offers something you have grown yourself—even if it's only a sprig of parsley nurtured in a small pot, *you* grew it. It's an experience unlike any other that life has to offer. Celebrate it!

Digging Around For Information

When nothing much is growing outside except drifts of snow, it's a perfect time to read. What follows is a list of books that I've found to be stimulating, informative and pleasant reading.

The Complete Vegetable Gardener's Sourcebook, Duane Newcomb (New York: Avon Books, 1980). A book intended primarily as a guide to help you choose from the enormous range of materials and tools available to gardeners. Paperback.

The City People's Book of Raising Food, Helga and Willaim Olkowski, (Emmaus, PA: Rodale Press, 1975). Some good sense along with some fun ideas for raising your own meat and vegetables in the city. The chapter on composting in the city is particularly good. Now out of print, but check your local library for a copy.

How to Grow More Vegetables, John Jeavons (Berkeley, CA: Ten Speed Press, 1982). Precise, step-by-step information with lots of demonstration drawings. Good for the organic gardener who wants to delve more deeply into intensive gardening techniques. Paperback.

The Self-Sufficient Gardener, John Seymour (NY: Dolphin Books, 1980). Seasonal information using the deep bed method. Exquisite drawings accompany this most detailed and informative book. A good view of what the insides of growing things look like. Paperback.

Vegetables: How to Select, Grow and Enjoy, Derek Fell (Tucson, AZ: H. P. Books, 1982). Both colorful, tempting photographs and drawings are perfect for the novice who likes to see how all vegetables actually look when they grow. Paperback.

Square Foot Gardening, Mel Bartholomew (Emmaus, PA: Rodale Press, 1981). A well-thought-out system of planning and producing vegetables based on a grid of 1 foot squares. Saving of space and work. Not for the instinctive or free-spirited gardener.

In and Out of the Garden, Sara Midda, (NY: Workman Publishing, 1981). A sheer delight of a book filled with delicate, charming, old-fashioned drawings. A book that makes you smile with pleasure as you turn its pages, and offers some good information, too.

Intensive Gardening Round the Year, Paul Doscher, Timothy Fisher, Kathleen Kolb (Brattleboro, VT: The Stephen Green Press, 1981). A comprehensive reference, particularly for those advanced gardeners who are interested in extending the growing season in cold climates and who do it in less space. Paperback.

Herb Gardening in Five Seasons, Adelma Grenier Simmons, (NY: Hawthorn Books, 1964). Written by a doyenne of herb gardeners, it includes lore, growing tips and some unusual recipes. Paperback.

The Organic Gardener's Complete Guide to Vegetables and Fruits, from the Editors of Rodale Press, 1982. A particularly good section on fruits and berries with explicit information on selecting the correct varieties for your growing zone and keeping fruit trees vigorous without the use of chemicals. For those gardeners who nostalgically remember and would like to duplicate what fruit used to taste like, before the onslaught of chemical sprays and the habit of picking before fruit is tree-ripened.

Index

Page numbers in boldface indicate charts and illustrations.

A

Acid-alkaline (pH) balance
  how to adjust, 157-59
  how to test for, 155-56
Aerobic compost, 172, 174
All-America Selection, definition of, 94
Almond shells, **199**
Aluminum foil
  as a mulch, 197
  used to reflect light, 19
Anaerobic compost, 171-72
Animal by-products, **163, 173**
Aphids, **208-9**
Apples, for containers and small
  spaces, **122-23**
Apricots, for containers and small
  spaces, **123**
Assassin bugs, **218**

B

Bacillus thuringiensis, 223, 225
Bacteria, **224-25**
Bagasse, **198**
Barberry, as a windbreak, 20
Vernon Barnes & Son Nursery, 98
Barriers, types of, to deter wildlife, 219-22
Basil, for containers and small
  spaces, **132-33**
Bayberry, as a windbreak, 20
Beach plum, as a windbreak, 20
Beans
  pollution and, 23
  watering of, 202

Beans, lima
  heat and, 21
Beans, pole
  used to screen sunlight, 21
Beans, snap
  for containers and small spaces, **102-3**
Bees, **217**
Beetles, **210-11, 216**
Beets
  amount of sunlight needed, 24
  for containers and small spaces,
    95, **102-3**
  moles and, **27**
Berms, 16
Biodegradable plastic, 197
Birds, benefits of, 211, 213-15, 218
Blackberries, for containers and small
  spaces, **128**
Blood, dried, **173, 178-79,** 221
Blueberries
  for containers and small spaces, **128**
  as windbreaks, **19**
Bone meal, 159, **173, 178-79**
Borage, for containers and small
  spaces, **132-33**
Borers, **212-13,** 223
Bottomless boxes. *See also* Raised beds
  advantages of, 29-31
  how to make, **30,** 31-34
  how used, 26, 28-29
Bountiful Ridge Nurseries, Inc., 98
Boysenberries, location for, 22, 24
Braconid wasp, **216**
Brittingham Plant Farms, 98
Broccoli
  for containers and small spaces, **102-3**

location for, 22
pollution and, 23
transplanting of, 190
watering of, 202
Brussels sprouts, for containers and small
spaces, **102-5**
Buckwheat hulls, **199**
Burgess Seed & Plant Co., 98
W. Atlee Burpee Co., 5, 67, 98, 232

C

Cabbage
amount of sunlight needed, 24
for containers and small spaces, **104-5**
pollution and, 23
watering of, 202
Calcic limestone, **158,** 159
Capriland's Herb Farm, 101
Carrots
for containers and small spaces, **104-5**
moles and, **27**
watering of, 202
Catalogs, seed
definitions used in, 94-95
how to select fruit from, 96-97
list of, 98-101
Caterpillars, **212-13**
Cauliflower
for containers and small spaces, **104-5**
pollution and, 23
transplanting of, 190
watering of, 202
Chadwick, Alan, 27, 166
Chamomile, for containers and small
spaces, **132-33**
Chapin Watermatics, 204
Cherries, bush
for containers and small spaces, **124**
Cherries, sour
for containers and small spaces, **123-24**
Cherries, sweet
for containers and small spaces, **124**
Chervil, for containers and small
spaces, 132-33

The Chinese Method, 27. *See also*
Raised beds
Chives
amount of sunlight for, 24
for containers and small spaces, **132-33**
Cilantro, for containers and small spaces,
134-35
Circle gardening, 38-39, 41
Cities and gardening, 3, **8-9,** 11
pollution and heat retention for, 18-19
Clay soil
definition of, 154
organic matter for, **160**
Climate. *See* Weather
Cloches, 230-32
Clothes, for the garden, 144-46
Cocoa bean hulls, **199**
Coffee grounds, **163**
Cold frames, 18, 232-33
Companion planting, 88-90
definition of, 151
herbs and, **133, 135, 137, 139, 141**
marigolds and, 88
nasturtiums and, 88-89
to repel insects, 209, 211
Compost
aerobic, 172, 174
anaerobic, 171-72
bins for, **169, 170,** 171, **175**
grass clippings and dry leaves as, **174**
how to make, 169, 171, 174-75
location for a, 24
as mulch, **198**
pollution and, 23
rooftop gardening and, **61**
trench, 175, 179
Compost tea, 182-83
Comstock, Ferre Co., 5
Containers
airborne, 62-68
chimney flue, 51, **55,** 57-58
cinder blocks, 51
clay, 51
color of, 52
concrete, 51

Containers *(Continued)*
    crop rotation in, 91
    drainage in, 51
    fruits for, **122-30**
    garbage pails as, **53**
    growing walls, 67-68
    hanging baskets, 64-65
    herbs for, **55,** 61-62, 131, **132-41**
    how to fill, 54, 59
    how to make portable chimney flue
      and sewer pipe planters, 57-58
    how to move heavy, 58-59
    how to select, 49-52
    locations for, 48
    modular boxes, **50**
    for mulch, **169, 170,** 171, **175**
    open wire basket, 65
    on paved surfaces, 52
    plastic, 51
    pressed-paper tubs, 51-52
    pyramid plantings, 66-67
    recycled, **54**
    rooftop gardening and, **60-61, 63**
    soil mixture and care of plants in,
      59, 61
    for starting seeds, 187-88
    strawberry jars or barrels, 65-66
    Styrofoam, 52
    types of, 49-52, **53, 54**
    vegetables for, 95-96, **101-21**
    watering in, 61, 65, 66, 205
    where to look for, **56-57**
    window boxes, 62-64
    wood, **49,** 50-51
Cooperative Extension agents. *See* United
    States Department of Agriculture
Copper naphthenate, 31
Corn
    for containers and small spaces,
      104-7
    pollution and, 23
    as sunscreens, 21, **22**
    watering of, 202
Corncobs, ground, **198**

Cottonseed
    hulls, **199**
    meal, **173**
County extension agents. *See* United States
    Department of Agriculture
Creosote, 31, 32, 221
Crop rotation, 90-91, 151, 209, 228
Cucumbers
    for containers and small spaces, **106-7**
    as sunscreens, 22
Cuprinol, 32, 51, 232
Currants, for containers and small
    spaces, **128**
Cutworm collars, 190
Cutworms, **214-15**

D

Deer, repellents for, 221-22
Deer-Away, 221
Desert Seeds Company, Inc., 98-99
Dill, for containers and small spaces, **134-35**
Diseases
    chart of common plant, **224-25, 226-27**
    how to control, 207, 209, 211, 226-28
    how to identify, **155**
Dolomitic limestone, **158,** 158-59
Drainage
    in containers, 51
    in different types of soil, 154
    raised beds and poor, 26
    slopes and, 15, 24
    test for, 24
Duncraft-For the Birds, 213
Dwarf plants
    definition of, 96
    fruit trees as, 96

E

Ecology Action Studies, 166
Edging, wood, **70**
Eggplant
    amount of sunlight needed, 24

for containers and small spaces, **106-7**
heat and, 21
pollution and, 23
Eggshells, **162**
Epicure Seeds, 99
Exercises, for the gardener, 146-49

F

Farmer Seed and Nursery, 99
Feathers, **163**
Fences
    electric, 219-20
    plastic pipe, 220
    as sunscreens, 21, **22**
    used to repel wildlife, 219-21
    as windbreaks, 20
Fennel, for containers and small
    spaces, **134-35**
Fertilizers
    animal manures, 180-81
    custom-blended, **182**
    dry organic, **178-79,** 179-80
    liquid supplements, 181-83
    when to apply, 183
Henry Field Seed & Nursery, 99
Figs, for containers and small spaces, **125**
Fish emulsion, 183
    for container plants, 59, 65
    as a source of nutrients, **173,
    178-79,** 200
Fish meal, **173, 178-79**
Fish scraps, **162, 178-79**
Flowers, edible, **46**
Dean Foster Nurseries, 99
Freeform beds, 34, **40, 44-45**
    definition of, 26
    how to plan, 35, **36**
Frost dates, 185
Fruits, chart of fruits for containers and
    small spaces, **122-30**
Fruit trees, **46,** 86
    chart of fruits for containers and
      small spaces, **122-30**

how to select and plant, 96-97
as windbreaks, 21
Fungi, **224-25, 226-27**

G

Gallatin Valley Seed Company, 93
Gallup poll, 2, 3
Garden(s)
    how to choose a site for a, 23-25
    locations for, 7-14
    vacation, 92
    vandalism of, 25, **40**
    vertical, 193-95
Garden, how to design a
    adding plants to a design, 74
    designs, **73,** 74-81
    drawing a plan, 72
    how to assess the site, 71-72
    materials needed, 71
Garden cress, for containers and small
    spaces, **134-35**
Gardening
    cost of, 3
    reasons for, 1-2
    statistics on, 2-3
Geranium, scented
    for containers and small spaces, **138-39**
Germination of leftover seeds, test for, 191
Gooseberries, for containers and small
    spaces, **128-29**
Gophers, use of wire mesh to deter, **27,** 29
Granite dust, **173, 178-79**
Grapes, for containers and small spaces, **129**
Grass clippings, **163, 174, 198**
Grasses, cured, **198**
Greensand, **173, 178-79**
Green stink bug, **210-11**
Ground covers, **46**
Growing season
    how to determine the, 16-17, **155**
    how to extend the, 229-33
Grubs, **214-15**

Gurney Seed & Nursery Co., 99
Gynoecious, definition of, 95

H

Hair clippings, **163**
Harlequin bug, **208-9**
Joseph Harris Co., 99
Hastings, 99
Hay, **162,** 197, **198**
Hedges, **46**
Herbs, **46**
    chimney-flue herb garden, **55**
    companion planting and, 89
    in containers, **55,** 61-62, 131, **132-41**
    how to select and plant, 97-98
    list of dealers in, 101
    sunlight for, 24
    tolerant to wind, 21
Fred P. Herbst Seedsmen, Inc., 99
Holly, as a windbreak, 20
Hops, spent, **198**
Hot caps, 230, **231**
Hulls, **199**
Humus, soil and, 160
Hybrid, definition of, 94

I

Insects. *See also under individual insects*
    birds and, 211, 213-15, 218
    box turtles and, **207**
    chart of common, bad, **208-9, 210-11,**
        212-13, 214-15
    chart of common, good, **216-18**
    companion planting and, 209, 211
    crop rotation and, 209
    how to control, 207, 209, 211
    how to identify, **155**
    intercropping and, 211
    lizards and, **207**
    pesticides and, 223, 225-26
    toads and, **207**
Intercropping
    definition of, 151

how to do, 87-88
in raised beds, 28
to repel insects, 211
Interplanting. *See* Intercropping

J

Jackson & Perkins Co., 99
Le Jardin du Gourmet, 99-100
Johnny's Selected Seeds, 99
J. W. Jung Seed Co., 99
Juniper, as a windbreak, 20

K

Kale, for containers and small spaces, **108-9**
Kelly Brothers Nurseries, Inc., 99
Kelp meal, **173**
Key-Lite, 231

L

Lacewing, **217**
Ladybug, **217**
Landscape, insulating material, 54
Langham, Derald G., 38
Lawns
    clippings from, 23
    growing vegetables on, 7-8
Leafhoppers, **208-9**
Leaves and leaf mold, **163, 174, 198**
Lemon balm, for containers and small
    spaces, **134-35**
Lettuce
    amount of sunlight needed, 24
    for containers and small spaces, **108-11**
    heat and, 21
    pollution and, 23
    watering of, 202
Henry Leuthardt Nurseries, Inc., 100
Lighting
    fluorescent, 188
    for seedlings, 188
Lime
    pH levels and, **158**

types of, 158-59
when and how to apply, 159
Living Wall Garden Co., 67
Lizards, **207**
Loam soil, definition of, 154
Lovage, for containers and small spaces,
136-37

M

Macroclimates, 14
Mail-order seed companies, list of, 98-101
Manures, **163, 173, 178-79,** 180-81, **198**
Manure tea, 181-82
Marigolds, companion planting and, 88
Marjoram, sweet
for containers and small spaces, **136-37**
Marl, 159
Maturity times, definition of, 94
Earl May Seed & Nursery Co., 100
MCK Big Game Repellent, 221
Mellinger Seed, Nursery & Garden Supply,
100, 231, 232
Melons
for containers and small spaces, 110-13
heat and, 21
Merry Gardens, 101
"The Method." *See* The Chinese Method
Michigan peat, 161, 163-64
Microclimates
definition of, 14
how to identify in your garden, 15-16
how to modify, **17, 22**
in raised beds, 30
J. E. Miller Nurseries, Inc., 100
Milorganite, agricultural, **173**
Mint
for containers and small spaces, **136-37**
location for, 22, 24
Mites, **208-9**
Moles
thorny branches to deter, 219
use of wire mesh to deter, **27,** 29
Mulch
advantages of winter, 196-97

containers for, **169, 170,** 171, **175**
organic, **198-99**
plastic as, 197, **200,** 230
purpose for, 22, 195-96
in raised beds, 29
used to extend the growing season,
229-30
watering and, 196, 201
what to use for, 197
when and how to apply, 200
Mushroom compost, **199**
Mylar, **17,** 18, 188

N

Nasturtiums, companion planting and,
88-89
The Naturalist, 101
Nectarines, for containers and small
spaces, **125**
Newspaper. *See* Paper
Nichols Garden Nursery, 101
Nitrogen, sources of, **173, 178-79**
Normal-size plants, definition of, 96
North American Fruit Explorers, 222
Nurseries, list of, 98–101
Nutrients
major soil, 161
soil nutrient test, 156
sources of, **173**
Nut shells, **199**

O

Oil sprays, 225-26
Okra
for containers and small spaces, 112-13
heat and, 21
Onions, green
for containers and small spaces, **108-9**
Open-pollinated, definition of, 94
Oregano, for containers and small spaces,
136-37

Organic gardening, 150-51
Organic matter
    soil and, 159-61
    sources of, **162-63, 173**
Organic mulches, **198-99**
Organic pesticides, 223, 225-26

P

Paper, **162-63, 199**
Parasites, **216**
Parking lot garden, **12**
Geo. W. Park Seed Co., 52, 100
Parsley
    amount of sunlight needed, 24
    for containers and small spaces, **136-39**
Patio Tower Garden, 67
Peaches, for containers and small
    spaces, **126**
Peanut hulls, **199**
Pears, for containers and small spaces,
    126-27
Peas
    for containers and small spaces, **112-15**
    pollution and, 23
    as sunscreens, **22**
    watering of, 202
Peat moss
    how to work with, 163
    as a mulch, **199**
    as a soil conditioner, 161, 163-64
    types of, 161
    used to lighten soil mixes, 25
Pecan shells, **199**
Peppers
    amount of sunlight needed, 24
    for containers and small spaces, **114-15**
Perlite, used to lighten soil mixes, 25
Pesticides, organic, 223, 225-26
pH
    factor test for, 156
    how to adjust, 157-59
    how to test for, 155-56

Phosphorus, sources of, **173, 178-79**
Pine needles, **162, 199**
Pines, as a windbreak, 20
Planting
    checklist for, 91-92
    companion, 88-90
    crop rotation, 90-91
    deciding on what to grow, 85-86
    paper plan, 82-85
    succession planting, 87-88
    for vacation time, 92
    when to start, 185-86
Planting techniques. *See also under*
    individual techniques
Plant protectors, 18, **190,** 230-32
Plant supports, 193-95, **196**
Plastic
    black and clear plastic used to absorb
        sunlight, 18, **200,** 230
    for cloches, 230-32
    as a mulch, 197, **200,** 230
    used under garden paths, 34
Plums, for containers and small spaces, **127**
Poisson, Leandre, 230
Pollution
    gardening and, 22-23
    retention of heat and, 18-19
Polyethylene films, 197
Pomace, **198**
Potash, sources of, **178-79**
Praying mantis, **216**
Pressure-treated lumber, 31, 32, 33
Privet, as a windbreak, 20
Propagation box, 188
Pyramid plantings, 66-67
Pyrethrum, 223

Q

Quassia, 225
Quicklime, 159
Quince, for containers and small spaces,
    127

R

Rabbits, repellents for, 221-22
Raccoons, fences for, 221
Radishes
    amount of sunlight needed, 24
    for containers and small spaces, **114-17**
    watering of, 202
Raised beds, 9, 170. *See also*
    Bottomless boxes
        advantages of, 29-31
        The Chinese Method, 27
        description of, 26, 27
        drainage and, 26
        fences and, 220
        how to make paths for, 34
        how to prepare, 27-28, **30, 33**
        intercropping in, 28
        microclimates in, 30
        mulch and, 29
        succession planting in, 28
        trellises in, **28**
        used to trap sunlight, 18
Raspberries, for containers and small
    spaces, **129-30**
Repellents, for wildlife, 221-22
Resistance, definition of, 94
Rhubarb, for containers and small spaces,
    116-17
Rice hulls, **199**
Rock phosphate, **173, 178-79**
Rock salt, 23
Rodale, J. I., 27
Rooftop gardening
    bottomless boxes and, 26
    compost and, **61**
    containers and, **60-61, 63**
    pollution and, 23
    safety of, 25
    soil for, 165
    stress and, 24-25
    watering and, 22, 204-5
Rosemary, 21
    for containers and small spaces, **138-39**

Rotenone, 223
Rowan, Lilian, 146
Russian olive, as a windbreak, 20

S

Safer Agro-Chem's Insecticidal Soap, 225
Sage, 21
    for containers and small spaces, **138-39**
Sandy soil
    definition of, 154
    organic matter and, **160**
Savory, for containers and small spaces,
    138-39
Sawdust, **199**
Seashore gardening, **176-77**
    windbreaks for, 20-21
Seaweed, **162, 173, 199**
Seeds/seedlings
    care and feeding of, 188-89
    containers for, 187-88
    hardening of, 189
    how to start seeds indoors, 186-89
    leftover, 191-92
    planting directly into garden, 190-91
    soaking of, **187**
    spacing of, 5, 190-91
    starting plants from, 184-85
    transplanting of, 188-90
Seed-starting mixes, 186-87
Sewage sludge, 23, **173**
Shemin Nurseries, 221
Shrubs
    as sunscreens, 21
    as windbreaks, 20
Shrubs, bushy, **46**
R. H. Shumway Seedsman, Inc., 100
Sizes, of plants
    definitions of, 96
    of fruit trees, 96
Sky gardeners, 11, 14, 24-25
Slopes
    types of, 15
    water drainage and, 15, 24

Slow-to-bolt, definition of, 95
Slugs, **210-11,** 222
Small plants, definition of, 96
Snails, **210-11**
Soil
    for balcony and rooftop gardens, 165
    for container plants, 59, 61
    cost of a soil test, 156
    drainage of, 154
    how to adjust acid-alkaline balance,
      157-59
    how to buy topsoil, 164-65
    how to dig a new garden, 166-67
    how to mix, 165
    how to prepare soil for planting, 165-66
    how to test for pH, 155-56
    lime and, 158-59
    nutrients in, 161
    organic matter and, 159-61, **162-63**
    peat moss and, 161, 163-64
    properties of, 154
    services from the USDA, **155**
    soil tests from the USDA, 156-57
    types of, 154
    worms and, **157**
Sorrel, French
    for containers and small spaces, **140-41**
Sphagnum peat, 161, 163
Spinach
    amount of sunlight needed, 24
    for containers and small spaces, **116-17**
Spot pockets
    definition of, 26, 35
    how to plan, 37
Spring Hill Nurseries, 100
Sprinklers, 39, 203
Squash
    for containers and small spaces, **116-19**
    as sunscreens, 22
Squash bug, **208-9**
Squash-vine borers, 223
Stark Brothers, Nurseries and Orchards,
    100
Stokes Seeds, Inc., 100
Stones, as a mulch, 229

Straw, **162,** 197, **198**
Strawberries, for containers and small
    spaces, **130**
Succession planting
    definition of, 151
    how to succeed with, 87-88
    in raised beds, 28
Sugar cane wastes, **198**
Sugar Snap pea, development of the, 93
Sunflowers, as windbreaks, 21
Sunlight
    amount needed for growing, 23-24
    how to determine amount received, 15
    how to filter, 21-22
    how to trap, 17-20
Swiss chard, for containers and small
    spaces, **118-19**

T

Tachinid fly, **216**
Tamarisk, as a windbreak, 20
Tarnished plant bug, **210-11**
Tarragon, French
    for containers and small spaces,
      140-41
Taylor's Garden, 101
Tea, **163**
Thompson & Morgan, 100
Thyme, 21
    for containers and small spaces, **140-41**
Times to maturity. *See* Maturity times
Toads, **207**
Tobacco stems, **198**
Tolerance, definition of, 94-95
Tomatoes
    amount of sunlight needed, 24
    for containers and small spaces, **118-21**
    pollution and, 23
    transplanting of, 190
Tools and equipment
    for the beginning gardener, 142, **143**
    how to buy garden, 142
    maintenance of garden, 143

salvaged, 144
sources of, 152-53
Topsoil, how to find and buy, 164-65
Transplanting
    to outdoors, 189-90
    into pots, 188-89
Trees
    as sunscreens, 21
    as windbreaks, 20, 21
Trellises, 9, 193
    in raised beds, **28**
    types of, 194-95, **196**
    as windbreaks, 20
Trichogramma wasp, **216**
Turnips
    for containers and small spaces, **120-21**
    watering of, 202
Turtles, box, **207**

U

United States Department of Agriculture
    (USDA), 2
    Cooperative Extension agents, 17,
        155, 156
    county extension agents and their
        services, **155**
    how to locate local offices of the, 156
    soil tests from the, 156-57
The Urban Farmer, 100

V

Vegescape
    in curved rows, **10, 40**
    definition of, 26
    how to create, 41-43, **46,** 47
Vegetable characteristics, definition of, 95
Vegetables
    chart of vegetables for containers and
        small spaces, 95-96, **101-21**
    space and, 95-96
Vermiculite, used to lighten soil mixes, 25
Vertical gardening, 193-95

Vines, **46**
Viruses, **226-27**

W

Walls, growing on, 67-68
Walnut shells, **199**
Wasps, **216**
Water drainage. *See* Drainage
Water/watering
    attachments for, 203, **204**
    in circle gardens, **38,** 39
    conservation methods of, **202**
    in containers, 61, 65, 66, 205
    drip irrigation systems, 204
    ground level, 203
    how much to, 201-3
    how to, 200-1, 203-4
    mulch and, 196, 201
    overhead, 203
    in raised beds, 28
    seasonal, 203
    of seedlings, 188, 189
    when to, 22, 201-3
Weather
    macroclimates, 14
    microclimates, 14-16
    zone maps, 16
Weeds, **163,** 195
Weyerhaeuser Company Research
    Department, 221
Whiteflies, **208-9**
White Flower Farm, 100
Wildlife and gardens, 218-22
Wind
    effects on plants, 16, 20
    herbs and, 21
Windbreaks
    berms as, 16
    blueberry bushes as, **19**
    fences as, 20
    herbs as, 21
    movable, 21
    shrubs as, 20

Windbreaks *(Continued)*
    stones as, 18
    sunflowers as, 21
    trees as, 20, 21
    trellises as, 20
Wireworms, **214-15**
Wood ashes, **158,** 159, **163, 173, 178-79**

Woodchucks, fences for, 221
Wood shavings, **163, 199**
Worms, **157, 212-13**

Z

Zone maps, 16